SOCIAL JUSTICE JESUS

Justice, Mercy, and Faith as Presented in the

Sermon on the Mount

By Edward S. Georgeson

Avinu Publishing

SOCIAL JUSTICE JESUS:
Justice, Mercy, and Faith as Presented in the Sermon on the Mount
Large Print Edition
Copyright ©2021 by Edward S. Georgeson
All rights reserved by the publisher.
Avinu Publishing
Freedom, California

Website: www.avinupublishing.com
Email: avinupublishingcompany@gmail.com

- - - - - - - - - - - - - - - - - - -

- - - - - - - - - - - - - - - - - - -

ISBN: 978-1-7364371-2-4
Library of Congress Control Number: 2021910078

Cover design by JD&J Book Cover Design
Edited by Rick Steele of Rick Steele Editorial Services and
Victoria Brock of The Word Tank
Formatting by JD&J Book Cover Design

FOR

the hungry,

the thirsty,

the naked,

the sick,

the imprisoned,

the widow,

and the widower,

the orphaned,

the abused,

the confused,

the robbed,

the war affected,

the strangers in a strange land,

and all who suffer and are dismayed and disheartened,

may this book perform a small role in inspiring citizens of the

kingdom of heaven to be a renewed and even greater blessing to you.

"We make a living by what we get,
we make a life by what we give."

−Winston Churchill

TABLE OF CONTENTS

PART III The Sermon on the Mount
This Is the Law and the Prophets

PART IV The Sermon on the Mount
    Justice, Mercy, and Faith

THE CURTAIN-RAISER

"Social Justice Jesus" has always existed. Faithful followers of Christ have always seen their Lord as a defender of the weak and oppressed—the helper of those in need of help. Likewise, the true followers of Christ have always responded to their Lord's call to duty to address disparities and injustice wherever they find them. For these faithful servants, social actions are not seen as works of salvation but as fulfillments of the tenets of the kingdom of heaven. The pursuit of equity and justice are not only actions requested within the teachings of our Lord, they are duties assigned by our King. As such, they do become part of one's salvation, because failure to be socially responsible and active—to love one's neighbor and even one's enemy—is grounds for denied entrance into the kingdom of heaven.

Nowhere is this more evident than in Jesus' epic sermon, the "Sermon on the Mount." Unfortunately, much of modern Christendom believes that this sermon is a remnant of an old covenant and that these epic words of Jesus no longer apply to us. Nothing could be further from the truth, and believing this erroneous deception has been spiritually lethal—both individually and corporately. What a tragedy! What terrible confusion this has produced within Christianity, and what a loss of opportunity for the Christian church!

This is why I have written **"Social Justice Jesus."** Jesus' Sermon on the Mount, as recorded in the Gospels, is a manifesto of the kingdom of heaven. It is a guide to how the followers of Christ are to live their lives. Within this sermon, Jesus indicates multiple times that his words—his instructions to his followers—remain valid far into the future, and that they are the pathway to current blessings and eternal life. Following them is faith in Jesus. Christians need to correctly understand this. Jesus' words shape the proper influence and impact that Christianity is to have on earth. Their implementation brings the peace of heaven to earth—a major objective of the kingdom of God. Failing to implement his words would be a form of taking God's name in vain—claiming to be a child of God but living as if one were free of the duties God desires us to perform. Calling oneself a Christian but failing to follow Jesus' words is a misrepresentation of Jesus' mission on earth, the nature of the kingdom of heaven, and God's character.

Many Christians have always intuitively understood their role as followers of Christ and have been active in the duties he has assigned. The words of their king are not taken lightly. The Sermon on the Mount greatly influences their lives. I know, because it has greatly influenced me. It has helped me see the value of every human life and has encouraged me to be active in service to others. It helped direct the course of my academic studies. It took me to Africa for seven years, where I helped meet the needs of war-displaced refugees and thirsty nomads. Jesus' sermon has been the material of many of my Bible study classes and the topic of multiple sermons of my own. Jesus' epic sermon is not a relic of the past. Correctly understood, it is a guide to Christian living. And the life he is directing us to live is exciting! This is what I want to share with you.

For well over two decades, I have been studying Jesus' Sermon on the Mount, collecting thoughts, jotting down notes, thinking, and rethinking its applications, and trying to see how each theme connects to the previous topic. When I began, I had preconceived ideas of what Jesus was trying to say, but I wanted to dig deeper into every word. Jesus gave us a clue that his sermon was the fulfillment of God's Law and Prophets. This means that his words are built upon past teachings. So, I took key words from within his sermon and tracked their usage in the Old Testament. For example: what is the meaning of someone who is "pure in heart"? Who are they? What do they believe? How do they live? Initially, I believed I knew the answers to these questions, but as I dug deeper into the Word of God, the revelations that I discovered took me in a direction I did not originally expect, and *Social Justice Jesus* began to take shape. These new discoveries profoundly called into question my own commitment to Christ. Was I really following him? Does he expect more from me than I have been giving? And if so, how do I put into action his request? My journey into God's word was a revelation to me, and I anticipate that what I am about to share will be a revelation to you as well.

On December 31, 2019, I made a New Year's resolution to put my research and knowledge to paper in the form of a book. I have written other books of a technical nature; they were tedious but not difficult to compile. I anticipated, however, that this book would be harder to complete. It would require more effort to organize and convey my knowledge and insights, and would be controversial to many Christians, but I felt I had to do it. I work full-time, so on weekends and evenings, when I had the time and strength, I attempted to write. Early on, it was slow going. Writing requires large chunks of time and mental energy, where one wrestles to analyze thoughts, and tries to conceive the best way to communicate ideas. By mid-March I had only completed two chapters, and I realized that fulfilling my New Year's resolution was going to take an exceedingly long time.

Then suddenly and unexpectedly, the world was hit with a new coronavirus. My employer deemed me nonessential and sent me home for weeks. The government told me to stay home and shelter-in-place. By a strange turn of tragic events, I suddenly had time on my hands. I knew what God wanted me to do, and I felt an urgency to complete the task. So, I began to write, and this book began to take shape in ways that have surprised even me.

Then, amid this world tragedy, multiple social injustices became public, and people around the globe began to cry out for justice with a fervor that has seldom been acknowledged in recent generations. Their cries should be heard and evaluated. Injustices need to be corrected. There is, however, a danger that the pendulum will be swung to its opposite extreme, and one set of injustices will be substituted with another set. What needs to occur is a stopping of the pendulum altogether. Society needs to see all humanity as the creation of God, and it must value every life. Without justice for all, injustice will always exist. True justice, however, requires a true standard, and we have a standard presented to us in Jesus' Sermon on the Mount.

Social justice and equity are dominant themes within the message of Jesus as found in the Sermon on the Mount. However, Jesus teaches that justice and mercy go hand in hand; correcting society's failures requires action, but it also requires forgiveness. This is a message that many do not want to hear, but for Christians it is the Word of our King.

Throughout my studies over the years, and while writing this book, I have often lamented the fact that if we Christians had taken Jesus' Sermon on the Mount literally, we would have had nearly two thousand years of leading the cause of social justice and equity, peace and love, to all the world. Where would the world be today if Christians, past and present, fully understood Jesus' words and diligently applied them? The world's social and equity disparities may have already been corrected by the actions of Christ's followers. The unrest we see today may never have been. Only the God of heaven knows for sure. What I know is that the Sermon on the Mount is an indispensable part of Jesus' gospel—it is God's word—and it too is to be preached to all the world.

It is my hope that as you read this book, you will see clearly what Jesus was trying to communicate to us that day on the mountainside. It is my hope that you will be surprised and convinced by what Jesus still has to say to us today. It is my hope that you will see its universal and eternal application. And finally, it is my hope that you will accept the themes of his message and become a devoted follower; putting his words into action and helping to build his kingdom of heaven here on earth.

INTRODUCTION

It was mid-August and 3:24 in the morning when I stepped out of the Lufthansa airliner and onto African soil for the first time in my life. The air smelled of dust, and the temperature was 93 degrees. Except for the abrupt change in people—their culture, their language, and their religion—I found the environment oddly similar to that from which I had departed. I had arrived from Barstow, California, and Barstow in mid-August is oppressively hot. I had left one oven to enter another. I was twenty-six years old, ten-thousand miles from home, in a strange new land, alone, but not lonely.

I had accepted a volunteer position to help participate in famine relief efforts in one of Africa's poorest nations. It was something I had longed to do for many years, and now, God had granted me the opportunity to serve him through service to others. Since I was a child, I intuitively knew that being a Christian required that we do what we can to help others in need. This is one of Christ's predominant messages throughout the Gospels. It is the message in the parable of the sheep and the goats, and the main theme of Jesus' epic Sermon on the Mount.

It was this desire to be of service that led me to study theology, which eventually morphed into a degree in international development. I had envisioned myself working as an agricultural developer in Central or South America. Instead, after graduation, I landed a job at an agricultural research facility in Barstow. It was the perfect place to prepare for where God was about to send me, though I did not know it at the time.

It was early August when I received a surprise phone call from a Christian international relief organization that had previously rejected my request for employment. Africa was in trouble; a severe famine had reached a crisis point, and the world was responding by sending food. The relief organization needed coordinators in place, and they needed them fast. Would I be interested in participating as a volunteer for three months? I was! So, I abandoned my job in Barstow and headed to Africa with only a promised two-hundred-dollar-a-month stipend, which would be enough to cover my student loan. It was a leap of faith, but I knew this was the Lord's work, and I was willing to give it a try.

As I exited the airport's customs office and walked out onto the street, a young Coptic Christian man walked up to me and questioningly spoke my name. "Yes, that's me," I replied.

He nodded with a grin of satisfaction. "Yes. I was sure you were the one." He looked tired and eager to get his assignment completed. "My name is Zaki. I have been sent to pick you up and take you to where you will be staying. Welcome to Africa!"

As we loaded my luggage into Zaki's vehicle, I must admit I felt disoriented, apprehensive, and even fearful. I was now in Africa, about to take on world-pressing responsibilities, the duties of which still had not been told to me. I could only hope and pray to God that he would be with me and guide me for the next three months. Little did I know that this poor, war-torn nation, plagued with social injustices and racial and religious misunderstandings, was going to be my home for the next seven years.

In today's world, the pursuit of equity within all sectors of society is known as "social justice." Social justice has many definitions, and its application means different things to different groups, but essentially it is the philosophical theory which asserts that there are dimensions of fairness—justice—

that go beyond those embodied in the principles of civil or criminal law, which themselves can be unjust. It looks to correct disparities that are perceived to exist in the communal distribution of wealth, opportunities, and privileges. It seeks to treat all people with equality, fairness, and dignity.

Social justice advocates can be viewed as heroes or terrorists, depending on their actions, underlying motives, and who they represent or who feels championed or threatened by them. Our whole world is divided by many political ideologies, races, cultures, and spiritual paradigms, and anyone who advocates a change to someone's norm is open to suspicion and initial resistance. And rightly so. A change advocated by one, can be the violation of another's sacred beliefs—a violation of their moral standards and taboos. Take, for example, the fight for marriage between same-sex couples, or the right for the terminally ill to end their lives. While some calls for justice will remain hotbeds of controversy, other battles for "justice" are eventually accepted and no longer questioned—like the right for women to vote.

This book is written primarily for a Christian audience, so certain assumptions are made regarding the mindset of my readers. However, the teachings of Jesus hold value to anyone, Christian or non-Christian, and what I have to present should be of interest to those who wish to study how Jesus interpreted the Mosaic Laws, and how he applied them to the social deficiencies of his time and to ours. There are limits, however, to how far Christians can use Jesus' message. The gospel messages, for example, cannot be used to extrapolate a position on the legalization of cannabis, or to gain insight on whether an electric car is good or bad for the environment. There are some things we must figure out on our own.

"Social justice", as referred to in this book, will be presented within the context of Jesus' time and culture, and to how he advocated for a greater compliance with God's fairness toward all sectors of his society. Jesus saw the law of God being incorrectly followed, and part of his ministry was to correct its misapplications. Jesus preached social justice, but he preached it within the context of his time and the laws of Moses that governed his community. Does this mean that Jesus' teachings are irrelevant to our present age? No, far from it! His teachings address social issues that are still plaguing us today, and his wisdom gives us valid solutions to these problems. So, the social justice teachings of Jesus are timeless and still relevant to anyone who wishes to be a part of his kingdom of heaven.

This book will focus on the teachings of Jesus as found in the Sermon on the Mount. Early in my Christian walk, I rarely considered Jesus to be the consummate social justice leader, but his equity themes became more and more apparent as my studies into this epic sermon deepened. They took me in directions that made it impossible for me to ignore Jesus' repeated social justice themes. The context of his sermon is a revelation of the nature of a kingdom of heaven forming in his time—not just a future kingdom. It is a kingdom to be put into action, now, by those who hear him. Kingdoms have manifestos—policies and principles to be followed. These are formed for the good of their communities. The Sermon on the Mount is a manifesto outlining Jesus' revelation of God's law in action. Social justice and social equity are major themes of that law, given for the good of all who live on this earth.

Much has been written about Jesus' epic Sermon on the Mount as recorded in the Gospels. It is a sermon that has fascinated me since I was a child, partly because, unlike other parts of the Bible that I have found difficult to understand, this sermon was understandable. Its concepts seemed straight-forward, and I could see the logic of applying its principles to my everyday life. However, as a child, I did fail to comprehend the broader applications of Jesus' message. I did not fully understand the context of the sermon or see how Jesus' words were often a rebuttal to the teachings of his day. I missed the way in which this sermon reframed the Old Testament Law and the Prophets in easy-to-understand terms. I missed that Jesus essentially declares himself to be the "prophet" promised by Moses in Deuteronomy 18:15–19. I missed that he puts his words, uttered that day, on par with the Law and the Prophets, and declares that his words, if obeyed, lead to safety and eternal life.

As a child, I also missed the fact that this sermon is about what Jesus calls the "weightier matters of the law: justice and mercy and faith,"[1] which Jesus says are not to be neglected. However, as I grew older and studied this sermon in depth, I began to see that its message is indeed the law of God, and its focus is the weightier matters of the law—justice, mercy, and faith. It is a message calling for social justice and *"equity,"* a word often used to define *"righteousness."* It is a message that calls disciples to take equitable actions, now, to begin the kingdom of heaven in their lives, for the benefit of themselves and for all who live on this earth. It is a message that has a cost to those who practice it, but calls for its disciples to have faith that God the Father will provide for their needs as they pay the price of implementing this kingdom in their lives.

Surprised? Yes, you should be surprised if no one has told you this before! It is sad that what is probably the most straight-forward aspect of Jesus' message is the one most often miscomprehended or ignored. Perhaps this is because our religious leaders over-spiritualize Jesus' teachings. For example, pastors often take the beatitudes and frame them

---

[1] Matthew 23:23

in terms of future benefits to members of God's kingdom. In so doing, they miss the immediate calls to action and the current benefits that Jesus is presenting to those who act now. And these benefits are not for followers only; they are for the blessing of all humanity.

Perhaps today's "faith alone" Christians find the works-oriented themes of the Sermon on the Mount too divergent from their mainstream Christian paradigms. Maybe the face value of Jesus' message is considered too radical or impossible to follow. Rest assured, this sermon was radical even in Jesus' day. Shortly into his equity message, Jesus has to detour and address his listener's concerns that what he is saying may be a violation of the Law and the Prophets, *as it has been taught to them*. Nearly one-third of this sermon is devoted to correcting the misguided instructions that the people have received from their religious leaders. Could it be that we also need similar correction today? Later, Jesus must balance his equity themes with encouragements that living a life of equity is not as hard as listeners might expect. And finally, Matthew's Gospel records that at the conclusion of Jesus' teaching, the people were "astonished" by what they had heard and the way in which Jesus presented his message.[2]

Let me show you what Jesus teaches, and I believe you will be astonished too. The logic and structure of his social justice and equity message will become remarkably clear. His message is brilliant. If taken literally and acted upon by the whole of our Christian community, Christianity would become a far greater force for good in this world. We would be a government that transcends those of the nations of earth, filling in the needs of humanity where earthly governments fall short. We would be the kingdom of heaven on earth as Jesus intended us to be. The word "intended" is the key point here.

---

[2] Matthew 7:28–29

The kingdom of heaven works through human agents, and it needs knowledgeable and committed followers working its tenets for the good of humanity.

In this book, I will start with some background information concerning the kingdom of heaven and its expected arrival. This will set the atmosphere within which the people heard the message of Christ. It is important contextual information and will give us vital clues for understanding the themes Jesus will be addressing.

Next, we will take an in-depth look at every verse of the Sermon on the Mount. This is not as dry as it might sound. Looking at each verse, comparing it to other parts of the Bible and tracing key words back into the Old Testament, unlocks new insights and revelations—wondrous concepts that are rarely shared in weekend sermons or Sunday School lessons. These new revelations will leave you shaking your head in amazement. I am positive you will have this experience multiple times.

The process of this study will be straight-forward as we progress through this sermon from beginning to end. Each new topic or theme will be treated as a separate chapter. Longer chapters will have divisions so you can take breaks in thought and later return to the book as your schedule permits. I do not expect you to read this book in one night. There is too much illuminating information to expose yourself to all at once. Feel free to pace yourself as you like.

As you read this book, you will frequently see the use of the word "equity." This term has often caused confusion for some readers and is mistakenly thought to mean *equality* or having a financial stake in some sort of property. "Equity" is more than this, and this book draws on one of the word's alternate means and signifies a *quality of being fair or impartial* in one's personal conduct with others. But it is also more than this. The Hebrew, Aramaic, and Greek words from which the Bible derives the English words for *right, righteous* and *righteousness*, are often defined using the word "equity." And the biblical definitions of these three words are matched with the equivalent words of *lawful, beneficence,* and *equitable deeds.*[3] These latter concepts of doing right, following the law of God, being charitable, fair, and just, on a personal level, are what best define my use of the word "equity."

So, is our Lord and Savior a social justice warrior? After comprehending the Sermon on the Mount, it will become clear that social justice is a tenet that has its origins in heaven. Its principles were set in stone by God and existed before the foundation of the world. However, the disciples of God's true social justice are not the same as the militant actors that we see in many of today's secular warriors. Like Jesus, Christian warriors will seek change and fulfillment of God's law by way of the same meekness and forgiveness displayed by their king. Like Jesus, they will not only advocate for change, but they themselves will be the solution that is needed.

There is a sad note, however. The unfortunate truth may be that the social justice turmoil of our day has arisen due to Christians failing to be the social justice leaders for which Jesus had advocated. The gospel message is about Christ's death and his forgiveness of our sins. It is also about his resurrection and victory over death, and his ability to grant us eternal life. But as you will soon see, the gospel message is also about the promotion of social justice and equity. All these elements are to be preached to all the world before the end comes. We have been strong in promoting Christ's grace, but too often deficient in participating in his calls for social responsibility.

The participation in the promotion of justice and equity are part of our great commission as faithful Christians. If Christians

---

[3] See Strong's Concordance words OT:6662, 6663, 6664, 6665, 6666 and NT:1342, 1343, 1345 and 1346

fail to preach this aspect of the gospel message, we could be in danger of being passed by, as God gives this message to others— to children, or even to the stones to cry out.[4] Perhaps this is where we are in history today. As Christians, it is imperative that we understand the full gospel message, and apply every aspect of it to our lives. By Jesus' own words, it is a matter of life or death.

So, I invite you to take a journey with me now, and take a closer look at a literal view of Jesus' Sermon on the Mount. Look at the information and determine for yourself how Jesus wants the followers of the kingdom of heaven to live. You will be surprised! You will be changed!

---

[4] See Luke 19:37—40. See also Habakkuk 2:9—12

PART I

The Kingdom of Heaven Is at Hand

CHAPTER 1

The Kingdom of Heaven

When investigating a social justice Jesus, it is particularly important to understand that a "kingdom" was at hand and this fact propelled Jesus' ministry. Not an earthly kingdom, but a kingdom from above. The Gospels of Matthew and Mark both record this fact as the first words introducing Jesus' ministry. Matthew records Jesus' proclamation as follows:

Repent, for the kingdom of heaven is at hand.[5]

Mark adds more detail, and writes:

The time is fulfilled, and the kingdom of God is at hand. Repent, and believe in the gospel.[6]

Jesus has not arrived on the scene to teach a new religious theory or a new rabbinical perspective. God promised long ago at Mt. Sinai to make the children of Israel a kingdom of priests and a holy nation.[7] Jesus has arrived to call the people to a renewal of faith in that promised kingdom. He is warning the people that this

---

[5] Matthew 4:17

[6] Mark 1:15 In Matthew's Gospel the kingdom is said to be "of heaven", while in Mark's Gospel the term "kingdom of God" is used instead. Both phrases are referring to the same realm.

[7] Exodus 19:6

1

kingdom is soon to be a reality, and the people need to change their ways—repent—if they want to participate in this kingdom.

That word "kingdom" implies that this soon-expected government, as with any kingdom, will have a king ruling over the people. And, yes, the kingdom will have rules. It will have expectations of loyalty from its subjects. The kingdom will have its own culture. It will be known for the ways in which its citizens live and conduct their affairs, both within the community and inter-communally. And Jesus gives his audiences a hint of these details and expectations by stating that the kingdom is from above. Thus, the king, the rules, the culture, and expectations are heavenly ones—its subjects will be servants of God.

Everyone gathering and listening to Jesus that day had come because of excitement generated by John the Baptist, who also had been preaching about the coming kingdom from heaven. The Gospel of Matthew records that people from Jerusalem, "all Judea," and beyond were responding to John's calls for repentance. Note the following:

> *In those days John the Baptist came preaching in the wilderness of Judea, and saying, 'Repent, for the kingdom of heaven is at hand.' . . . Then Jerusalem, all Judea, and all the region around the Jordan went out to him and were baptized by him in the Jordan, confessing their sins.*[8]

As John's fame grew, he began directing his ministry toward Jesus, who was also preaching a soon-coming kingdom of heaven. Almost immediately, the crowds followed Jesus. Their curious minds were filled with questions. *Will this kingdom free us from Roman tyranny? How do I become a member of this kingdom? What benefit is it to me? What are the principles of this kingdom?*

---

[8] Matthew 3:1–2, 5–6

What will be expected of me if I become a member? How will it change my world and the world at large? The answers to these questions would be addressed by Jesus in his epic Sermon on the Mount—a manifesto of the kingdom of heaven. The answers, however, would be far different than what most of the population had been eagerly expecting.

This concept of a kingdom from above was not at all new to any of Jesus' listeners. The Hebrew nation started out as a theocracy when it entered the land of Canaan after its exodus from Egypt. During that exodus, God met with the people at Mt. Sinai and began to speak his laws to them. The event proved to be far too distressing for the people—they were scared beyond their wits—so they begged Moses to go up into the mountain and hear God on their behalf. They suggested that it would be better for Moses to hear God and then relay His laws and words back to the people.[9] Those words from God formed the Torah and began the theocracy of the nation of the Israelites—a kingdom directed by heaven.

The Israelites, however, over time, failed to live up to the codes and expectations of this heavenly kingdom and were often temporarily given up by God to their own failures. They desired more than a theocracy and wished to be like the surrounding nations. They sought an earthly king, and pursued the pleasures of idolatry, immorality, and wealth, which would lead to their repeated alienation from their God. In the coming centuries, their nation would be conquered by other nations; the people would be dispersed, the land left in ruin. Nevertheless, God continued to honor his promise to Abraham to make a great nation through his offspring. As the people repented and turned their hearts back to God, he would reestablish them in their promised land. Their failures, however, took their tolls. By the time of Jesus, the Israelite nation had been reduced from twelve tribes to two, and a foreign power controlled their land.

---

[9] See Exodus 20:18–22; Deuteronomy 5:4,5; 18:15:16

Nevertheless, during the time of Jesus, a strong hope and belief existed that God was still working on behalf of the remnant of Israel. Many anticipated that God would reestablish his kingdom—a kingdom of heaven—first among his people and eventually covering the whole earth. Old Testament prophets had repeatedly spoken on this theme and had pointed to future events where God's kingdom would be reestablished. Perhaps the most prominent of these predictions is found in chapter two of the book of Daniel. Here Daniel retells, and interprets, a dream given to Babylonian King Nebuchadnezzar—in the sixth century BCE.

The king's dream was of a large image made of various metals from head to toe—a head of gold, chest and arms of silver, belly and thighs of bronze, legs of iron, and feet of mixed iron and clay. Each metal represented an earthly government in its succession in time, from the golden head—representing the kingdom of Babylon—until the end of earthly governments. In the dream, the last of the earthly reigning powers—the feet of iron mixed with clay—would be struck by a stone cut from a mountain without hands. The force of this stone would grind all the metals of the statue to dust, and then the stone itself would grow into a mountain and fill the whole earth. Daniels' interpretation of the dream tells us that the "stone" represents a kingdom set up by the God of heaven and that this kingdom would replace all previous kingdoms and will stand forever.

I find this dream worthy of mentioning primarily because the succession of kingdoms that it portrays is easily tracked by other prophecies within the book of Daniel. The head of gold was the kingdom of Babylon. The silver represented the Medo-Persian Empire that followed. Greece is determined to be the belly and thighs of bronze, and the Roman Empire is represented by the legs of iron. This brings us to the time of Jesus who lived during the Roman period, but does it bring us to the time of the reestablishing of the kingdom of heaven? Would not Jesus' proclamation that the "time is fulfilled" be out of place by preceding the predicted earthly kingdom of mixed iron and clay?

The above questions are ones that are up for debate, but I would claim that from the perspective of those living in Jesus' time, and shortly before, the people could easily see themselves as living during a period of "mixed" rulership. The reason for this is that Rome had expanded greatly by the first century BCE. Its expansion, it can be argued, had outpaced its ability to control the new territories with administrators of solely Roman ancestry. To maintain control, Rome adopted a strategy of giving conquered regions some degree of autonomy. Local leaders still ruled local governments in a form of co-rulership with Rome. These leaders received power at the blessing of the Roman emperors and could remain in power so long as they remained loyal to the emperors, kept the peace, and paid their tributes to Rome. We can think of the system as one similar to that of the United States, where individual states can make their own laws and decisions, but still operate under the umbrella of a federal government.

Any region that failed to meet Rome's requirements would be subjected to the full force of Rome's powerful armies—which themselves had become a conglomerate of Roman and foreign soldiers directed and financed by Rome. Any Jewish student of prophecy living around the year 25 CE could easily surmise that the "iron legs" of Rome had become the feet "mixed with clay." The time would have seemed right, from their perspective, for the intervention of a major disruption to earthly powers by an external kingdom of heaven. Many Jews in Jesus' day would be living with an expectation of an imminent, world-changing event. For them, the time was, indeed, at hand.

Enter John the Baptist, Jesus' cousin and elder by six months. In the Gospels, John is the forerunner of Jesus' ministry. It is John who sets the stage and prepares the people for the soon-coming of the promised kingdom of heaven. From where does John get this idea? Is John a student of prophecy? Why does he think the time is at hand? And why does he think his cousin Jesus is the leader of the coming kingdom of heaven?

Answering these questions may take some speculation but they are not too hard to understand if we place ourselves inside the stories of the Gospels and the history of the first century CE. The Gospels tell us that the births of both John and Jesus are due to miracles. John's parents were older, and his mother was beyond childbearing age. Nevertheless, an angel of God reveals to John's father—the priest Zacharias—that his wife Elizabeth would have a son.[10] Zacharias expresses doubt that this can be possible given his wife's age, and is told he will not be able to speak until after the child is born.

Meanwhile, several months later, one of Zacharias or Elizabeth's relatives—a young girl by the name of Mary—is also met by an angel and told she will miraculously have a child. Mary is more trusting and compliant to God's will even though she is a virgin and wonders how she could possibly have a child. The angel encourages her by informing her that her elderly relative Elizabeth is also pregnant with a miraculous child—and he closes his announcement with the

---

[10] This story is recorded in Luke 1:5–25. John's father Zacharias is met by an angel with this news while he is serving in the temple at Jerusalem. From the book of Numbers (Numbers 8:23–26) we learn that Levites were to stop working in the Temple at age fifty. John's father is said to be old, but he is still working in the temple. Therefore, his age, as well as his wife Elizabeth's age, could be near this fifty-year-old threshold.

proclamation that nothing is impossible for God. Shortly afterward, Mary travels to visit and stay with Elizabeth for three months. The timelines given by the Gospels indicate that Mary was probably with Elizabeth when baby John was born. More than likely Mary was also present at the time of John's circumcision—eight days later—and the miraculous return of his father's voice and the subsequent praises Zacharias gave concerning his son John and the child that Mary was still carrying.[11]

No doubt both children grew up with the knowledge of these family stories, and the continual affirmation that they were destined for leadership roles among God's chosen people. These miraculous events, and the faith and support of their parents, would foster a keen interest in spiritual knowledge and the study of the Torah and the Prophets. John, the son of a priest, would seemingly have had an educational advantage over his cousin Jesus, the son of a carpenter. We do not know what contact the two children might have had during their earlier years. They lived in separate towns, but they no doubt had occasions to spend time together, even if this was only at the annual feasts in Jerusalem.

The book of Luke records that John eventually resides in the wilderness, and when he reappears and begins his ministry, the Gospel of Mark describes him as a man who survives by living off the land.[12] Our western minds conjure up a picture of a hearty soul living alone in the desert, sleeping on the ground, foraging among the plants and communing with God. John's life was probably not quite so austere. More than likely the Gospel accounts could be making references to John's association with a pious community of Jews known as the Essenes.

---

[11] See Luke 1:59–79

[12] Mark 1:6 and Luke 1:80

The Essenes viewed the rest of Jewish society as having drifted from the principles of God, and felt that fidelity to God's worship necessitated a withdrawal from the less moral lifestyles of urban life. Small Essene communities were scattered primarily in the Judean wilderness, mostly in the Dead Sea areas. The most famous of these sites is the Qumran site where the Dead Sea Scrolls were found in 1946. Indeed, it was the discovery of these scrolls that is helping to shed light on the Essene communities and their beliefs.

The Jewish historian Josephus writes of their piety, their absence of personal property and of money, their belief in communality, and commitment to a strict observance of Sabbath. He further adds that the Essenes ritually immersed themselves in water every morning, ate together after prayer, devoted themselves to charity and benevolence, and forbade the expression of anger and the act of swearing oaths. Repentance from evil was a prerequisite to baptism. They chose not to possess slaves but to serve each other.[13]

Essenes should not be thought of as a small group of uneducated, hermit-like, curmudgeons. On the contrary, they appear to have been very literate and spent much of their time copying and preserving Jewish literature. This included not only the books of the Bible's Old Testament, but volumes of other Jewish writing, prophecies, and records as well. Their communities were not hideouts, but fully functioning communities with families, small farms, and places of worship. While wishing to withdraw from mainstream Jewish life, they still interacted with Judea and were dependent upon trade with outside communities. They just believed that the preservation of their view of true Judaism necessitated their need for isolation.

---

[13] See Titus Flavius Josephus, *The Jewish Wars* (c. 75), book II, 119-161. Also see Philo of Alexandria, *Every Good Man Is Free*, 75-79.

The descriptions of John and his teaching appear to closely parallel the culture and philosophies of the Essenes. While we cannot say with certainty that John was an Essene, his residence in the wilderness probably brought him into close association with this group. It is not too hard to imagine the young John, perhaps now without his parents, seeking to study the spiritual literature of the Jews. After all, he is the son of a priest, who knows he has been assigned a role in history. The Essenes were known for their piety and their preservation of Jewish spiritual literature. What better place to reflect on one's divine destiny but with these Essenes in the safety and solitude of the desert?

Found among the Essene's collection of literary documents was the book of Daniel with its prophecy of a succession of earthly kingdoms ending with a time of "iron mixed with clay." John's ministry, as recorded in the Gospels, uses imagery similar to this prophecy found in the book of Daniel—the book that predicts the coming of the kingdom of heaven, which John knew he was destined to preach. For example, Daniel 2 pictures the kingdom of heaven as a stone cut without human hands, an indication that God does not need to build on existing empires. John, in his sermons, tells the Jews they should not feel privileged just because they are descendants of Abraham, because God can easily ignore them and make a kingdom from the stones surrounding them.

John also speaks about the coming kingdom of heaven as a wind that will blow away the chaff of a winnowed crop—the chaff being those who are not accepted into the kingdom. Daniel's prophetic image uses similar terms by describing the metals symbolizing the fallen empires as being ground to dust by the stone of the heavenly kingdom, and blown away by the wind. Daniel presents the coming kingdom of heaven as an everlasting kingdom. John, too, speaks of the coming kingdom as imminent and perpetual.

The book of Daniel is also laden with themes of loyalty to God's laws, of repentance, and of remembering the poor. In fact, in Daniel 4, after King Nebuchadnezzar is befuddled by yet another dream concerning his reign, Daniel advises the king that he may be able to postpone God's judgments by telling him, "break off your *sins* by being righteous, and your *iniquities* by showing mercy to the poor."[14] Some six hundred years later, John the Baptist, will make similar statements when he tells his listeners that preparation for the coming kingdom of heaven requires repentance from one's past evil deeds and a change in one's conduct toward others, especially those who are weaker. When asked by the crowds what they must do to be ready for the kingdom, John replies with calls to clothe and feed the poor, to practice honesty and integrity, to show respect for others and live moral lives.[15] All of John's points are themes of justice and equity within society, which Jesus will continue in his ministry—a ministry that continues to proclaim the imminent coming of a kingdom of heaven.

---

[14] Daniel 4:27

[15] Luke 3:10–19. See also Matthew 14:3,4

CHAPTER 2

A Mountain, a Stone,
and a Kingdom from Heaven

The prophetic dream of Daniel 2 depicts God's coming kingdom of heaven as a stone, cut from a mountain without hands. This stone is seen as traveling toward, and striking, the controlling kingdoms of earth and destroying them. The stone then begins a period of growth and continues to grow until it, itself, becomes a large mountain and fills the earth. We are then told that this kingdom mountain will never be replaced and will last forever.[16] While King Nebuchadnezzar did not fully understand the implications of the "mountains," the "stone" and a kingdom from the God of heaven, Daniel no doubt did. After all, Israelite history is replete with images of mountains, stones, and an everlasting kingdom. What Daniel did not tell King Nebuchadnezzar was that these symbols could represent his own nation—the Israelites. King Nebuchadnezzar correctly saw the dream as a message that the God of heaven chooses who rules the earth. Daniel, on the other hand, could have had an understanding that the final ruling power was to be his own nation—an understanding that Daniel would prudently avoid sharing with the king.

Think about these connections for a moment. The Hebrew nation begins with a promise from the God of heaven to

---

[16] Daniel 2:34–35, 44–45

their patriarch Abraham. God promises to make Abraham a great nation and a blessing to all the nations of the earth.[17] God carried on this promise to Abraham's descendants, promising to multiply them as well.[18] However, years later, the descendants of Abraham find themselves multiplying as slaves in the land of Egypt. Not to worry, however, the God of heaven sends Moses to lead the people out of Egypt to the land that God promised to Abraham. Their release from bondage is a miraculous one, and Moses, at God's direction, leads the people to a mountain—Mount Sinai. Here, God calls Moses up into the mountain and instructs him to give the following message to the people of Israel:

> *Now therefore, if you will indeed obey my voice and keep my covenant, then you shall be a special treasure to me above all people; for all the earth is mine. And you shall be to me a kingdom of priests and a holy nation.*[19]

After a bit of preparation, God begins to speak the words of His covenant directly to the people of Israel. The event, however, proves to be far too frightening for the people. Indeed, the scene is terrifying. The mountain is quaking; thunder and lightning and the sounds of loud trumpets are on dramatic display. Smoke is ascending like a furnace, while God, in the form of a fire, descends upon the mountain.[20] And if that is not terrifying enough, the people then hear the voice of God coming from the mountaintop, giving the Ten Commandments. Although God had much more to say

---

[17] Genesis 12:2; 18:18

[18] Genesis 21:18; 32:11

[19] Exodus 19:5–6

[20] Exodus 19:16–19

directly to the people, the Bible records that the people feared for their lives, and asked Moses to intervene on their behalf. The elders feel it would be far safer for God to speak to Moses and then for Moses to relay His words to them.[21] God Himself hears this request and agrees that it is a good idea.[22]

So, we have a historical account of the God of heaven associated with a mountain upon which Daniel 2's dream can reference, but what about the stone cut without human hands? You are probably thinking ahead of me at this point, and if so, great! Billions of people on this earth are familiar with the Mount Sinai story and know very well that the mountain is the place where Moses is given the law written on tablets of stone. However, what they might have overlooked is that the original stone tablets are provided by God Himself.[23] God, or at least heavenly beings, cut the stone. The stone is not cut by human hands! What is equally as interesting is we find that not only is the stone cut by the provision of heaven, but that God engraves upon this stone, with His own finger, laws, and commandments.[24] Again, another image of stone being cut by God's hand, not man's hand.[25]

The connection of the God of heaven's word—His laws and commandments for human beings—being set into stone that was

---

[21] Deuteronomy 5:23–31

[22] Deuteronomy. 5:28

[23] Exodus 24:12

[24] Exodus 31:18; 32:16

[25] The Bible records that there were two sets of stone tablets containing the Word of God. The first set was made and engraved by God himself. However, Moses, in anger, destroyed this set when he discovered the Israelites worshiping the Golden Calf when he descended from the mountain. The breaking of the tablets was his way of symbolizing that the people were breaking the covenant that God was establishing (see Ex. 32). Shortly afterward, God tells Moses to "cut" two tablets of stone and bring them to God, and He will rewrite His words on the tablets (see Ex. 34:1–4). This blank, second set of tablets, though "cut" by Moses, were again engraved by the hand of God.

not cut by human hands and its relationship to Him establishing a kingdom on earth is not to be overlooked. Recall that the very purpose for the Israelites being at Mount Sinai was for God to offer them the opportunity to be a "kingdom of priests and a holy nation." They were to be the kingdom of heaven's representatives on earth—an extension of heaven on earth. There was a condition, however. The Israelites—the descendants of Abraham—would need to "obey [*God's*] voice and keep [*His*] covenant." The words of that voice from the mountain and the covenant of which He spoke were engraved on the stone cut without human hands. Those words were to guide them in how they should live individually and together as a community. The words on the stone provided a framework for the kind of kingdom heaven wants to establish here on earth.

As I mentioned earlier, I find it hard to believe that the prophet Daniel, in revealing the king's dream, would not have noticed that the dream ends with symbols so closely tied to his own nation's history. Daniel would be prudent not to mention this observation to the king, after all King Nebuchadnezzar had conquered the Hebrew nation, and Daniel was a captive from that nation. Now was not the time to tell the king that his dream appeared to depict that the Hebrew nation was to eventually destroy his kingdom. But would Daniel have been correct if that were the conclusion he drew from the dream's symbols? The answer is, maybe "yes," and maybe "no."

I say maybe "yes," because in the future that may still be the case. After all, God's many promises to the people of Israel do present them as having a leading role in an everlasting kingdom. However, I can also say "no," because the dream of King Nebuchadnezzar depicts a "stone," cut without human hands, as being what eventually dominates the earth and lasts forever. So, the real question is, "What does the stone represent?" Is it the nation that originally received the God-given information on the stone? Or could it be the God-given information on the stone itself, which any nation or individual can accept as one's foundation for the rule of law on earth? Does the stone represent the nation of Israel, or does it represent the principles of heaven that eventually dominate in the future? As you will soon see as you progress through this book, it appears to be the latter.

If one accepts the premise that the stone represents the Law of God coming to and being established on earth, then King Nebuchadnezzar's dream chronicles the complete destruction of five successive forms of government being replaced with an everlasting government with heavenly rules. This indicates that the stone contains important information that is superior to past forms of government. The dream is explicitly implying that not only are God's laws and commands superior to other forms of government, but that ultimately, they will form an everlasting, heaven-based government on earth. Likewise, the dream implies that past forms of government—all five in the dream—were inferior to God's design. After all, if they had met God's standards, why replace them?

The laws and commands given by God to the children of Israel contain a wide variety of instructions to the people. Some of these instructions seem harsh and outdated to us today, and I would agree that many of them do not apply specifically to us. Communities and nations were more myopic and racial twenty-five hundred years ago, and God had to work within the boundaries of the cultural environments faced by His chosen people. However, the principles of the law were to lay a foundation for the cultivation of a society more just than what Israel had experienced as slaves in Egypt. The laws given at Mount Sinai were not God's last words. Even within the Torah, God announces that He has more to tell the people, and they have more to learn.[26] God ultimately wants to bring humanity to a point of understanding that fully

---

[26] Deuteronomy 18:18–19

comprehends the governing principles of His heavenly realm. King Nebuchadnezzar's dream indicates that nations fall due to their failure to meet these heavenly principles.

Is there any indication of the aspects of God's laws which may be most important, and lacking, in those nations that God eventually destroys? I would say that there is. Take, for example, a case found in Daniel 4. Here is recorded another dream by King Nebuchadnezzar and its interpretation by Daniel. In this dream the king sees a mighty tree, which, at the direction of a heavenly being, is cut down. Daniel interprets the tree to be the king, and the reason for the tree being cut down is that the king has failed to acknowledge that it is the God of heaven that bestows a kingdom to him. The root of the tree is allowed to remain, and after seven years, when the king comes "to know that Heaven rules,"[27] his kingdom is to be returned to him.

This is not good news to give to one's king, and Daniel quickly tempers the message with a word of advice. Daniel tells the king that perhaps there can be a lengthening of his prosperity—or in other words a delay in God's judgment. The king is advised to "*break off your sins by being righteous and your iniquities by showing mercy to the poor.*"[28] By implication of this advice, we can see that Daniel considers the king at risk due to the way he has been conducting his affairs, and part of that conduct is his lack of mercy for the poor. This advice clearly has social justice overtones.

If we look at the words Daniel uses in his advice to the king, we can glean more details regarding the king's shortcomings. The phrase, "*break off your sins by being righteous,*" is composed of three Aramaic words.[29] The words literally mean "*discontinue your offense by being beneficence,*"

---

[27] Daniel 4:26

[28] Daniel 4:27

[29] Strong's Word OT:6562, 2408 and 6665

that is, by being charitable or kind to others. Aramaic is an ancient language that is similar to Daniel's native Hebrew. The Hebrew word equivalent for the Aramaic word for "*righteous*"[30] carries with it the connotation that one's right deeds are being done for the sake of equity or fairness to others. In other words, the charity or kindness of one's "*righteous*" action carries with it an implication that one is correcting a social imbalance.

The phrase, "*your iniquities by showing mercy to the poor*" is also composed of three Aramaic words.[31] These words literally mean that the king should discontinue his "*perverseness by showing favor to the poor.*" These words, too, have Hebrew equivalents which are more descriptive.[32] The combination of these equivalents suggest Daniel's intended meaning is that the king should discontinue his "*misdirected ways by stooping to give favor to an inferior such as those who are browbeaten or depressed in society.*"

Daniel's advice to the king shows he felt the Babylonian society had social imbalances that needed attention. These imbalances could have been due to race or social class, and no doubt led to unfairness in financial and judicial areas as well. Daniel's advice implies that the king's administration of government is out of line with those of heavenly ideas, and he calls for the king to align himself closer to the principals espoused by the God of heaven in order to delay judgment.

This was not an issue isolated only to Babylon. Nations being judged by God due to social imbalance is a common theme in the Old Testament. Even the nation of Israel itself was guilty of ignoring God's requirements of equity and

---

[30] Strong's Word OT:6664

[31] Strong's Word OT:5758, 2604 and 6033

[32] Strong's Word OT:5753, 2603 and 6031

exposed itself to God's judgments. For example, the book of the prophet Zechariah records that one reason Israel is a captive in Babylon is for this very issue of social injustice.

> *Then the word of the Lord came to Zechariah, saying, "Thus says the Lord of hosts:*
>
> > *'Execute true justice,*
> > *Show mercy and compassion*
> > *Everyone to his brother.*
> > *Do not oppress the widow or the fatherless,*
> > *The alien or the poor.*
> > *Let none of you plan evil in his heart*
> > *Against his brother.'*
>
> *But they refused to heed, shrugged their shoulders, and stopped their ears so that they could not hear. Yes, they made their hearts like flint, refusing to hear the law and the words which the Lord of hosts had sent by His Spirit through the former prophets. Thus, great wrath came from the Lord of hosts. Therefore, it happened, that just as He proclaimed and they would not hear, so they called out and I would not listen . . . and I scattered them with a whirlwind among all the nations which they had not known."[33]*

Clearly, God's law has a desire for social equity within all areas of community, and in all communities. Heeding that law—keeping that Mosaic covenant—was one of the conditions for Israel becoming a kingdom of priests and a holy nation and remaining such a kingdom. The book of Daniel reveals that these

---

[33] Zechariah 7:8–14

principles within God's law impact other nations as well. Babylon would be judged by God and would fall, in part, due to its social imbalances.

These are examples of God's social justice and equity requirements on past governments and kingdoms. This book, however, is about the coming kingdom of heaven which was at hand in the first century CE. Is there a thematic connection to this kingdom, as preached by Jesus in his ministry, and to that of the social justice requirements of the Torah? If the equity components of the Mosaic covenant were still valid and necessary for participation in this arriving first century kingdom, what evidence do we have that Jesus taught these themes? And did Jesus have any legal basis or divine authority to uphold and teach them?

This book is about how Jesus upholds the equity themes of the Torah, even elevating them far beyond the understanding of contemporary Jewish sages. So, those questions will be answered in the coming chapters. As for Jesus' authority to teach, this was a point of contention throughout his ministry. The four Gospels record numerous times when the religious leaders asked Jesus by what authority he taught or worked his miracles. They were constantly frustrated by what they considered to be his indirect or evasive answers, and Jesus was often frustrated by their inability to comprehend his responses.

In Jesus' day there was an expectation for a "prophet" to appear and teach the words of God, and the religious leaders knew this well. Moses had predicted that God would send someone in the future, like Moses, to speak God's words. The prediction is recorded in the Torah and reads as follows:

> *The Lord your God will raise up for you a Prophet like me from your midst, from your brethren. Him you shall hear, according to all you desired of the Lord your God in Horeb in the day of*

the assembly, saying, "Let me not hear again the voice of the Lord my God, nor let me see this great fire anymore, lest I die." And the Lord said to me: "What they have spoken is good. I will raise up for them a Prophet like you from among their brethren, and will put My words in His mouth, and He shall speak to them all that I command Him. And it shall be that whoever will not hear My words, which He speaks in My name, I will require it of him."[34]

When the ministry of John the Baptist began, the religious leaders questioned whether John might be this "prophet," and so they asked him if he was.[35] John replied, "No," and directed their attention to the one who would come after him—Jesus.

The Torah contained the words of God, and was—and still is—held in reverence by the Jews. These words are lifesaving, so for Moses to predict that a future prophet would come and continue to speak God's words meant that his words would be equally lifesaving. Identifying that future prophet, when he does appear, is crucial to any Jew. As per Moses' prediction, identifying this prophet correctly means you will hear his lifesaving teachings. Getting it wrong means God will hold you accountable.

Jesus, in the Sermon on the Mount, as we will see, boldly claims that his teachings are from God and are lifesaving words. He will even liken the following of his words to one being safely established on a "stone" foundation—imagery of the lifegiving law set in stone. He will claim to uphold and fulfill the Law and the Prophets, but his teachings and actions, in the minds of the religious leaders, will appear to be inconsis-

---

[34] Deuteronomy 18:15–19
[35] John 1:19–26

tent with both. But are they? Or is it possible that the religious leaders misunderstood the laws? Once again, the Sermon on the Mount will address this very issue. Jesus will inform his listeners they have been incorrectly taught by their religious leaders, and he will use this point to give authority to his sermon's social justice themes.

To fully comprehend Jesus' message in the Sermon on the Mount we need to look at the social equity and justice requirements found within the laws given to Moses and supported by the prophets. Let us do this now by taking a one-chapter detour to help set the stage for the chapters to come. It is an interesting detour into an area of the law that many of today's Christians have ignored. This ignorance has led to the failure of many Christians to see the social justice foundations of Jesus' message.

CHAPTER 3

The Law, Social Justice, and Faith

There is no better way to start this chapter, but to point you in the direction of a story in the Gospel of Matthew. This is a short account of a lawyer—an expert of the Torah—coming to Jesus with a question that he regards as a test of Jesus' knowledge of the law. The lawyer asks, *"Teacher, which is the great commandment in the law?"* Jesus replies:

> *"You shall love the Lord your God with all your heart, with all your soul, and with all your mind." This is the first and great commandment. And the second is like it: "You shall love your neighbor as yourself." On these two commandments hang all the Law and the Prophets.*[36]

In an almost identical story found in the Gospel of Mark, we find a scribe approaching Jesus with the same question, and Jesus gives the same answer as above. In Mark's story the scribe agrees with Jesus and, adding his own comments to Jesus' reply, he states:

> *Well said, Teacher. You have spoken the truth, for there is one God, and there is no other but*

---

[36] Matthew 22:36–40 Jesus is quoting two texts from the Torah in his answer. They are found in Deuteronomy 6:5 and Leviticus 19:18.

He. And to love Him with all the heart, with all the understanding, with all the soul, and with all the strength, and to love one's neighbor as oneself, is more than all the whole burnt offerings and sacrifices.[37]

Jesus replies to the scribe's comment by telling him, *"You are not far from the Kingdom of God."*[38] These two accounts (possibly one in the same) tell us volumes about the law of God and Jesus' view of it—not to mention that of this scribe's. The Torah[39] contains the stories of the earth's origin and then covers the lives of the patriarchs. It also contains the complete law of God given to Moses. In it one will find numerous commandments, statutes, and ordinances. The lawyer wanted to know which commandment—singular—is the greatest of all those recorded in the Torah. Jesus, however, gives him two commands saying that the second is "like" the first. The word "like" that the Gospel uses to tie the two together is the Greek word *"homoia."*[40] It means, *similar in character*, at the *same place or time*, or basically *together*. Jesus places "love to God" as the greatest commandment, but he is also making the point that "love of one's neighbor" is not to be separated from one's love to God.

One of the best and simplest commentaries on this gospel story is one I heard told by Mother Teresa. She stated that *"we demonstrate our devotion to the first*

---

[37] Mark 12:32–33

[38] Mark 12:34 Note: In Mark's Gospel, the term "kingdom of God" is synonymous with Matthew's term the "kingdom of heaven."

[39] The first five books of the Old Testament: Genesis, Exodus, Leviticus, Numbers and Deuteronomy.

[40] Strong's Word NT: 3664

commandment by our actions in fulfilling the second."[41] I would say she was right. How better to give love to our unseen God than to love our visible neighbors, created in the image of God, and for whom God died because of His love for them. As Jesus intended, she connects the two together as inseparable, and places love and service to others as the best practical way to love and serve God.

The scribe's comments following Jesus' answer is also full of meaning. The law of God can be reduced to two basic themes: our relationship to God and our relationship to our neighbors. In the law, much of our relationship to God deals with the offerings and sacrifices required to atone for one's wrong doings, which we have committed against our neighbors—and by extension against God. The scribe's point is that if we followed God's laws regarding our relationships to Him and our neighbors there would be no wrong doings to atone for with offerings and sacrifices. In short, if there were no sins, there would be no need for atonements.

The intent of all of God's "neighbor" laws is to create patterns of conduct that help define our love and respect for our fellow citizens within our community—and in so doing reflect our respect for God. Nothing in the law prevents us from going above and beyond what the law requires. Jesus, in stating that the scribe is "not far from the kingdom of God," is telling His listeners that the law's connection between one's relationships to God/neighbor is the focal point of being a member of the kingdom of God. Love and service to our neighbor is love and service to our God, and vice versa.

This balance of love to God and love to our neighbor is seen from the beginning of God's law given on Mt. Sinai. Recall that when God met with the people and began to speak His law, His first words were what we call the Ten

---

[41] Mother Teresa's quote is paraphrased.

Commandments.[42] These ten commands would form a framework upon which all of God's other laws would hang. It has been widely observed that these ten commandments start by establishing man's relationship to God. For example, love only God, do not make idols, and do not take His name in vain. This is followed by commandments regarding man's relationship to his fellow man—his neighbors. For example, honor parents, do not kill, do not commit adultery, steal, lie or covet. These six commands clearly have social overtones calling for everyone to respect each other's lives, families, reputations, and property.

You may have noticed that I have left one of the Ten Commandments out of the examples above. It is the traditional fourth commandment—the Sabbath command.[43] Pastors generally present this command as one of the four commandments that defines our relationship to God. I would disagree. While the Sabbath command holds directions for honoring God as creator and redeemer, its benefit is directed toward His creation—man, land, and beast.

I wish to focus on this law for the remainder of this chapter because the Sabbath law, more than any other, is the one which has the most profound social justice overtones. It is perhaps the most misunderstood of the Ten Commandments given by God. The underlying principles of this commandment were a point of contention between Jesus and the religious leaders of his day. His interpretation and practice of the Sabbath was widely divergent to that of the leaders. They saw Jesus as a law breaker, especially on this one law, and Jesus saw them as ignorant and arrogant.

The Sabbath themes, rightly perceived by Jesus, would serve as the basis for much of His social justice preaching

---

[42] Exodus 20:1–17; Deuteronomy 5:6–21
[43] Exodus 20:8–11; Deuteronomy 5:12–15

during the Sermon on the Mount and the rest of His ministry. It is the Sabbath principles that call for respect for laborers and support for the poor, and for the periodic redistribution of the nation's wealth. The Sabbath themes are also tied to the death and resurrection of Jesus, and the rest we receive from our bondage to sin. Let us take a closer look and you will see what I mean.

Prior to the Sabbath commandment given at Mount Sinai, the Bible records two earlier references concerning a seventh-day rest. The first is found in the creation story where we are told:

> *Thus, the heavens and the earth, and all the host of them, were finished. And on the seventh day God ended His work which He had done, and He rested on the seventh day from all His work which He had done. Then God blessed the seventh day and sanctified it, because in it He rested from all His work which God had created and made.*[44]

This statement in the Bible has created a lot of discussion among theologians and layman alike. Why would an all-powerful God need rest? How would He rest? What does "blessed" a day mean? And why would a day need sanctifying? After all, the word "sanctified"[45] used in this text means to *be clean*, *make holy*, or *to purify*, or *consecrate*, or *set apart* as special. How would this apply to a day—the seventh day?

I will not deal with those questions now, but the answers should become clear as you read further in this book. Suffice it to say that, traditionally, Christians and Jews alike have seen the

---

[44] Genesis 2:1–3

[45] Strong's Word OT:6942

Sabbath day as a time to temporarily cease from our labors and come into the presence of God. It is a day to worship God and be present with Him, without the distractions of worldly cares. The rest that this day affords is a blessing but that blessing in our fallen world—as we will soon see—comes with duties that are tied to the concepts of sanctification, and those concepts have close biblical ties to social justice themes as a prerequisite for entering God's presence. One does not enter God's presence unless they are clean, or pure—"sanctified." There is a close connection between Sabbaths, social justice and preparing oneself for coming into God's presence. This will be seen in the coming chapters.

The next appearance of a seventh-day rest comes shortly after the children of Israel have been freed from slavery in Egypt. They are in the wilderness, before reaching Mt. Sinai, and they are hungry. The book of Exodus records that God miraculously intervenes with the creation of food (bread or "Manna") that falls from heaven each morning, except on the seventh—Sabbath—day. I invite you to read the whole account as found in Exodus 16, however, following is an excerpt of some of its important points.

> *Moses said to* [the Israelites], *"This is the bread which the Lord has given you to eat. This is the thing which the Lord has commanded: 'Let every man gather it according to each one's need, one omer for each person, according to the number of persons; let every man take for those who are in his tent.' . . . So they gathered it every morning, every man according to his need. And when the sun became hot, it melted. And so it was, on the sixth day, that they gathered twice as much bread, two omers for each one. And all the rulers of the*

congregation came and told Moses. Then he said to them, "This is what the Lord has said: 'Tomorrow is a Sabbath rest, a holy Sabbath to the Lord. Bake what you will bake today, and boil what you will boil; and lay up for yourselves all that remains, to be kept until morning.'" So they laid it up till morning, as Moses commanded. . . . Then Moses said, "Eat that today, for today is a Sabbath to the Lord; today you will not find it in the field. Six days you shall gather it, but on the seventh day, the Sabbath, there will be none."[46]

I would like to direct your attention to two important points in this story which set up themes that will be found in future Sabbath laws. First, everyone was to collect only what they needed for their household for that day. They were not to collect more, or to store it, except on the day before the Sabbath. And second, they were not to worry about their future needs but trust that God would provide what they needed each day with a double portion on the sixth day so that they could rest on the Sabbath. This command laid down a pattern of having faith in God for your daily need and not hoarding more than you needed. These two points will help you see the intentions of future Sabbath commands. They hint of social justice and the fact that implementing this kind of justice requires faith.

Next comes Mt. Sinai and the giving of the Ten Commandments. The Bible records these Commandments twice—once in the book of Exodus and once in the book of Deuteronomy. Interestingly, the Sabbath command is worded differently in each of the two presentations. They are similar and ask for the same reverence of the seventh day, but they differ on reasons for the basis of keeping the Sabbath. One

---

[46] Exodus 16:15, 16, 21–26

points to the creation story and God's blessing and sanctifying the day, while the other points back to the deliverance from the burden of slavery. Here are the two versions for your review:

> *Remember the Sabbath day, to keep it holy. Six days you shall labor and do all your work, but the seventh day is the Sabbath of the Lord your God. In it you shall do no work: you, nor your son, nor your daughter, nor your male servant, nor your female servant, nor your cattle, nor your stranger who is within your gates. For in six days the Lord made the heavens and the earth, the sea, and all that is in them, and rested the seventh day. Therefore*[47] *the Lord blessed the Sabbath day and hallowed it.* (Exodus 20:8–11)

> *Observe the Sabbath day, to keep it holy, as the Lord your God commanded you. Six days you shall labor and do all your work, but the seventh day is the Sabbath of the Lord your God. In it you shall do no work: you, nor your son, nor your*

---

[47] The use of the English word "therefore" may not be the best interpretation of the Hebrew words used by the author. The Hebrew words are `al and *ken* (Strong's Word OT:5921 and 3651). Together they convey a variety of different meanings. "Therefore" can be an acceptable interpretation, meaning that God's "rest" was a cause for him to bless and sanctify the day. However, `al and *ken* convey a passage of time and the setting up of something. The author could be saying that *after* God's rest on the seventh day, He saw fit to *establish* it as a memorial of rest and *set* the seventh day apart as a continual Sabbath—a day of rest and blessing. In its context of the creation story, God has just finished His creation and given it to man for his enjoyment and upkeep. It is a gift from God and is to be remembered as a wonderful gift. Likewise, the same word "therefore" as used in the Deuteronomy version of the Sabbath command would in context mean that God's freedom from the burden of slavery was a gift and a blessing, and he commands that this be memorialized on a weekly basis as well. In essence we are to remember to give to others just as God has given to us.

daughter, nor your male servant, nor your female servant, nor your ox, nor your donkey, nor any of your cattle, nor your stranger who is within your gates, that your male servant and your female servant may rest as well as you. And remember that you were a slave in the land of Egypt, and the Lord your God brought you out from there by a mighty hand and by an outstretched arm; therefore the Lord your God commanded you to keep the Sabbath day. (Deuteronomy 5:12–15)

While many theologians view these as laws commanding our service to God, I like to look at the Sabbath command as a labor law, at least at face value. While both versions ask us to acknowledge God and the role He plays in our lives, the main action being required is for us to rest from our labors. But that is not all, we are also being asked to give rest to everyone—man and beast—over which we have authority. By this law God has set aside a day by which He gives us rest, and by this law we have a day in which we are to give rest to others. God is appealing to us to accept His gift of rest, and at the same time appealing to us to be like Him by sharing that rest with others. Just as God has authority over us but seeks to ensure that we are not overburdened, so He asks us to care for those who are under our authority or within our "gates" and not overburden them.

Before I move on, I would like to point out that the Exodus version of the commandment starts with the word "remember"[48] while the Deuteronomy version begins with the word "observe"[49]. Though they may seem slightly different, both words are conveying the meaning that the Sabbath is to be a continual event as time goes on. It is to be marked, protected,

---

[48] Strong's Word OT:2142 "zakar."
[49] Strong's Word OT:8104 "shamar."

recounted into the future; it is a celebrational memorial of past events—the "rest" and "gift" of creation and the "rest" and "gift" of deliverance from bondage.

While both versions of the Sabbath command are to be kept as a weekly memorial—one day in seven—they are only an introduction to what the Sabbath is to be to the people of Israel.[50] Within the Torah, God commands that during each year there will be seven additional Sabbaths that generally do not fall on a weekly Sabbath. These Sabbath days are referred to by God as "My feast."[51] They are to be an assembling of the people together before the Lord—once again a coming into his presence. They are additional holy days for the remembrance of God's provisions to His people—in the past and for the current year. They include Sabbath days within the Passover Feasts (Feast of Unleavened Bread), and what is called The Feast of Weeks, The Feast or Day of Trumpets, The Day of Atonement, and the Feast of Tabernacles.[52]

God will also command other cycles of seven to be observed. There is to be a sabbatical year of rest after each sixth year. During this seventh-year, agricultural lands are to be left uncultivated (at rest),[53] and all personal debts are to be forgiven (debtors receive forgiveness and rest).[54] Another example is that Israelites who fall on hard times can sell themselves into servitude to others, but their term of service is limited to only seven years, to which afterward they can go free. This seven-year limit need not parallel the sabbatical year cycle. A seven

---

[50] Details of the days and years are recorded, in part, in Leviticus chapters 23 and 25 and Deuteronomy chapter 15.

[51] Leviticus 23:2

[52] The Jewish names are *Passover* (*Pesach*), *Shavuot, Rosh Hashanah, Yom Kippur, Sukkot.*

[53] Leviticus 25:1–7

[54] Deuteronomy 15:1–11

year "service contract" could begin at any time and would continue for seven years regardless of which year within the sabbatical cycle it began. At the end of the seventh year, one could choose to remain a servant to his master and not take his freedom. There are various reasons for doing this: security, loyalty and friendship being a few.

In addition, at the end of a cycle of the seven sabbatical years (after forty-nine years) there is to be a Year of Jubilee. At the beginning of this year (the fiftieth year of a fifty-year cycle) anyone serving as a servant/slave is to be freed. This would include anyone who started, but has not finished, a seven-year service contract, and those who chose to remain as servants to anyone at the end of their seven years. All are set free. There is no provision to continue as a servant within the fiftieth year. Also, in the fiftieth year, any agricultural land that has been sold in the past forty-nine years is to be returned to its original owners.

This is just a brief overview of how the weekly Sabbaths provided a model or starting point for a much greater system of Sabbath rest. All these additional Sabbaths and cycle of "seven" laws either provided opportunity to come into God's presence or to be freed of the burdens of personal work, servitude, debt, or poverty. These laws mirror the reasons given within the original Sabbath laws of the Ten Commandments—*receiving* and *giving* rest to others, as God has given it to you. The sabbatical years also expand the concepts of those inherent in the wilderness provision of bread from heaven. The people are not to take more than they need, and they are to have faith that God will provide.

There is a cost in forgiving debts every seven years or in surrendering one's purchased land every fiftieth year. However, by doing so, creditors or landowners are freeing someone from a disadvantage which is preventing a family from advancing in society. The sabbatical cycles help prevent runaway poverty and runaway accumulation of wealth into a few hands. Can you see the social justice foundations within these Sabbath laws? The provisions and limits are designed to help equalize wealth and opportunities every seven days, every seven years, and within each generation.

There is also a component of faith in all these laws. It takes faith to set aside one day in seven and trust that God will meet your needs. It takes sacrifice and a leap of faith to forgive debts and to let your land lay fallow one year in seven and trust that God will meet your needs during that year. During the sabbatical years and the Year of Jubilee, people were to pick from the fields only what they needed to survive. God promised they would have enough but believing this would take faith. Creditors or landowners who had to forgive loans or return land had to have faith that they could survive without the additional income or assets. And more importantly, they had to have faith that this social system of redistribution of wealth and opportunity was wise and just to the whole community, and a benefit to themselves.

It would be easy to not want to participate in such a system if you were part of the wealthy sector of society and destined to lose part of your wealth. But the Torah commands us to be considerate of the poor, and encourages us to trust that God will bless us for honoring his laws. One such admonition, along with encouragement, is recorded in the book of Deuteronomy, and reads as follows:

> *If there is among you a poor man of your brethren, within any of the gates in your land which the Lord your God is giving you, you shall not harden your heart nor shut your hand from your poor brother, but you shall open your hand*

wide to him and willingly lend him sufficient for
his need, whatever he needs. Beware lest there
be a wicked thought in your heart, saying, "The
seventh year, the year of release, is at hand,"
and your eye be evil against your poor broth-
er and you give him nothing, and he cry out to
the Lord against you, and it become sin among
you. You shall surely give to him, and your heart
should not be grieved when you give to him, be-
cause for this thing the Lord your God will bless
you in all your works and in all to which you
put your hand. For the poor will never cease
from the land; therefore I command you, saying,
"You shall open your hand wide to your broth-
er, to your poor and your needy, in your land."
(Deuteronomy 15:7–11)

God's laws in terms of economics have a design that
defends and favors the poor. Those who are not poor,
however, are assured blessings for remembering the poor
and addressing their needs. While on the other hand, God
hints that withholding support for the poor and needy can
become a sin for those who could be of help.

In closing this chapter, I have added an imaginary story to illustrate how these sabbatical principles based on the
fourth commandment may have worked in biblical times.

Reuben and the Hard Times

Reuben was the only son of a poor farmer from an area
northeast of the town of Jericho. Reuben was only fourteen
when his father was injured by an animal. Sadly, his father
passed away after several months of prolonged suffering.
Reuben, along with his widowed mother and a cousin, con-

tinued to work the farm, but production was never as good as when it had been managed by the skilled hands of his father.

By the age of nineteen, Reuben had married Miriam, a neighboring farmer's daughter. She was the joy of his life and a great blessing to his aging mother. Before long, Miriam blessed the family with the birth of twin boys. They named them Eliezer and Jehiel.

Not long after the birth of the boys, Miriam became sick and her health progressively worsened. Reuben found it almost impossible to care for the farm, his aging mother, his young family and his sick wife. The situation was getting harder to manage day by day, and he had no means to hire additional help. So, Reuben made the difficult decision to sell his family's farm. The money would let him move to nearby Jericho, buy a small house, start a new trade and get care for his wife and family.

Life in Jericho did not go as well as planned. Miriam's recovery was slow and expensive, and Reuben's aging mother, needing a watchful eye herself, was not able to help care for everyone adequately. Reuben's business of making and repairing farm tools was not producing as much money as he had hoped. Fortunately, the house in the city was a good one and it was paid off with the money from the sale of the farm. However, before long, Reuben again found himself in hard times, financially. He borrowed money from a friend and began working longer hours to pay back the loan, but the strain was hard on the whole family.

Originally, Reuben had agreed to pay off his loan to his friend before the Year of Release arrived, but his situation made payment difficult, and he fell short of full repayment. By the end of the sabbatical year, his creditor was upset and demanded that he pay the balance, even though it was a Year of Release. Reuben turned to the elders of Jericho for their input on the issue, and they defended his legal right to have the debt forgiven.

A great financial burden was lifted from Reuben's shoulders, though it strained his relationship with his friend.

As time went on, Reuben continued to struggle financially and decided that his best option, for himself and his small family, was to accept an offer to become one of Obadiah's servants. Obadiah was a wealthy merchant in Jericho, and he had several successful businesses and two farms on the edge of town. He knew that Reuben's skills and honesty would be a great asset to his own family and enterprises, and offered Reuben an opportunity to work for him. Reuben agreed and began a seven-year long contract as one of Obadiah's servants. Reuben's wages would care for his family and alleviate the stress of financial instability. With the advance he received for selling himself as a servant, Reuben made good on his old loan to his disgruntled friend. It did not need to be repaid according to the law, but Reuben was happy to do it and hoped it would pacify his old friend's bitterness.

Years passed, and Reuben, Miriam, and the boys lived a happy, stable life. Miriam's health returned, and she soon gave birth to a baby girl whom they named Naomi. The only sad time during those seven years was the passing of Reuben's mother.

Reuben's skills, good work ethic, and kind personality did prove to be valuable to Obadiah. The relationship, however, was mutual, and the two men quickly became good friends, and Reuben was encouraged to help out in any of Obadiah's enterprises. Reuben especially enjoyed working with Obadiah's farm manager. His name was Jethro, and he was a truly knowledgeable farmer. He could make anything grow and had invented many techniques to make the labor of farming more efficient. From Jethro, Reuben began to see things he could have done better when he ran his family farm.

At the end of Reuben's seven-year term as Obadiah's servant, he had a difficult decision to make. He could take his freedom and venture out on his own again, or he could give up his freedom and remain a servant for Obadiah until the Year of Jubilee, which was only nine years away. After discussing the situation with Miriam, he felt she had sound advice worth following. Miriam had pointed out that Reuben enjoyed working for Obadiah. They were friends, the wages met their needs, and he was learning many new skills that would be valuable in the future. She also reminded Reuben that the Year of Jubilee was coming relatively soon, and they would have their farm returned. By that time, the two boys would be strong young men—good farm hands—and Naomi would no longer be a baby. Reuben decided to remain a servant to Obadiah.

Meanwhile as the years passed, Daniel, the owner of Reuben's old farm, was doing very well. Reuben's farm was one of three that Daniel owned and worked, and he and his cousins were skilled at their trade. They had dug a new well, planted a vineyard on the hill behind the farmhouse and built a barn for the oxen and donkey. They had also repaired the threshing floor and built a canal which brought water to the farm during the spring and early summer from a nearby stream. The farmhouse was expanded with an additional room, and new trees were planted in the olive orchard to replace old ones that had died. The farm had never looked so good, or been so productive.

Finally, the Year of Jubilee arrived, and Reuben and his family were free to return to their farm. Obadiah was sad to see his old friend and trusted servant leave, but he wished him well and gave Reuben a generous parting gift. Jehiel, Reuben's son, had recently married his sweetheart and asked to remain in Jericho. He would live in the family house and start his new home. So it was that Reuben, Miriam, Eliezer, and Naomi packed up their belongings and made the trip back to the family's old farmstead.

Daniel was at the farm to greet Reuben and his family. He excitedly took the men on a tour of all the changes and filled them in on how the crops had performed over the recent years. Reuben was filled with nostalgia as he remembered the years working there with his father, followed by the struggle of trying to keep the farm. He was grateful for all that Daniel had done and noticed that Daniel, too, had a look of pride in his own eyes as he handed Reuben the deed to the property. As Reuben walked back to the house to Miriam and Naomi, he realized that he had a deep sense of peace and belonging in his heart. He was home again. His soul was at rest. The hard times were in the past, and the future had never looked better. God was caring for them and blessing them. He was happy.

CHAPTER 4

The Blessings

Over the last three chapters, we have looked at several key pieces of information that can help us better understand Jesus' Sermon on the Mount and its social justice themes. The first piece was that Jesus begins, and continues, his ministry with the revelation that a "kingdom of heaven" is at hand. A "kingdom" implies structures, policies, rules and creeds—citizens working together. It survives when its citizens follow the kingdom's tenets. The Jewish people had laws from God, but they also had a promise that God would send to them further commands via a future prophet. He would have God's words and commands, as did Moses, and they would need to obey his commands.

We also looked at the probability that the people of Jesus' day had good reason to believe that this kingdom was at hand. Jewish prophecies had been predicting it, and the prophecies of this kingdom in the book of Daniel appeared to point to the time around Jesus' birth. Daniel's prophecy also indicated that there was a strong relationship between the final kingdom of "stone" and the law of God given from His holy mountain. Jewish history recalls God's people being given the laws on stone tablets while God met with them at a mountain. Jewish poetry cites God as a "rock" of refuge and salvation, and frequently calls His place of residence a mountain.

Finally, we looked at the laws and discovered that their commands—especially the Sabbath commands—have a foundation of social justice. God's law is concerned with those in society who are suffering or have fallen behind and are now disadvantaged. He commanded that we remember these suffering neighbors and give them rest. He has encouraged and created systems to periodically balance disparities of power and equity.

If Jesus is the "Prophet" like Moses, and the one ushering in this predicted kingdom of heaven, we can expect that he will teach true to the law of God.[55] He will support the law, and we should expect to see that his teachings will reveal its tenets. My position is that Jesus does do this, and that the Sermon on the Mount is a foundational manifesto of this kingdom that undoubtedly reveals Jesus' support for God's law and its social justice themes. Our background investigation is finished. Now, we need to look forward and see how Jesus launches us into his epic sermon.

Jesus' Sermon on the Mount, as it is recorded in the book of Matthew, begins with a series of nine encouraging statements.[56] These statements are directed to a wide variety of life circumstances, from poverty to wealth, mercy to persecution. Each of these statements begins with the same Greek word, "*Makarios*,"[57] meaning "supremely blessed." These nine blessings from Jesus Christ have become known as the "Beatitudes," an English word which means "utmost bliss" or "supreme blessedness." The word "supreme" (or "supremely") is a word that references something of the highest possible rank or quality or finality. In other words, it does not get any better than whatever is labeled *supreme*. *Supremely blessed* is as good as a blessing can get.

Most English translations of the Bible generally prefer to translate *makarios* using the word "*blessed*" or "*happy*."

---

[55] Deuteronomy 13:1–4; 18:18–19 and Isaiah 8:20

[56] Matthew 5:3–11

[57] Strong's Word NT:3107 meaning "supremely blessed," "fortunate," "well off."

But do either of these words truly capture the meaning within Jesus' mind as he spoke these blessings? I believe both fall short of the idea that the word *makarios* appears to be encapsulating. Even Jesus' pronouncement of a supreme blessing often seems to be contradictory to the situation to which he connects it. After all, Jesus' nine statements are all framed with the implication that the supreme blessings or happiness comes to us despite the wide variety of deficient circumstances of which he speaks. Does happiness really come from being poor, or a mourner? Are the persecuted really expected to be in a happy state of mind? Of course, the answer is "no," at least not at face value. However, Jesus constructs each of his nine statements with balancing outcomes which serve to trigger the reason for one to be blessed regardless of his situation. For example, Jesus states: "Blessed are those who mourn, for they shall be comforted." The blessing is not found in the "mourning," but in the fact that they will be "comforted." It is the action of being comforted that results in their blessed state. The blessing, a supreme one, is in the comfort they receive. Pain and suffering are a reality of life, but they can be mitigated by actions to relieve them. It is the action that brings about the blessing.

All nine of Jesus' statements have some balancing condition that will make the life situations he mentions "blessed." He does not elaborate on those conditions for the most part, but it is not hard to deduce that a change will need to take place for the individual to be blessed. In short, a blessing follows as an outcome of an action—either by God or by one of His followers. The mourner is blessed because of comfort he receives; the merciful is blessed through his giving of mercy, which in turn results in his receipt of mercy. The peacemaker is blessed in his efforts to make peace. The word *makarios* is therefore more than a state of mind; it is the fruit of the effort to bring about goodwill to other individuals. It is a supreme blessing that we experience internally, but we obtain it through our external actions of benevolence. Jesus' audience, educated in the words of the Old Testament and its laws, would have understood Jesus' connections between the stated blessings and their related required actions. The Old Testament is filled with examples of these connections, as we will soon see.

As we look more closely at each of Jesus' nine beatitudes, it will become clear that his statements are not pacifying symbolisms of future hope. Not at all! They are, instead, calls for the members of the kingdom of heaven to be socially active in creating the blessings Jesus is revealing; the members of this kingdom of heaven will be the blessings. The beatitudes are nothing short of a rallying cry for Jews and Christians to be social justice practitioners and advocates. This will become obvious very soon. Before we get there, however, let us take care of some prerequisites.

Our translations of this sermon come from Greek texts, but it is not likely that Jesus spoke this sermon to the local people of his day in the Greek language. Jesus' audience was not Greek, but instead made up of common folk of Judea and Galilee. Most likely he used the local Aramaic language or its close relative, Hebrew. So, our English versions of this sermon are translations of translations. This is not necessarily a problem. We have a wealth of information today to help linguists derive accurate meanings of ancient texts. That process, however, is not the scope of this book. Suffice it to say, I believe that the English words "blessed" or "happy" are good, though somewhat weak, equivalents for the word Jesus used. Nevertheless, to get a better understanding, we do need to dig deeper into the language and the sermon's context to crack the meaning of Jesus' message. Jesus' word choice for these nine opening statements was deliberate.

That word's historical use helps shape the meanings of Jesus' nine statements. When traced back to the Old Testament, that word reveals a social justice link, which is the scope of this book. So, let us take a closer look at Jesus' word "blessed."

The equivalent Hebrew word that is used in the Old Testament, and perhaps by Jesus, for *blessed* is "*esher.*"[58] It merely means "happiness" and is translated into English as "blessed" and "happy." *Esher*, however, is derived from a more primitive root that implies the origin of the happiness. That word is "*ashar.*"[59] Its meaning is a bit more varied and complex. It means "to be straight," but its use implies being "correct," "level," "honest" and "happy." It also carries with it the figurative implications of guidance and relief. Visually, this is not hard to comprehend. People traveling on a straight, level, well-marked pathway are relieved to know they are not lost. They are "happy" that their destination lies at the end of a good path, and they move forward in confidence.

This illustration of a safe pathway is one that is frequently used throughout the Old Testament to indicate that one is safe when walking within the law of God—trusting the guidance that God has given. The word "*esher*", in its various grammatical forms, is often combined with these illustrations. For example:

> Blessed (*esher*) is the man who walks not in the counsel of the ungodly, . . . but his delight is in the law of the Lord, . . . he shall be like a tree planted by the rivers of water. (Psalm 1:1–3)
>
> Blessed (*esher*) are the undefiled in the way, who walk in the law of the

---

58 Strong's Word OT:835
59 Strong's Word OT:833

Lord! . . . Then would I not be ashamed.
(Psalm 119:1, 6)

"Now therefore, listen to me, my children: for blessed (*esher*) are those who
keep my ways. . . . For whoever finds me,
finds life, and obtains favor from the Lord."
(Proverbs 8:32, 35)

To comprehend the length and breadth of the word
esher, I identified that it is used forty-five times in the Old
Testament. By reviewing each of these references, I observed
that the word is used in association with approximately nine
different themes. On many occasions the use of the word in
a verse can likewise fulfill the intent of multiple themes. So,
I listed the meaning of each of the forty-five verses into one
or more of the themes, to see if I could discover the most
common usage. Below is a summary of my top four rankings
in descending order from most used to least used.

Happy (*esher*) are those who obey the law of God.
Happy (*esher*) are those who have the Lord as their
God—a source of safety.
Happy (*esher*) are those who trust in God.
Happy (*esher*) are those who are guided (corrected) by
God.

These four were the dominant themes but happiness was
also afforded to those who resided in God's presence, had been
forgiven of their iniquities, had family stability, victories in battles, and to those who have competent national leadership. All
of these are worth remembering.

It is clear to see from these dominant themes that happiness
(*esher*) has a direct connection to one's belief in God, and

more importantly, one's belief that God is trustworthy and His guidance, via His laws, is the best course in life. Trust and obedience are what makes the individual "happy." There is safety in following God's law. His path is the best path.

This strong connection between happiness and following God's laws, His path, as seen in the Old Testament, begs the question as to whether, Jesus—a Jewish rabbi—might also be making the same connection between happiness and obedience to God's law when he spoke the Beatitudes. I would argue that he is, and yet he does it without ever mentioning a direct reference to God's law. Instead, he includes with each blessing a condition for the blessing, which upon closer inspection reveals the law of God in action. Implementation of the condition, on someone's part, is implementation of the law, which brings about the blessing.

The connection between happiness and God's law requires a closer look at God's law. How does following God's law make an individual happy? How does following God's law make for a happier community? This can best be illustrated by focusing on a specific example and seeing how a law's implementation affects society. Let us take, for example, the eighth command of the Ten Commandments: "You shall not steal." Imagine a society where everyone always follows this commandment faithfully. In such a society, an individual would no longer be afraid of any of his belongings being taken. He would have trust in his neighbors, and his neighbors would have trust in him. There might not be a need for locksmiths in such a society. Why lock a door if no one is going to take what is behind the door? This level of peace, from not having to worry about thieves, would be a blessing—it would foster happiness.

But the words "You shall not steal" can, and do, have implications that far exceed the safety of our personal belongings. For example, an employer can be tightfisted in what he pays an employee. If the withholding of a fair wage is being done simply due to the greed of the employer, the employer is stealing from the laborer. One might also attempt to elevate one's status by taking credit for something he was not fully responsible for. This would be the theft of someone else's credit and respect.

The words, "You shall not steal" call for individuals to have the highest level of respect for a neighbor's possessions, their welfare, and dignity within our community. You, as an individual within such a community, benefit from the implementation of everything this law implies. When a community follows this law implicitly, everyone is a blessing to all their neighbors, and all their neighbors are a blessing to them. They are all much happier. This one law, when implemented by everyone, becomes a blessing—a supreme blessing— to the whole community. So, the law, even though it is stated as a command for personal application—a standard *you* are to live by—it is made with the benefit of the community in mind. It is to be implemented individually but experienced corporately.

OK, fine, but let us say that you live in a society where you are the only person following God's commandment, "You shall not steal." You might still find some peace of mind—happiness, blessing—in knowing you have been faithful to your God and have obeyed His command. Nevertheless, you will need to install locks on your doors, watch your neighbors, check your paycheck, and mistrust the motives of others in your community. The greater blessing and happiness that comes from community participation of the axiom "You shall not steal" will not be realized. You cannot, therefore, fully experience the blessing that this law holds unless the entire society participates in the condition of not stealing.

I would argue that this is true of any one of God's laws. They were designed as commands that individuals should apply to their lives, but the greatest benefit to the community comes from the sum of all individuals following the same law. Justice—fairness, equity, righteousness—therefore is experienced when a community accepts its individual obligations to create a corporate lifestyle that blesses all individuals. In short, I have been commanded to "not steal," and as all my neighbors and I participate in "not stealing," we all benefit with a supremely blessed and happy community.

Jesus' Beatitudes, as we will soon see, are presenting this corporate concept of right doing as beneficial to all members of society. Blessings arise from the actions taken by members of the kingdom of heaven. These blessings, though felt individually, have a far greater effect when kingdom members act to benefit their communities. The communal blessings are the result of the implementation of societal justice—the implementation of righteousness and its equity obligations within our communities. What you will soon see is Jesus teaching the obedience to God's law embedded within statements of encouragement and blessing. We may have difficulty seeing the obvious connections today, but in the mindset of the religious faithful of Jesus' audience, the connection of happiness and obedience to God was not lost. Happiness was always connected to faith in, and obedience to, God. It still is!

We are about to embark on an in-depth investigation of Jesus' Sermon on the Mount and discover its overtly social justice implications. But I want you to be aware of something first. Jesus' Sermon on the Mount appears twice in the Gospels. It is found in the book of Matthew chapters five to seven, and again in the book of Luke chapter six. Matthew's version is far more detailed. Luke's version is abridged but has details that are not found in Matthew's version—this is especially true of Luke's Beatitudes and his inclusion of a group of counterbalancing "woes." While some people have difficulty with this and consider it a reason to discredit the Gospel accounts, I have no problems with a dual record. In fact, I consider it a benefit to those of us who want to truly understand the words and intents of Jesus' teachings.

The Gospels plainly show that Jesus traveled about teaching the people concerning the kingdom of heaven (or the kingdom of God, as referenced in several of the Gospels). I personally believe that the Sermon on the Mount was a regular dissertation given by Jesus as he traveled from town to town, region to region. To think that he only gave the sermon once is a dubious position to take. In Jesus' day there were no audio recorders, no video cameras, no podcasts, no live streaming, and no real-time dictation of the sermon by a scribe. So how did we get this sermon in such detail? Simple, the Sermon on the Mount's themes were the basis of Jesus' teaching of the kingdom of heaven. As he traveled from town to town, he repeated these themes (with variations) to many new crowds of listeners over and over again. His disciples would have heard this message repeatedly, and just as *repetition is the mother of all learning*, Jesus' repetition of these themes would have cemented his teachings in the minds of his followers.

On this deduced basis, I believe that the book of Matthew merely records this epic, widely repeated, sermon as it is re-called from one, or more, of Jesus' disciples, while the book of Luke records the sermon themes as it was recalled by his source materials. The sermons, though similar and different, are com-plimentary. The details of each will benefit our investigation.

One last point needs to be made regarding this sermon before we start. Many Christians take the position that this sermon is a "spiritual" one, and that a direct literal interpretation of the actions Jesus requests is not humanly possible. They also argue that trying to follow a literal interpretation of this sermon is an act of self-righteousness that will exclude your entrance into the kingdom of heaven. Thus, Jesus' plain and straight-forward sayings are said to mean something other than his plain and straight-forward sayings. "Spiritual" interpretations tend to focus Jesus' message to one that only benefits a select class of Christians, and they water down Jesus' universal calls for faith and social action.

Others argue that Jesus is only speaking to his disciples and the listening crowds of his day, and that his message is a pre-crucifixion/resurrection message. His message was only true, it is argued, for his time and his people. His message, therefore, should not be seen as having universal or present-day application. This is the view that Jesus' message is for an earlier dispensation of time.

I do not take either of these positions, because I find them to be dangerously reminiscent of the serpent's ploys to deceive Adam and Eve in the Garden of Eden. As you can recall, the serpent's deception was based on statements that God's word was not valid. The above arguments likewise imply that Jesus does not mean what he says. This is a dangerous position to take. Nevertheless, I do not object to the spiritualized interpretations of this sermon and feel that these Christianized interpretations do have value, but they are only one layer of a multi-layered onion. I also understand that much of what Jesus said does concern future followers experiencing the blessings of which he spoke. However, there are also literal meanings to Jesus' words, backed by the teachings of the Old Testament, and these should never be diminished. A careful analysis of these blessings, and the supporting details of Jesus' sermon, will show us that what Jesus taught in this sermon has literal benefits to Christians and nonbelievers alike. It benefitted the people in his day and continued to benefit readers of this sermon throughout the centuries. And now, his sermon is a present-day call to action. It always has been that way.

We should not bend the words of Jesus to fit modern Christian paradigms. We should let Jesus talk through scripture and then try to understand what he meant for the generation he addressed in person and what he meant for future generations. For example, within Jesus' sermon he calls for his disciples to be *"perfect, just as your Father in heaven is perfect."*[60] Many theologians today point to this as evidence that Jesus' sermon asks for impossible standards, and it is therefore a sermon based, supposedly, on an outdated Old Testament covenant. However, in the context of this command, we will see that Jesus portrayed the Father as the giver of sunlight to the good and to the evil, and rain to the just and to the unjust. Jesus' point, in the context of his command, is that the Father's generous gifts are not limited to only those who follow him. Being *"perfect"* like the Father, therefore means to be generous like the Father—giving without bias. Certainly, this is a standard we too can reach.

Likewise, we should not consider Jesus' message as being directed to only his disciples. The books of Matthew and Luke both record that the sermon was given with his disciples present, but both Gospels make it known that large crowds were also present to hear. Matthew ends his account by emphasizing that the crowd was intently listening to Jesus' sermon and that they were *"astonished at his teachings."* Jesus was not hiding anything from them while attempting only to speak to his disciples. His message was, and still is, for anyone willing to listen.

Before Jesus' ascension back to heaven, Matthew and Mark record that Jesus tells his disciples to go into all the nations and teach them what he has taught. This command is for the purpose of making more disciples, but in order to do this, the teachings of Jesus need to be spoken to non-disciples

---

[60] Matthew 5:48

first. But first, these teachings of Christ must also be lived by his disciples, if the appeal of the gospel is to reach the nations. And the living out of the gospel—following the teachings of the Sermon on the Mount—will have benefits for believers and nonbelievers, the just and the unjust, and for those living today—post crucifixion and resurrection. This will become clear in *Social Justice Jesus* chapters to come. Are you ready? We are about to jump into a fascinating study!

PART II

The Sermon on the Mount
The Beatitudes:
They Are About Equity

CHAPTER 5

Blessed Are the Melancholic Beggars

"Blessed are the poor in spirit,
for theirs is the kingdom of heaven."

Matthew 5:3

This introductory beatitude, and its promise, is foundational to the rest of Jesus' sermon. It sets a tone for the whole of the sermon, and we need to get it right if we are going to comprehend the reasons for everything else Jesus has to say. We have a lot of fascinating ground to cover. To make things easier for the reader, I will break the chapter up into several progressive topical sections, so you can stop at one thought and later pick up again at the next, if you need to take a break.

So, let us begin our study of the Sermon on the Mount and attempt to find its true and deep meanings as Jesus had intended the crowds to comprehend it. To do this, however, I ask that you participate with an open mind to what I have to say. Remember this sermon was given before there were any Christian theologians or denominations. This sermon was given to Jewish men and women, some of whom are new disciples of Jesus and others are just crowding around to discover what they can about this new rabbi's teachings. Most of them are poor, hardworking folk, trying to survive and care for their families. You will get a better understanding of this sermon if you join them—if you become one of them. So, put yourself into a dusty robe, strap sandals onto your feet, and walk on over to that hill where the new rabbi is about to begin speaking about the kingdom of heaven. Do not worry about the fact that it is a one-hour walk to your village and the sun is beginning to drift to the west. This is Jesus, the one that John the Baptist has been saying was going to come after him. You are lucky to have crossed his path today, and you do not know when this itinerant rabbi will be back in this region again. You should stay! This is your chance to hear what he has to say.

Those first words that come from Jesus' mouth, *"Blessed are the poor in spirit, for theirs is the kingdom of heaven,"* are packed with meaning. Jesus intended them to be that way, for the most part he is speaking to the poor, and he wants to have their attention. Since this sermon was first uttered, we seem to have lost this simple fact. Nearly two thousand years have passed, and numerous Christian theologians and denominations have had their chance to bend its meaning until it complies with their Christian paradigm. It is not that our modern interpretations and applications are bad, or even wrong for that matter, it is merely that many of us have forgotten that the original audience was poor. We internalize Jesus' words within the context of our present-day reality, and within the teaching of our Christian faith. Jesus, however, for the most part, was speaking to Jews—poor Jews.

Let me give you a few examples of how we change this message: here is an explanation from the website of well-known evangelist, Dr. Billy Graham, that answers the question, *"What does it mean to be poor in spirit"*?

> Simply this: We must be humble in our spirits. If you put the word "humble" in place of the word "poor," you will understand what [Jesus] meant. In other words, when we come to God, we must re-

alize our own sin and our spiritual emptiness and poverty. We must not be self-satisfied or proud in our hearts, thinking we don't really need God.[61]

This answer has excellent spiritual points, and it is worth heeding Dr. Graham's advice regarding how we should approach God. Dr. Graham, however, is clearly focusing on a spiritual interpretation rather than a literal one, but is this what Jesus is telling his audience? We will soon look at the meaning of some of the key words that Jesus used, but at the moment I am asking myself whether or not it is a good idea to substitute Jesus' word "poor" for the word "humble." After all, the authors of the books of Matthew and Luke, where this beatitude is recorded, chose a particular Greek word for "poor." They chose not to use a Greek word for "humble." This would seem to highlight their understanding of what Jesus is saying, and their choice of word indicates material poverty, as we will soon see.

Another site answers the question *"What does it mean to be poor in Spirit?"* this way:

> To be poor in spirit is to recognize your utter spiritual bankruptcy before God. It is understanding that you have absolutely nothing of worth to offer God. Being poor in spirit is admitting that, because of your sin, you are completely destitute spiritually and can do nothing to deliver yourself from your dire situation. Jesus is saying that, no matter your status in life, you must recognize your spiritual poverty before you can come to God in faith to receive the salvation He offers.[62]

---

[61] https://billygraham.org/answer/what-does-it-mean-to-be-poor-in-spirit-as-jesus-said-we-ought-to-be/

[62] https://www.gotquestions.org/poor-in-spirit.html

This answer certainly fits modern Christian paradigms, but I would like to point out that we do have something of worth to offer to God—ourselves. After all, Jesus suffered tremendously—willingly sacrificing his life—because of the high value he and the Father placed on humanity. Some would also argue that there is something one can do to improve their "spiritual poverty." They can follow the promptings of God's Spirit and accept His gifts of repentance and forgiveness, and begin walking with God. This answer is subject to numerous theological debates. Suffice it to say, I question how anyone within Jesus' audience that day would have extracted such a complex, spiritual meaning from his simple statement.

Dietrich Bonhoeffer when writing on this beatitude wrote, in part, the following:

> Privation is the lot of the disciples in every sphere of their lives. They are the 'poor' tout court. . . . For [Jesus'] sake they have lost all. In following him they lost even their own selves, and everything that could make them rich. . . . They have their treasure in secret; they find it on the cross. And they have the promise that they will one day visibly enjoy the glory of the kingdom, which in principle is already realized in the utter poverty of the cross.[63]

Bonhoeffer's comments are quite poetic, but they are clearly placed in the context of a post resurrection understanding. Such meaning would have been incomprehensible to Jesus' audience sitting on a mountain on that long-ago day. All three of these examples have merits but they demonstrate the modernization of Jesus' words and the spiritualization of

---

[63] Dietrich Bonhoeffer, *The Cost of Discipleship* (New York: Simon & Schuster, 1959), pp. 107, 108.

his message. What we really need is information that will help us comprehend what the common people sitting before Jesus would have understood him to be saying. Let us place this beatitude back into its first century CE context.

The key words we need to look at are "poor" and "spirit." What do they tell us and the people of Jesus' day? Let us start with the word "poor." The word used for "poor" in this passage is the Greek word "*ptóchos*"[64] It means to be a beggar or a pauper and denotes that one is in that condition because of no other alternative. It pictures a person crouching or cringing as a beggar being timid and hopeful for the goodwill of others. This is a picture that Jesus' audience can identify with.

The Greek language has another word that translates into English as "poor." The Gospel writers could have used it. It is "*penes*"[65] and it means one who toils for daily subsistence, a hungry person working to feed himself, an indigent person. The picture here is of a poor person, but one who has enough capacity to do something to help himself. The author, however, chooses the word that pictures someone who has sunk to an even lower state of capacity and now must beg for their subsistence.

The word "spirit" or "in spirit" comes from the Greek word "*pneuma.*"[66] It literally means a current of air, a breeze, or a breath. All three are invisible but essential for life. The word can also mean angels or demons, again something invisible but having an influence on the visible world. Figuratively, the Greeks saw the rational and irrational aspects of the human soul or emotions as an invisible but tangible part of life. These qualities are driven by *pneuma* as well. "Spirit"

---

[64] Strong's Word NT:4434

[65] Strong's Word NT:3993

[66] Strong's Word NT:4151

is therefore one's mental disposition, as in one being in *good spirits*, or *poor spirits*.

The two words "poor" and "spirit" in this beatitude are tied together with another Greek word. It is the word *"to"*[67] (not to be confused with our English preposition with the same letters). The word is in a dative form. It is an adjective and a common technique used to indicate that the word "spirit" is describing, or adding, something more to the word "poor". In our case, our "beggar" is in some condition of "spirit." The context of the beatitude would logically dictate that we consider beggars to be depressed and sorrowful individuals— melancholic beggars. This is understandable given their status in life. However, Jesus' pronouncement is that poor, depressed beggars have a reason to be happy—"for theirs is the kingdom of heaven."

Is it possible that what Jesus is saying in this first beatitude is that poor, depressed beggars have a reason to be happy because they are going to have a part of the coming kingdom of heaven? Is Jesus actually describing a particular sector of society that is to be a beneficiary? The answer is "Yes," especially when one looks at the parallel Sermon on the Mount given by the Gospel of Luke.

Luke's Sermon on the Mount is recorded in chapter six of his Gospel. Like Matthew's sermon the first beatitude deals with the poor. It reads as follows:

Blessed are the poor, for yours is the kingdom of heaven[68]

Luke uses the same Greek word for "poor," meaning beggars or paupers. Note, however, he ignores making any mention about their mental (spirit) state. Luke's source material understood this beatitude to be simply about the poor.

This is further strengthened by the fact that Luke's sermon

---

[67] Strong's Word NT:3588
[68] Luke 6:20

has Jesus including a list of contrasting "woes" which off-set each beatitude. The woe that counterbalances the phrase "Blessed are the poor" is as follows:

> *But woe to you who are rich, for you have received your consolation.*[69]

The word "woe"[70] means "grief," and the word "rich"[71] means someone who is *wealthy*; they have *money, possessions, fullness.* There is nothing in Luke's recorded beatitude or its contrasting woe that implies that these two groups are anything other than the "poor" versus the "rich."

When considering the details of both Matthew and Luke's Sermon on the Mount, there really is no reason to assume that Jesus' first beatitude is speaking of anyone other than the lowest poor of his society. Matthew's inclusion of Jesus' qualifier of the beggar's mental state does however have value. Presenting the beggars as mentally depressed or anxious— *poor in spirit*—deepens their plight, but it also amplifies the degree of happiness that Jesus is promising.

Jesus' statement that the lowest of the poor are going to be happy because theirs is the kingdom of heaven is a pro-found and provocative opening statement. Jesus' audience would have understood him to be speaking of beggars, but his association of them as the "blessed" of the kingdom would be a cultural shock to their minds. The Jewish paradigm of Jesus' day was that wealth was an indication of God's favor or blessing. Poverty, or worse yet, something that led to one having to be a beggar, was an indication of God's displeasure or judgment on that person.

---

[69] Luke 6:24

[70] Strong's Word NT:3759

[71] Strong's Word NT:4145 from 4149

We see this belief revealed in the Gospels. On one occasion Jesus' disciples see a beggar who was born blind, and they ask Jesus if the man's blindness was due to his personal sin or the sin of his parents.[72] They see his blindness, and the poverty it led to, as a judgment of God. Wealth in their minds is a blessing. On another occasion Jesus tells his disciples that *"it is hard for a rich man to enter into the Kingdom of God."*[73] In astonishment his disciples ask, *"Who than can be saved?"* In their minds a rich person is already well on his way into the kingdom, his wealth is proof of that—God has been blessing him.

There was good precedent for these beliefs. The Torah promises good fortune and health to the Israelites if they obeyed God. It likewise lists poverty and disease as the results of not following God as he commanded. The words "blessed' and "cursed" are associated with these possible outcomes. The wise Jewish King Solomon once gave the proverb that, *"The blessing of the Lord makes one rich, and He adds no sorrow with it."*[74]

For Jesus to proclaim, from his opening statement no less, that the depressed beggars are to be happy because the kingdom of heaven is for them, puts the present-day Jewish values on its head. It was an inversion of what people would have expected Jesus to say. It would seem to defy the law of God as they knew it. Nevertheless, at the same time, it is exciting news for Jesus' poor audience. It meant that the coming kingdom of heaven is within their reach, too—despite their poverty. They had a chance to participate and to benefit. Likewise, Jesus' "woe" to the rich was an inversion of Jewish values. It viewed one's wealth as a possible liability, not an asset. In contrast to the first beatitude, it appears to exclude the rich from the happiness of the kingdom to come.

---

[72] John 9:2

[73] Matthew 19:23

[74] Proverbs 10:22

I see no reason to modernize or spiritualize the words of Jesus when trying to understand his meaning of this beatitude. In fact, I think doing so detracts from his message. It puts a person on a wrong footing and sets them in a direction that Jesus is not intending. This could be dangerous to our relationship to God. We need to be correct here from the beginning. So, are there other reasons why we can believe that this first beatitude is about the "poor" and not about the spiritual mindset of prospective members of this soon coming kingdom of heaven? The answer is, "Yes," and we will begin by looking now at several of these circumstantial pieces of evidence.

A. Parallel Beatitude in the Book of Luke

We have already looked at Jesus' first beatitude as recorded by Luke, that corresponds to Matthew's *first beatitude* concerning the poor. We also saw that Jesus adds a counterbalancing "woe" that is critical of the rich and is not found in Matthew's version of the Sermon on the Mount. Shortly, we will take a quick look at *another beatitude* that is found only in Luke. This is the second beatitude in his series. But first, let me ask you a question. When you think of someone who is impoverished, what pictures come to your mind? One of your thoughts may be of someone who is hungry—a person or family who does not have enough food. Well, this is the topic of Jesus' *second beatitude* as recorded by Luke. It reads as follows:

Blessed are you who hunger now, for you shall be filled.[75]

Should it come as any surprise that immediately after Jesus addresses the "poor," he would also address a major concern of the poor, which is being hungry? No, it is not a surprise, but it is a proof that the first beatitude is indeed being directed to a physical state of being, more so than a spiritual condition.

---

[75] Luke 6:21

Jesus also has a counterbalancing woe for this second beatitude, it reads as follows:

Woe to you who are full, for you shall hunger.[76]

This woe reverses the tables on the rich and the poor, the full and the hungry. It might be incorrect to read too much into these passages, but my first instinct is to conclude that the food that fills the hungry could be the food that was once filling the full. In short, the resources of the rich will be taken to meet the needs of the poor.

This picture does not appear here for the first time in the Bible. You might find it interesting to learn that two different women in the Bible, both of whom were mothers of children with miraculous births, share a similar praise to God and mention these very themes. It is worth sharing. The first woman is Hannah, the mother of Samuel, the Old Testament prophet. When she gave the young Samuel to God's service in the Temple, she gave a prayer of thanksgiving which includes these lines:

> *The Lord makes poor and makes rich; He brings low and lifts up. He raises the poor from the dust and lifts the beggar from the ash heap, to set them among princes and make them inherit the throne of glory.*[77]

Years later, Mary, the mother of Jesus, will echo these words in her praise to God for choosing her to be the mother of our Lord. She states the following:

> *He has put down the mighty from their thrones and exalted the lowly. He has filled the*

---

[76] Luke 6:25

[77] I Samuel 2:6–8

hungry with good things, and the rich He has sent away empty.[78]

It appears that those who follow God are aware that God routinely confounds the conventional wisdom of people. He likes to bring about the opposite of what we expect. Jesus himself is famous for saying many variations of *the last shall be first, and the first shall be last.* God finds irony in reversing the roles of men. I see no reason to not take Jesus literally and conclude that the kingdom of heaven is elevating and benefiting the literal, and even the lowest, poor of the community. Why can't Matthew's first beatitude be about depressed beggars and the fact that the kingdom of heaven is for their benefit now?

B. The Poor in the Torah and the Prophets

When one reads the entire Torah and the other books of the Old Testament, especially its prophets and psalms, it will be noticed that God has much to say about the poor. He has made multiple commands regarding how the poor should be treated. If convicted for a crime, they are to be treated as any other man, but civilly they are to be assisted with special attention and care so that they are not neglected or abused by others.

In chapter three we looked at one of the Sabbath laws that required the forgiving of debts every Year of Release. We quoted a portion of the book of Deuteronomy that forbids the withholding of loans just because the Year of Release was nearing. God referred to this as doing *"evil against your poor brother."* This law, however, was prefaced by a command that required assistance to the poor, regardless of when he needed assistance. Here it is again.

---

[78] Luke 1:52–53

If there is among you a poor man of your brethren, within any of the gates in your land which the Lord your God is giving you, you shall not harden your heart nor shut your hand from your poor brother, but you shall open your hand wide to him and willingly lend him sufficient for his need, whatever he needs. Beware lest there be a wicked thought in your heart, saying, "The seventh year, the year of release, is at hand," and your eye be evil against your poor brother and you give him nothing, and he cry out to the Lord against you, and it became sin among you. You shall surely give to him, and your heart should not be grieved when you give to him, because for this thing the Lord your God will bless you in all your works and in all to which you put your hand. For the poor will never cease from the land; therefore I command you, saying, "You shall open your hand wide to your brother, to your poor and your needy, in your land."[79]

You might recall that the laws were given to the Israelites for the purpose of making them a *"kingdom of priests and a holy nation."*[80] It is interesting to note that within this kingdom God foresaw the existence of both rich and poor. And He commanded that those with means were to be the ones to provide for those without means. It was the duty of the rich to alleviate the suffering of the poor. This was part of the structure of the kingdom that the God of heaven was trying to build here on earth through the Israelite nation. Jesus' first beatitude echoes this plan.

---

[79] Deuteronomy 15:7–11
[80] Exodus 19:5–6

Besides the above, the Torah has numerous references regarding special attention given to the poor. The poor are not to be cheated. They are to be judged fairly and correctly. They are not to be charged interest on a loan. A poor person's pledge is to be returned each night, and wages are to be paid daily so that person can eat. Poor people are allowed to glean the fields and orchards as needed to meet their needs. Farmers are to intentionally leave some of their crops for the poor to glean. And as we have noted earlier, those in need are to be assisted as much as they need.

The "poor," however, are not the only ones the law cares for; it adds other groups as well—the fatherless, the widow and the stranger (or foreigner in need). All these classes of individuals are to be given special attention, and those who are to meet the needs of these individuals are the ones who have the means to help. The Torah plainly demonstrates that God's kingdom has a special concern for the disadvantaged sectors of society. And it offers blessing to those who heed and address His concerns.

This concern, however, is not limited to the Torah only. The book of Psalms repeatedly mentions God's concern for the poor and how he will defend them. The Old Testament prophets are also filled with repeated calls to care for the poor, but more often they reveal that God's judgments are, in part, the result of failures to properly care for the poor, fatherless, widows, or strangers.

You might recall the story in the book of Genesis, where God destroys the city of Sodom with fire. Nearly all Christians will state that this was done due to the city's excessive sexual immorality. However, few Christians are aware of the reasons that are given by the prophet Ezekiel. Sexual immorality was only one of its sins; its pride and the failure to equitably care for others was the bulk of its immoralities. Ezekiel records the following:

> *Look, this was the iniquity of your sister Sodom: She and her daughter had pride, fullness of food, and abundance of idleness; neither did she strengthen the hand of the poor and needy. And they were haughty and committed abomination before Me; therefore, I took them away as I saw fit.*[81]

I can only scratch the surface of this subject in this small section. I would invite you to do a concordance word search on the words, "poor," "fatherless," "widow(s)," and "stranger(s)," and review your results line by line. God's concern for the disadvantaged, and the duty He places on others of means to assist them, will become abundantly clear. So too, will the fact that His kingdom—His people—are to be the means by which He defends and cares for the disadvantaged.

C. The Poor and Rich in Jesus' Day—Hillel the Elder

I would now like to bring to your attention a curious and unfortunate event that occurred in the generation prior to Jesus' birth. I consider it a profoundly serious collapse of Jewish law and faith in God.[82] It would impact the people of Jesus' day, and I believe it was a subject of Jesus' ministry, though he never refers to it by name. It is called the *Prosbul.* Have you ever heard of it?

The *Prosbul* (from Greek, meaning *before the assembly of counselors*, or *in front of the court*) was a legal procedure introduced into Judaism by Hillel the Elder in the first century BCE. It permitted the making of personal loans to people in need without fear, on the part of the lender, that his debt

---

[81] Ezekiel 16:49–50

[82] This is my opinion, which I will argue soon, but let it be understood that others consider the *Prosbul* to be a valid implementation of Jewish law that was of great help to Jewish society.

would be legally cancelled at the end of a Year of Release. In short, it was a way to circumvent the requirements of forgiving debts as instructed in the Torah.[83] The procedure allowed creditors to register loans before the courts thus transferring a personal loan into a corporate, or civil debt which was considered to be exempt from the requirements of the law. Civil authorities would then collect payments on behalf of the creditor. No doubt there were fees for this registered transfer and the related collection services, so civil administrations benefited from the Prosbuls.

Now, one might wonder how such a blatant violation of the Torah could be enacted, especially at the direction of one of Judaism's leading religious leaders of the day. It is actually quite logical, and I will explain how. In the first century BCE, Jewish commerce was experiencing a lending liquidity problem. People in need would seek a loan from someone, but lenders, fearing that they would lose property, especially if a Year of Release were near, would refuse to give loans. As a result, loans were not being made, and individuals and the economy were suffering. The issue was becoming a serious one until Hillel the Elder stepped in with a solution.

Hillel noticed that the Torah's command that debts be forgiven at the end of a Year of Release pertained to personal debts made to a "neighbor" or "brother." Civil and corporate debts were debts to the entire community and were not, therefore, subject to the Year of Release's injunction—at least that was Hillel's interpretation. So, while all personal debts needed to be forgiven, any loan registered with a court would need to be paid in full over the course of its agreed upon term. A *Prosbul* was the documentation of a loan with a recognized legal authority, thus transferring a personal debt to the civil authorities for collection.

---

[83] Deuteronomy 15:1–11

This solution was not without merit given the spiritual climate of the day. Lenders could now make loans without fear of losing their property (wealth), and people in need found it easier to get loans to address their needs. Initially, the *Prosbul* could only be issued if the debtor had some real property to serve as collateral for the loan, but eventually the system deteriorated to the point where even the ownership of a flowerpot, or a small parcel of land lent to the debtor by the creditor was considered valid collateral. The *Prosbul* was a legal loophole, but it did solve an economic problem and got money flowing more freely.

I said earlier that I felt this event was a profoundly serious collapse of Jewish law and faith in God. You may already see why, but here is my opinion. The legal requirement made by God to forgive debt at the end of each Year of Release—a sabbatical year—served three purposes. One, it released the debtor of a financial burden in keeping with the Sabbath law's intentions of releasing individuals from burdens, thus giving them rest. Second, it clearly functioned as a wealth redistribution vehicle within society to prevent increasing disparities between the needy and those with the means to meet their needs. Third, the law itself foresaw that the rich would balk at this principle, and commanded that they do not harden their hearts and refuse loans as a Year of Release approached. God promised to "bless" those who continued to loan to the needy.[84] Thus the practice of giving loans to the needy is an act of faith, both in the merits of the Year of Release's benefits to society and in God to compensate for one's participation in sharing their wealth. Wealth sharing is an opportunity to be blessed by God! So, my final point would be that the *Prosbul* made the exercise of one's faith impotent.

The *Prosbul* undermined all these intended purposes of the law. It kept the needy (the debtor) under continued financial

---

[84] Deuteronomy 15:9–11

burden (no rest); it allowed the wealthy to keep control of their wealth, and it prevented the benefit of redistribution of wealth within society. This resulted in the poor getting poorer and the rich richer. And spiritually, it removed from the rich a need to trust God for His promised blessings. Faith is grown by testing, and the *Prosbul* removed the test. The very existence of the *Prosbul* reveals that those with means had, as the book of Deuteronomy warned, "wicked thoughts in their hearts" and they were "grieved" by the thought of lending to the poor, the very thing that God warns against. The *Prosbul* is a sad commentary on the spiritual condition of the rich (and perhaps the spiritual leadership) during the generation leading up to the ministry of Jesus.

Besides heavy taxation by the Romans, which might have necessitated the need for loans, the *Prosbul* was part of the financial situation that shaped the landscape of Jesus' day. The old laws of God's *kingdom of priests and holy nation*[85] as recorded in the Torah, had been circumvented, and the poor had no legal escape from loan obligations—except to make a loan with a righteous, law abiding, brother or neighbor who would be willing to forgive a loan in the Year of Release. Jesus' first beatitude's blessing to the poor, and his statement that the coming kingdom was theirs, can be viewed as a condemnation of society's then-present financial climate and an encouragement that things will be reversed.

Within the Sermon on the Mount, Jesus will state his famous "Lord's Prayer," which has imbedded in it a request that God forgive our debts, just as we forgive the debts of others. Was this inclusive of financial debts? Was this intended, in part, as a statement against violations of the sabbatical years as allowed by the *Prosbul*? In this same sermon, Jesus will appeal to his listeners to lay up treasures in heaven, not on earth. He will later reveal that one way to do this is to distribute one's wealth

---

[85] Exodus 19:5–6

to the poor. We will be looking at these topics in greater detail in coming chapters.

Before we move on to the next section, it would serve us well to take a closer look at Hillel the Elder and a contemporary rabbinical leader named Shammai. These two men were the great religious minds shaping the world of Judaism into which Jesus would arrive. Parts of Jesus' Sermon on the Mount appear to address these men—particularly Hillel—and a little knowledge of them will help us better understand Jesus' message.

Hillel was a Jew born in Babylon but moved to Jerusalem in the first century BCE. He studied the Torah and eventually rose to become one of the great sages of his day. He is believed to have had a long life and passed away sometime around 10—12 CE. In his later years he served as the president (*nasi*) of the Sanhedrin. He established a rabbinical school, known as the House of Hillel, which taught students his interpretations of the Torah and related Jewish writings. When he died, his school was continued by his grandson, Gamaliel—the same Gamaliel who would serve as the teacher of Saul of Tarsus, also known as the apostle, Paul.[86]

A contemporary of Hillel, yet many years younger, was another great rabbinical sage by the name of Shammai. He is said to have lived from about 50 BCE to 30 CE. He took Hillel's place as president of the Sanhedrin after Hillel's death. Shammai also had a prominent school of Torah instruction, which was known as the House of Shammai. Hillel and Shammai differed on various interpretations of the law, with Hillel generally taking more liberal views, thus making the laws fit the realities of present day. Shammai viewed things more conservatively. This led to a widely circulated saying among the Jews that stated:

Hillel loosens and Shammai binds.

---

[86] Acts 22:3

In later years, the men's two "schools" of thought became more polarized, so much so that people coined the lamenting saying that:

The one law has become two.

For the most part, however, the two men, themselves, appear to have worked together well, and their differences did not polarize them as it would eventually polarize their followers. We will later see how these men may fit within the framework of Jesus' Sermon on the Mount.

D. Parallel Teachings in the Sermon on the Mount

Another reason why it is not hard to accept Jesus' saying of *"Blessed are the poor, for theirs is the kingdom of heaven"* as meaning the literal poor, lay in the fact that the poor and their support is a major theme within this sermon itself. This is what we are going to explore during the coming chapters, however, let me give you a few advance glimpses.

Aside from the poor that are featured in the remaining beatitudes, Jesus addresses the topic of debt forgiveness within his famous "Lord's prayer." This prayer is part of the Sermon on the Mount, and it is more than an instruction on how to pray to the "Father." It serves as instruction on how members of the kingdom of heaven should live. We will look at this in detail later.

Jesus also brings up the topic of fasting in this sermon.[87] He does so as a rebuke to incorrect fasting techniques and calls upon his listeners to fast correctly and in secret before God. To any well-educated Jewish individual (anyone who attended synagogue) this should have conjured up memories of how the prophet Isaiah defined correct fasting that was acceptable to God. Isaiah, in recording God's words, stated the following:

---

[87] Matthew 6:16–18

Is this not the fast that I have chosen: to loose the bonds of wickedness, to undo the heavy burdens, to let the oppressed go free, and that you break every yoke? Is it not to share your bread with the hungry, and that you bring to your house the poor who are cast out; when you see the naked, that you cover him, and not hide yourself from your own flesh?[88]

True fasting to God is the practice of assisting those in need. It is the lifting of others' burdens and the giving of rest to these same people through the support of our personal resources. It is sabbatical laws in action.

As mentioned earlier, Jesus will call on his listeners to store up treasures in heaven, not on earth, and one definition of doing so is the distribution of one's wealth to the poor.[89] Jesus follows this statement with the pronouncement that one cannot serve two masters—God and money. The implication is that we must choose one or the other, and Jesus clearly suggests that the choice be God.

The context of Jesus' sermon at this point is that we need to share our wealth—or at least part of it—to those in need. Any listener of this sermon, upon comprehending what Jesus is saying, would most logically react by mentally questioning, "If I do that, how am I going to support myself and my family?" Interestingly, as if on perfect cue, Jesus answers this unspoken question. He immediately turns his topic to "faith" and points out to the listeners that God feeds the birds and clothes the flowers of the field.[90] He concludes with the words:

---

[88] Isaiah 58:6–7

[89] Matthew 6:19–20 and Matthew 19:21 and Luke 18:22

[90] Matthew 6:25–30

O you of little faith? Therefore, do not worry, saying, "What shall we eat?" or "What shall we drink?" or "What shall we wear...?" But seek first the kingdom of God and His righteousness, and all these things shall be added to you. Therefore, do not worry about tomorrow....[91]

No doubt, a person somewhat resistant to this philosophy that Jesus is promoting, might try to give the following often-heard reasons for not participating. They will state defensive questions such as, "How do I know who to give help to? Are they really in need? Can I trust them? What if they misuse what I give them? Maybe I will be making things worse?"

Again, as if he were reading the minds of his listeners, Jesus answers the unspoken questions with the immediate reply of:

Judge not, that you be not judged. For with what judgment you judge, you will be judged; and with the measure you use, it will be measured back to you.[92]

Jesus' dialogue is directed toward encouraging his questioning listeners to carry out the provisions of the Sabbath commandment's direction to relieve burdens and give rest, and to exercise faith in God while one does so. This is a major theme of the sermon, so why should Jesus' opening beatitude not introduce the topic of the physically poor and their relation to the kingdom of heaven from the start. I might add before closing, however, that Jesus does give some qualification regarding who should not be helped. Judgment and discretion

---

[91] Matthew 6:30–34
[92] Matthew 7:1–2

are needed when assisting others. We will be looking at that in later chapters.

E. Parallel Teachings Throughout the Gospels

The theme of the poor and the need to support them occurs repeatedly throughout the four Gospels. Many times, the instruction is subtle, but often it is very straight forward and unavoidable. Let us take a brief look at some examples, to establish, once again, that this is a major topic of Jesus' kingdom of heaven.

The ministry of Jesus began with the ministry of John the Baptist announcing that the kingdom of heaven was at hand. John called for his listeners to repent in preparation for this kingdom and the coming king. People flocked to him for baptism and asked direction regarding what they needed to do next. This conversation is recorded in the book of Luke, and John's answer was as follows:

> *He answered and said to them, "He who has two tunics, let him give to him who has none; and he who has food, let him do likewise."*[93]

John's primary suggestion for appropriate action after one has repented from sin was to address the needs of the poorer sectors of one's community. John mentions giving away one of your two tunics—or fifty percent of your "tunic" wealth. What if a person has three or four tunics? What if they have three or four cars or houses? What would John say to them? Obviously, questions like these are not addressed, so I will leave it to you to speculate on how John might reply to them.

---

[93] Luke 3:11

The Gospel of Luke records a story of a short-in-stature tax collector named Zacchaeus, who lived in the city of Jericho.[94] The story goes that one-day Jesus is passing through the city, and Zacchaeus has to climb into a tree to see over the crowds' heads. Jesus sees him and stops. He then tells Zacchaeus to come down from the tree and then invites himself to spend the day at Zacchaeus' house. Zacchaeus is delighted, but the crowd is offended because Zacchaeus is a tax collector.

The Bible does not record the conversation that Jesus had at Zacchaeus' house that afternoon, but what we do know is that it prompts Zacchaeus to pledge half his wealth to the poor and to right any wrongs he may have committed. This prompts Jesus to proclaim:

> *Today salvation has come to this house, because he also is a son of Abraham; for the Son of Man has come to seek and to save that which was lost.*[95]

I find it interesting that Jesus makes no statement regarding Zacchaeus' spiritual condition until after Zacchaeus makes his pledge. It makes one wonder what the conversation was about that afternoon. What did Jesus say? What did Zacchaeus hear? Did the conversation involve themes of social justice and mercy for the poor? Why did Zacchaeus choose to respond to Jesus' message by giving to the poor? Why fifty percent? The results of Jesus' visit seem to have evoked a response reminiscent of John the Baptist's instructions to his new converts.

Luke also records one of Jesus' parables concerning giving to the poor, or more correctly, not giving to the poor. The

---

[94] Luke 19:1–10
[95] Luke 19:9–10

story tells of a farmer who has a remarkably successful crop, so much so that his current barns cannot hold all the grain he has produced.[96] His solution is to pull down the old barns and build even greater ones so that his entire valuable crop can be stored. His plan is to keep the grain and monetize it over the coming years so that he can be free of labor, and eat, drink, and be merry. Jesus concludes the story with these words:

> But God said to him, "Fool! This night your soul will be required of you; then whose will those things be which you have provided?" So is he who lays up treasure for himself and is not rich toward God.[97]

Jesus' point is that in God's eyes, the rich farmer should have shared his wealth rather than hoarding it for himself. Giving to the poor would have laid up treasures in heaven and been a much safer long-term investment—both on earth and in heaven.

Luke and Matthew also have a curious story that Jesus gives, regarding a servant's duty to an absentee master. It is recorded in Matthew, in part, as follows:

> Who then is a faithful and wise servant, whom his master made ruler over his household, to give [those in the household] food in due season? Blessed is that servant whom his master, when he comes, will find so doing.... But if that...servant [being evil] says in his heart, "My master is delaying his coming," and begins to beat his fellow servants, and to eat and drink with the drunk-

---

[96] Luke 12:16–21
[97] Luke 12:20–21

*ards, the master of that servant will come on a
day when he is not looking for him and at an hour
that he is not aware of, and will cut him in two
and appoint him his portion with the hypocrites.
There shall be weeping and gnashing of teeth.*[98]

The picture Jesus creates is one of a good servant caring for the physical needs of others in the household (or community). He will be rewarded. But if the servant were to become evil-hearted and begin abusing the others of the household and hoarding the rations for his own pleasure, he will be caught and punished by the master.

Matthew has another well-known story concerning God's future judgment of mankind, and it also reveals Jesus' value on the kingdom's requirements to care for the poor.[99] In this parable, Jesus has the good and bad of humanity divided into two groups, one referred to as sheep (good), and the other as goats (bad). The sheep are told by the king to enter the kingdom they have inherited, because in the words of the king:

*I was hungry and you gave Me food; I was
thirsty and you gave Me drink; I was a stranger
and you took Me in; I was naked and you clothed
Me; I was sick and you visited Me; I was in prison and you came to Me.*[100]

The story tells us that the sheep are not aware that they have done these good things to the king himself, who was disguised as everyman in need. They are rewarded with an invitation to enter the kingdom of heaven. The story con-

---

[98] Matthew 24:45–51. See also Luke 12:41–48
[99] Matthew 25:31–46
[100] Matthew 25:35–36

cludes by revealing that the entrance into the kingdom is equated with being "the righteous" and being given the gift of eternal life.[101] Therefore, in this story, the socially equitable sheep are the righteous; they enter the kingdom and have eternal life.

The goats, on the other hand, failed to respond to the needs of their fellow citizens and thereby failed to respond to their king as well. Their fate is exclusion from the kingdom, and everlasting punishment.

I could go on with numerous examples to help you get the point. However, let me close with only one more example that takes place after the ascension of Jesus. Here, we find the young Jewish church in its infancy in Jerusalem, and just beginning to put into practice all that they have learned from Jesus. What have they learned from him that now shapes their new movement? How are they responding to their interpretation of Jesus' kingdom message now that they are on their own? The book of Acts recalls those early days as follows:

> *Then those who gladly received* [Peter's] *word were baptized . . . and they continued steadfastly in the apostles' doctrine and fellowship, in the breaking of bread, and in prayers. . . . Now all who believed were together, and had all things in common, and sold their possessions and goods, and divided them among all, as anyone had need.*
>
> *So, continuing daily with one accord in the temple, and breaking bread from house to house, they ate their food with gladness and simplicity of heart, praising God and having favor with all*

---

[101] Matthew 25:46

*the people. And the Lord added to the church
daily those who were being saved.*[102]

Keep in mind, in this story, Peter's words were calling for people to accept Jesus as the Christ and to follow his teachings. I find it interesting that, to this early church, those teachings are acted upon by a redistribution of wealth and meeting the needs of all within the young community. This is not by accident. It is their view of what Jesus was calling them to do.

Now, in closing, let us look at one final point I feel supports the opinion that the first beatitude concerns the literal poor more so than a mental or spiritual condition of a prospective member of God's coming kingdom of heaven. This final point is the character of God, Himself. And the Sermon on the Mount even hints at this, too. We will see more on that topic in later chapters.

F. The Character of God

The Sermon on the Mount is a message about the kingdom of heaven. The Gospels of Mark, Luke, and John use the term the "kingdom of God." Both references are for the kingdom of the same divine entity—the God of heaven. This is important to us because it gives us a way to get insight into the mind and characteristics of God. When one makes a kingdom, or any proclamation at all, it is done so with that individual's paradigm behind its construction. An analysis of the tenets of the kingdom or proclamation will reveal the character of the individual who makes it. Likewise, if you know the character of an individual you should also be able to deduce what is important to them and what kind of values they will portray. This is true of God, too.

---

[102] Acts 2:41–47

One of the best revelations of the character of God is found within the first few chapters of the Bible. This would be the creation story itself. What we see here is that God is first and foremost "generous." Everything is made for the benefit of something else, and ultimately, He makes man—who shares the image of God—and gives man the care of the earth. The earth itself is a gift—an act of generosity. And God has a mind for detail and beauty, for He makes for man a pleasant garden in which to reside. Everything man needs to survive comfortably is provided freely as a gift.

From the creator's perspective there is nothing in existence that is greater than Himself. All creation is inferior and yet all His generosity is for the purpose of making the inferior safe, comfortable, fulfilled, and prosperous. And He wishes to spend time associating with His creation. His desires are not selfish, for He commands them to be fruitful and multiple, whereby they, too, will have the opportunity to be generous to those that they create—and to provide them with safety, comfort, and community as well.

God is a giving God. Generosity is His first revealed trait. He is generous to all His creation and sees each of them as equally in need of His provision of sustaining life. Inequalities, classes, and divisions, as well as rebellion against God, are manmade qualities that came into existence during and after the fall of man. And yet, even then we still see that God is giving, in that He continues to care for man, and does not withhold the gift of His earth to them.

The fall of mankind changed the nature of God's relationship with man, but it did not change God's generous character or make Him abandon humanity to suffer the fate of their complete self-destruction. The glory of God had to withdraw from visible earth, but the interest of God in His creation was perhaps heightened by a desire to rescue humanity from its self-imposed bondage. No, abandonment was not on God's mind. Instead, God had a plan to return the presence of His heavenly government to a corrupted

earth. Through a select family, God would reestablish His kingdom and it was to be an example to all the people of the earth and
the beginning of a return to the way things were meant to be.

This was God's purpose when He chose to dwell with the children of Israel and reveal to them His laws. Those laws further reveal the character traits of God. He now has to establish His role as
leader, and command that His people pledge loyalty to and faith in
Him, for if His kingdom is going to be present, they need to be focused on the roles He needs them to live. He also must command
the people to respect, honor, and care for those within the community—to see each person as valuable, as He sees them.

On one occasion during the giving of the law, Moses asks God
if he can see God's glory. His reply is that man (perhaps in his
current fallen state) cannot see the face of God and live. God, however, partially grants Moses' request, telling Moses that He will
place him in the cleft of a rock and cover him with His hand. He
will then let Moses look at Him from behind. This small glimpse,
however, reveals a partial view of God's character, and Moses records the following:

> *Now the Lord descended in the cloud and stood
> with him there, and proclaimed the name of the
> Lord. And the Lord passed before him and pro-
> claimed, "The Lord, the Lord God, merciful and
> gracious, longsuffering, and abounding in good-
> ness and truth, keeping mercy for thousands, for-
> giving iniquity and transgression and sin, by no
> means clearing the guilty, visiting the iniquity of
> the fathers upon the children and the children's
> children to the third and the fourth genera-
> tion."*[103]

---

[103] Exodus 34:5–7

From this, we see once again that God's nature is good, and that He preserves the works of His creation which He loves. And yet at the same time, He reveals that He is a just God, needing to punish and stop those who mistreat His creation. His many laws given within the Torah delineate the nature and substance of those mistreatments. A close examination of those laws demonstrates God's concern that the poorer and weaker sectors of human societies are neither abused nor neglected, as we have reviewed in earlier chapters.

Given this knowledge of the character of God, I find it easy to accept that His approaching kingdom, as preached by Jesus, would focus on these themes. Its very introduction should frame the nature of the problem and the solution to come. And I feel it does just that. There are poor people in the community; they are distressed and discouraged, but the kingdom of God is for their benefit, their rescue.

The bombshell of Jesus' introductory first beatitude is this; those who appear to be not blessed by God (according to the present-day cultural mindset) are actually—surprise—the objects of God's kingdom. In essence, the poor are present for the benefit of the rich. Equity cannot take place if there is no one to be equitable to. You need someone with no coat in order for you to give one of your own coats away to him who has none. The needy are needed to reveal the true character of the members of the kingdom. One's love for God is revealed by his service to his neighbor. A person in need can be a test of our love and loyalty to God. By love for God, and the emulation of His generous character, the poor are blessed by His kingdom, and the giver, in turn, is accessible to the blessings God promises those who are generous.

If, in the kingdom of heaven, the poor are to be happy, then it means that their deficiencies are going to be addressed.

The generosity of God is going to be extended to them. And as we will see, these deficiencies are addressed primarily by those who have the will and resources to address them. In short, the poor will be happy because of the generosity of someone with means—someone sharing the very character of God. People responding to the message of the kingdom of heaven will act to make the poor happy. The message of the kingdom of heaven is then, by its very nature, a message directed to those who can help. The happiness of the poor comes as others respond to the message and act upon it by helping those in need. They assimilate the generous character of God because of their love for Him, and their desire to be like Him. They give, and in so doing, reflect God's image. And as we will see, these helpful individuals will have their own blessings.

CHAPTER 6

Blessed Are Those Who Mourn

*"Blessed are those who mourn,
for they shall be comforted."*

Matthew 5:4

If you were to look at a comparative listing of what various Bible commentaries say about this verse, you would find that nearly all interpret Jesus' words in the context of Christian principles.[104] This is also true of numerous websites devoted to explaining the meaning of this verse. Mourning is taken to mean one's genuine sorrowing for their sins and the sin of the world. It is a sorrowing that leads one to repentance and thus avails them of the comfort of forgiveness that only God can give.

These sites and commentaries often link this beatitude to the first. Some have argued that the first beatitude concerns the "poor in spirit," which are those who see their spiritual poverty in comparison to God's character. Such individuals, if truly honest in heart, would naturally be led to a state of mourning concerning their wretched position. The two beatitudes are seen as steps in a process; realization of one's shortcomings, followed by a sorrow for those shortcomings. The two lead to a need for spiritual and physical comfort, and the promised

---

[104] https://biblehub.com/commentaries/matthew/5-4.htm

happiness implies that God will forgive, and this will be of comfort to the mourner.

The above spiritualized view of these two beatitudes has an element of truth, and I would not want to disparage those who find "comfort" in this interpretation of Christ's words. I, myself, find comfort in this interpretation of the beatitude, however, I would not limit the words of Christ to only this view. When I consider the whole of the Sermon on the Mount, I see its theme supporting a more literal interpretation. As I mentioned earlier, this can be a case of a message having more than one meaning—like an onion having many layers. The layer I see most clearly, however, is the one that first comes to mind at face value.

I agree that the first and second beatitudes can be seen as intricately linked. If one takes the position that the first beatitude is about the literal poor—the lowest sectors of society—then it is not hard to imagine that these individuals have reason to mourn and need comfort. However, this second beatitude implies much more than the mourning of the lowest of the poor. It does not specify who is mourning and thus allows the mourner to be anyone in pain—poor or rich—and in this way the two beatitudes are not linked. Mourning is not the sole possession of beggars. The pain of loss by injustice, violence, tragedy, disease or death, to name a few, can happen to anyone at any time—poor or rich, and everyone in between.

The Greek word that is used for "*mourn*" in this verse is the word "*pentheo.*"[105] It means "*grief,*" but not simple grief. It is *manifested grief.* Grief so severe it takes possession of a person and cannot be hid. This is an important distinction because anyone of us can be suffering grief that we hide within ourselves. No one around us may ever know that we have buried sorrows in our souls. This beatitude's grief, however, is the grief that has boiled over to the surface and is now in plain sight for all to

---

[105] Strong's Word NT:3996

see. If one interprets this beatitude as solely spiritual comfort from God, then one would be saying that God only comforts those who boil over in spiritual grief. Would not this imply that the silent, inner suffering of a soul is ignored by God until it boils over? If so, one would be inclined to question why is it that Jesus would limit God's comforting to only those who are visibly in grief?

For me, the answer is straightforward. Jesus is talking about physical and emotional grief that is in plain sight for anyone who is willing to look. The fact that the grief is visible is what leads to the one grieving being given comfort. But where does this comfort come from? God directly? Or can it be that the comfort comes from God through the subjects of his kingdom of heaven? Is it not that the members of the kingdom, sharing the character of God, will have sympathy on the suffering and seek to comfort them? My position on the first beatitude is that the members of God's kingdom will be active in supporting the needs of the poor, thus making them happy. Likewise, I see here the members of the kingdom of God actively comforting those whom they see *manifesting grief*, thus making them happy.

Luke lists this beatitude as Jesus' third in his record of this sermon, and this beatitude also has a counterbalancing woe. Jesus' words, as recorded by Luke, hint of "justice" rather than solely comfort. The beatitude reads as follows:

Blessed are you who weep now, for you shall laugh.[106]

The Greek word used for "*weep*" is the word *klaio*,[107] and it means to sob or wail audibly. The weeping is there for all to see. Jesus' counterbalancing "woe" for this beatitude, reads almost in reverse.

---

[106] Luke 6:21
[107] Strong's Word NT:2799

Woe to you who laugh now, for you shall mourn and weep.[108]

Interestingly, Luke's record of this woe has Jesus using both the word "mourn" (same as in Matthew) and the word "weep." It is a common linguistic tool in Hebrew literature to repeat ideas with different but similar words (like saying, "the poor and the needy"). It is used to give emphasis to the action or object being described. In short, Jesus is saying that the future is very bleak for those who laugh now.

I mentioned that Luke's version of this beatitude and its counterbalancing woe are hinting of "justice," because Jesus is describing a reversal of fates. It leaves us wondering if the "weepers" of the beatitude are made happy because of retribution against the "laughers" in the woe. Is there a direct relationship between the two events? You might recall the song of praise given by Jesus' mother Mary when speaking of God's care for mankind, in which she states:

He has filled the hungry with good thing,
and the rich He has sent away empty.[109]

Might it be that God could implement equity by emptying the rich in order to fill the hungry? Who then would laugh and who then would cry?

While Jesus does not elaborate on this issue in his sermon, he may have hinted at the relationship in his other teachings. On one occasion, Jesus visited his hometown of Nazareth on a Sabbath day, and he gave a Sabbath-focused message. He was handed the scroll of Isaiah, and he turned to and read the following words:

---

[108] Luke 6:25
[109] Luke 1:53

The Spirit of the Lord is upon me, because He has anointed me to preach the gospel to the poor; He has sent me to heal the brokenhearted, to proclaim liberty to the captives, and recovery of sight to the blind, to set at liberty those who are oppressed; to proclaim the acceptable year of the Lord.[110]

Curiously, Jesus did not complete the entire passage of Isaiah on this theme. Following the words *"to proclaim the acceptable year of the Lord,"* Isaiah continues with:

And the day of vengeance [revenge] of our God; to comfort all who mourn, to console those who mourn in Zion, to give them beauty for ashes, the oil of joy for mourning, the garment of praise for the spirit of heaviness...[111]

Jesus' public reading and his following comment did not go over well with his hometown, and they attempted to stone him to death. The reasons for this are beyond the scope of this book, although it is a relevant topic. For a good explanation of the events and the motivations, I would recommend you turn to Kenneth Bailey's book *Jesus Through Middle Eastern Eyes*.[112]

Notice in the verses of Isaiah that were left unsaid by Jesus, we have a completed picture of God exacting justice on others, and its resulting comfort to those mourning and heavy hearted. God's vengeance releases the poor, the oppressed and the sick, and brings comfort and healing to them. Would not God be bringing His ven-

---

[110] Luke 4:18–19 (quoting from Isaiah 61:1–2 and Isaiah 42:7.)

[111] Isaiah 61:2–3

[112] Kenneth E. Bailey, *Jesus Through Middle Eastern Eyes*, (Westmont, IL: InterVarsity Press, 2008), Chapter 12, "The Inauguration of Jesus' Ministry."

geance upon those who had oppressed the poor, held others captive, or ignored the plight of the disabled? This structure follows very closely Luke's blessing and counterbalanced woe.

Isaiah's statements of justice follow the philosophy of captives and the oppressed being given liberty, that is reminiscent of the sabbatical years of release and the Year of Jubilee. These years were designed to turn the tables of misfortune and level society's wealth disparities.[113] Jesus was aware of the full message of this portion of Isaiah but chose to limit the amount of information given to his community on that day. The beatitude and woe recorded in the book of Luke are essentially an abbreviated version of Isaiah's prophecy. Matthew's version of the blessing abbreviates the concept one step further in that it only addresses the comfort to the mourners.

On another occasion, Jesus gave a parable about an unnamed rich man and a poor beggar named Lazarus, who sits daily at the rich man's gate begging for assistance.[114] When both men pass away, Lazarus finds himself in the equivalent of heaven next to Abraham of old. The rich man finds himself in the equivalent of hell. When the rich man cries out to Abraham for mercy, Abraham replies as follows:

> *Son, remember that in your lifetime you received your good things, and likewise Lazarus evil things; but now he is comforted and you are tormented.*[115]

---

[113] Isaiah uses the term "the acceptable year of the Lord." This is a reference to the Year of Jubilee. What makes it "acceptable"? Recall that in Isaiah 58, God outlines what makes a fast acceptable to him. It is not going without food, it is the care for the poor, the release of the oppressed—in short, social justice. We can therefore conclude that an "acceptable year" would have the same social justice implications.

[114] Luke 16:19–31

[115] Luke 16:25

The rich man, seeing that his plight cannot be changed, then asks that Lazarus be raised from the dead and that he go warn his living brothers so that they do not end up in hell with him. But Abraham tells the rich man,

> *If they do not hear Moses and the prophets, neither will they be persuaded though one rise from the dead.*[116]

Jesus' message is clear. The rich man's fate is due to his neglect of the beggar, and God in the afterlife, has reversed their fortunes. What is also clear is the fact that the teachings of Moses and the prophets have already instructed those with means what their responsibility to the poor is. The instructions are available for anyone to follow.

While some might argue that this story speaks only of future rewards and punishments, I would remind them that the conclusion of the story speaks of present actions needed to avoid future fates. The rich man's brothers are still living in the present and if they heed the teachings of Moses and the prophets, they can avoid their rich brother's judgment. And what was the rich man's failure in this story? He failed to give comfort to the beggar when he had the opportunity to do so. The story is eerily similar to Jesus' beatitude and counterbalancing woe.

Perhaps we can deduce a few more lessons from Jesus' words. If the story had been different, and the rich man had been the one giving Lazarus comfort in his earthly life, would he not have been awarded the same reward of eternal life as the "sheep" in Jesus' parable[117] of future judgment? Would there be any justification for God to reverse the fates of the two men if the rich man had been more generous? Perhaps not, the rich man would only have made

---

[116] Luke 16:31
[117] Matthew 25:31–46

himself slightly poorer, and Lazarus would have had comfort and less to mourn about.

Here is my point in this deduction; just because one laughs now does not mean that they must cry later. There is joy in helping others, so those who act to comfort others now can also experience the happiness that God offers to those who mourn. The woe pronounced by Jesus appears to be in the context of those ignoring the suffering of others, or worse yet, those laughing at the expense of those who are suffering. The woe need not apply to those who are now actively comforting those who mourn. The statement, *"Blessed are those who mourn, for they shall be comforted,"* can be a present reality made true by the members of God's kingdom comforting those who are visibly experiencing grief. Quite literally, the kingdom of heaven is at hand when people reach out to comfort those in pain.

Relevant questions for this beatitude would be, "What kind of comfort? What do we do to comfort mourners?" The answer lies in the Greek word the Gospel author used for *comforted*. This is the word *"parakaleo."*[118] It is a construction of two Greek words; the first is *"para"*[119] which means *from beside* or *by the side of* someone or something. The second word is *"kaleo,"*[120] which means *I call, summon,* or *invite.* Jesus has created the picture of the comforter as someone who will come to the side of the mourner and will be close to them. The comforter also makes a personal invitation to the sorrowing individual—an implication that the comforter wishes to host that person as they, together, move to a place of safety or resolution of the mourner's pain. The blessing of happiness that the grief-stricken person will receive comes as a direct result of the comforter who is tangibly active in resolving the mourner's pain.

---

[118] Strong's Word NT:3870

[119] Strong's Word NT:3844

[120] Strong's Word NT:2564

It is true we should sorrow over our own sins and repent, and seek the forgiveness and comfort that God only can give, but the second beatitude, literally not figuratively, is a call of action to the members of God's kingdom to be observant of others' grief and to draw near to them during their time of emotional pain. The comforters are to be inviting the mourners into a place of physical or emotional security that they can provide for them, even if it is only a temporary solution or an act of direction pointing them toward safety. The beatitude implies an acute sense of loss, and that loss needs to be met with an equally matched effort to comfort. Like the first beatitude, the second is also asking God's people to alleviate the real and present burdens of others within our community—or as the Sabbath commands state, those *"within your gates."*[121] We can be the earthly tools in God's hands that carry out His promise below.

*"For the oppression of the poor, for the sighing of the needy, **now** I will arise," says the LORD. "I will set him in the safety for which he yearns."*[122]

---

[121] Exodus 20:10

[122] Psalm 12:5

CHAPTER 7

Blessed Are the Meek

"Blessed are the meek,
for they shall inherit the earth."

Matthew 5:5

This third proclamation of Jesus is a clear equity statement. Think of it. If the meek are to inherit the earth during the coming kingdom of heaven, then they must not possess it at the time of this statement. Otherwise, the statement would be meaningless. But as Jesus points out, the inheritance of the earth is to the meek, not to the domineering. This proclamation is again a picture of a disparity being righted—the earth taken from those who now possess and control it and being re-proportioned to those who do not now possess it.

The Greek word translated "*meek*" in this text is the word "*praus.*"[123] This word and its variants mean, *mild, gentle,* or *humble.* English dictionaries also define the word "meek" with a variety of mild characteristics. The meek are humble, timid, submissive, yielding, compliant, acquiescent, un-protesting.

So why is it that the meek do not now possess the earth? The answer is because they are meek! These are not the people one expects to find among the CEOs of today's Fortune 500 companies. On the contrary the meek are the people who will not fight

---

[123] Strong's Word NT:4239

to be first in line. They will step back when others push to get ahead. They are passive, not aggressive, and as a result they must settle for something other than first or second place. More aggressive people will step over, or past, them and seize the opportunities for gain in this world. Meekness of spirit and temperament often results in the loss of opportunity, position or income, and the meek will accept this fate, even if it is unjust. The meek are most easily shortchanged, exploited—even abused. But in Jesus' kingdom of heaven to come, the meek will be given their equitable share in the inheritance of the earth.

Jesus' use of the word "meek" is remarkably interesting. Why? It is because Jesus refers to himself as being among the "meek." In Matthew 11:29, when Jesus advises his followers to take up his yoke and learn from him, the reason he gives is that he is "meek and lowly in heart." He therefore associates himself with the meek and asks his followers to share this character trait with him. To Jesus, it is a positive trait, not a negative one. And just like the meek in the beatitude, Jesus himself, being one of the meek, is also inheriting the earth. It is a kingdom that he is going to receive from someone else—his Father.[124] As the inheritor of the earth, Jesus is free to re-proportion it as he wishes, and those of meek and lowly temperaments are the ones whom he chooses to be his co-beneficiaries. What an honorable blessing!

But the story does not end here. Jesus has lifted the phrase *"The meek shall inherit the earth"* from Psalm 37:11. Several verses earlier, we find that the psalm defines those that inherit the earth—the meek—as those who wait patiently on the Lord. We could, therefore, use the Bible's definition to rewrite Jesus' beatitude as follows:

---

[124] See Luke 10:22; Luke 19:12; Matthew 16:28; Matthew 25:31–34; and John 18:36–37.

> Blessed are those who wait patiently on the Lord, for they shall inherit the earth.

A study of Psalm 37 results in a list of characteristics of the meek. It also gives us a list of characteristics concerning the wicked who oppress the meek. I recommend that you read this psalm in its entirety, but here is a summary of many of the points. The meek, often referred to in the psalm as "righteous," are as follows:

- Trusting the Lord   (vv. 3, 7, 40)
- Poorer than the wicked   (v. 16)
- Merciful   (v. 21)
- Generous   (v. 21)
- He delights to walk in God's way   (v. 23)
- He may fall, but will not be utterly cast down   (v. 24)
- He speaks wisdom and justice   (v. 30)
- The law of God is in his heart   (v. 31)

These higher qualities of character are not appreciated by the wicked that oppose the meek. Their list of offenses is long and disturbing. Here is a listing of their faults from the psalm:

- They are workers of iniquity   (v. 1)
- They prosper in their way (as opposed to God's way)   (v. 7)
- They bring wicked schemes to pass   (v. 7)
- They plot against the just   (v. 12)
- They gnash at the just with their teeth (i.e., angry)   (v. 12)
- They draw weapons to cast down the poor and needy   (v. 14)
- They draw weapons to slay those of upright conduct   (v. 14)
- They borrow and do not repay   (v. 21)
- They watch the righteous and seek to slay (destroy) him   (v. 32)

As you can easily see, the meek are up against some intense and dangerous opposition. Nevertheless, the psalm instructs the meek to be patient; do not resist; the Lord will take care of you, and you will inherit the earth—and the inheritance is eternal.

I mentioned earlier that Jesus calls himself meek, and indeed he does display all the qualities of the meek listed in this psalm. He also faced all the listed oppressions that this psalm records coming from the wicked. The God-fearing meek of the earth and Jesus share a bond of experience, and it is no wonder that he promises to make them co-inheritors of the earth.

To some people this beatitude appears to offer only a future blessing to the meek, so it would be logical for them to question whether my position that God's kingdom of heaven, which was at hand in Jesus' time, offers a present-day benefit. However, I would maintain that it does for two reasons. The first is that, even with the future hope of inheritance, Psalm 37 indicates that the meek are presently under the care of the Lord. They are told that they will be satisfied in days of famine. They are not going to be forsaken, and their children will not beg for bread. My second reason stems from the fact that the rest of the beatitudes to come specifically focus on blessings for those who come to the rescue of others under oppressions, such as the meek listed in this psalm. Others in the kingdom are blessed for their defense of the meek; therefore, the meek are not left to suffer alone until the time of their inheritance. This will become evident in the following chapters.

CHAPTER 8

Blessed Are the Seekers of Right

"Blessed are those who hunger and thirst for righteousness, for they shall be filled."

Matthew 5:6

I will need to get somewhat academic here in order to explain this rather simple statement of Jesus. Yes, this statement is actually quite simple if you ask a child to explain it to you. However, ask Christian theologians to explain it to you, and soon your head will begin to spin. It is an unfortunate reality of Christianity that we are not united in thought. There is no doubt in my mind that the enemy of God is behind this sword of division—it is a "divide and conquer" technique as old as the first rebellion.

Here is where the problem lies: the term "righteousness" has evolved, since the time of Jesus' ministry, and now has two theological definitions. One refers to a person's good, moral actions. The other, a post-Christ meaning, refers to Jesus' justification of a sinner apart from the sinner's actions—good or bad. These two meanings are assumed by many theologians to imply opposition to each other. So, what meaning of "righteousness" did Jesus intend his listeners to understand in his Sermon? Did he use the first definition? The one that the common people and his disciples would have understood. Or was he using the future definition of the spiritualized Christian paradigms? We have theologians who come down on either side of the question.

So, let us take a closer look at the two definitions to get a better understanding of the issue. The Greek word that is translated *"righteousness"* in this verse is *"dikaiosune."*[125] The primary meaning of this word is *"equity,"* implying that a person or action is of good moral conduct, just, and charitable. That is the Greek word, but what if Jesus spoke his sermon in Hebrew? If so, he would most likely have used the word *"tsedaqah."*[126] This Hebrew word means *rightness, rectitude, justice, moral virtue.* However, we still have one more option, what if Jesus spoke this sermon in Aramaic, the common rural dialect of his day? If so, he would have used the word "tsidqah."[127] This word means *"beneficence,"* that is, *the quality or state of doing good, performing acts of kindness or charity.*

It should be plain to see that all the above definitions of the word *righteousness* would be describing a person that is of good moral character, doing the right thing, making just judgments, being charitable and acting in kindness to others. It is not hard to imagine that such a person would be concerned for the welfare of others, and that they would wish for others in their community to share this concern. After all, the above descriptions imply treatment of others. Righteousness is therefore an active consideration and outreach to those around us. This is an apt description of the "righteous" life and ministry of Jesus. Who better exemplifies the meanings of the word righteousness? This definition was the understood meaning of *righteousness* in Jesus' day.

---

[125] Strong's Word NT:1343
[126] Strong's Word OT:6666
[127] Strong's Word OT:6665

Of the three languages we looked at above, only the Greek word *"dikaiosune"* evolved a modern, post-Christ definition. In fact, the Christianized definition of this word does not appear to have been used until many years after the resurrection and ascension of Jesus. After his time on earth, this Greek word for *righteousness* morphed into a specialized Christian meaning that refers to *"justification."* This is a word that means *the action of declaring or making a person righteous in the sight of God.* The theology behind justification is that Jesus' perfect, righteous life—his righteousness—is now imputed onto his followers. Rather than seeing a believer's sins; God only sees the righteousness of His son Jesus. Jesus' righteousness covers the sinfulness of the believer's shortcomings.

Many Christians carry with this concept the notion that one's good (or righteous) works have no merit on one's salvation. Salvation is seen as stemming only from one's faith in Jesus and that nothing we do, or do not do, can change our status with God. If one is to choose this Christianized meaning of "righteousness" that developed after the time of Jesus, we end up with the verse in Matthew 5:6 meaning something like this following example from a Christian website:

> In summary, *blessed are those who hunger and thirst for righteousness, for they will be filled* could be paraphrased as follows: "Deeply joyful and spiritually whole are those who actively seek a right relationship with God and, in so doing, discover that He alone can completely save and satisfy their souls."[128]

Shortly before this quote, the author of this website's article defines righteousness as a "right relationship with God." This is

---

[128] https://www.gotquestions.org/blessed-hunger-thirst-righteousness.html

equating it to a right standing with God, which is further defined as God's "gift of salvation given through faith in Jesus Christ to those who believe in Him."[129] Under this interpretation, the act of hungering and thirsting for "righteousness" is nothing more than the desire to be saved by God. In short, we should therefore be hungering and thirsting to "believe" in Jesus. But does this make sense? One either does or does not believe in Jesus. I question whether there is room for hungering or thirsting to believe.

A similar difficulty can be seen in the following site's interpretation of Matthew 5:6 that also uses the modern Christianized definition of "righteousness." It reads, in part, as follows:

> Christians know that salvation is through faith in Jesus Christ alone, and that when by faith we receive [Jesus'] sacrificial death and resurrection nothing that we do or don't do can change our status with God. . . . So why hunger and thirst for righteousness if we already have it by faith? How can we hunger for something we've already been given? This is a major challenge [the author means conundrum] of the Christian life. We are saved by faith alone, yet we are called to grow, to mature, to live a more upright, more righteous, life.[130]

The "challenge" or conundrum here, is that the modernized definition of *righteousness* stigmatizes the value of works in salvation, and yet God's word, in both the Old and New Testaments, is replete with admonitions to do good works—to be **righteous**. Jesus, later within the Sermon of the Mount, will even be critical

---

[129] The website's author cites Romans 3:22.

[130] https://unlockingthebible.org/2017/05/what-does-it-mean-to-hunger-and-thirst-for-righteousness/

of believers in him that fail to do righteous works. In other parts of the Gospels, the failure to do good works results in exclusion from the kingdom of heaven, which Jesus will define as the loss of eternal life.

Even those who wish to interpret Matthew 5:6 using the modern Christianized definition of the word *righteousness* must concede that the God who saved them by faith wants them to live in accordance with His standards of conduct and justice after they have been saved. To do anything short of this would be a form of taking God's name in vain—claiming to be a child of God but living as if one were free of the duties God desires us to perform.

So where does this leave us in terms of what Jesus meant when he said, "*Blessed are those who hunger and thirst for righteousness*"? It brings us back to the primitive meaning of the word that all of Jesus' disciples and listeners would have comprehended. The *righteousness* that they were to hunger and thirst for was that of a life of good moral character, doing the right thing, making just judgments, being charitable and acting in kindness to others. It implies living one's own life correctly and seeking justice and fairness for others.

Those listening to Jesus that day would have understood him to be saying that those who are longing for good conduct, fairness, justice, kindness, and a more charitable distribution of their resources (equity) will see their longing fulfilled. In modern parlance we would hear Jesus saying:

> Blessed are those who hunger and thirst for *equity*, for they shall be filled.

The statement makes sense in the sermon's context and is a logical progression of what has been proclaimed earlier. Would not the poor, sad, and the oppressed meek—those in need—feel a hunger and thirst for a fairer world? Would not a more equitable mindset alleviate their poverty, afford comfort, and bring justice? These groups would be no stranger to the desire for a kinder, balanced society. But these feelings need not be limited to only those in need. A longing for a kinder, equitable, and just society can also be in the hearts of the rich and in those who have positions of authority. The realization of a world of hardships and injustices, and the desire to see them righted can awaken in anyone who has respect and love for his fellow man. Indeed, history is filled with the stories of numerous individuals from all walks of life who recognized injustices and disparities, and began actively righting the wrongs.

This fourth beatitude confirms to us that there is a class of people who currently comprehend that righteousness is absent or insufficient in this world. Fortunately, there are those who hunger and thirst for a better world. In the context of equity these are the individuals who see the disparities around them. They see that their world has been unjust to some individuals or groups. They desire to see a kinder society that is more equitable. They may not oppose the rich—they may even be the rich—but they do lament the plight of the weaker sectors of society. This longing for righteousness is the spark that motivates individuals to bring about change—change within themselves and within their communities. One soon realizes that within their own selves they hold the beginning of the solution to the world's disparities. They can bring a measure of equity into the lives of those with whom they come into contact. In so doing, they become active agents in the fulfillment of not just the fourth beatitude, but of all the beatitudes.

Jesus' promise within this beatitude is that people who long for righteousness—whether they are those in need or those with something to give—will be filled. This is a promise that righteousness, in all its pre-modern definitions of the word, can be realized in time. There can be equity. There can be justice.

There can be right doing. When one hungers and thirsts for it. The act of hungering and thirsting is the catalyst for meaningful action leading to positive results.

Jesus' stated condition creates a picture of dire need. The Greek word translated "hunger" means to be *famished*, or to be *craving* food.[131] When one is in such a state of hunger or thirst, they set aside everything to care for their physical needs. Food and water become their highest priority. The same is true according to Jesus if one's hunger for righteousness is to be filled. Do any of us long for righteousness with such intensity—whether it be spiritual, moral, or societal righteousness? Jesus' word can actually be a bit discouraging—too many of us seem to be content with or ambivalent toward the injustices that may surround us.

There is encouragement though! This sermon is about the principles and tenets of the coming kingdom of heaven. Daniel's prophecy of this coming kingdom presents it as a stone which grows into a mountain to eventually fill the whole earth. Jesus, likewise, used a parable in his ministry to compare the kingdom of heaven to a small amount of leaven in bread. It is the least of the ingredients, but it grows to fill the whole loaf. He also compares the kingdom to a small mustard seed that eventually grows into a large tree. And finally, within this very sermon he will tell his listeners that they are like a candle and like salt—a small light that penetrates the dark night, or a little seasoning that makes a meal taste better. His point is clear, even the little we do is of value, and eventually it changes the world.

In closing this chapter, I would like to give you some insight on what is to come. This fourth beatitude has something philosophically more than the first three. It serves as a transition, or bridge, from those before it to those that follow. The first three beatitudes speak of poverty, discomfort, and the oppressed—

---

[131] Strong's Word 3983

those faced with problems and opposition in our society. The following beatitudes begin to outline solutions to those problems—the merciful, the pure in heart, the peacemakers, and those willing to stand up for righteousness even in the face of persecution. Much of Jesus' Sermon on the Mount after this beatitude will focus on calling his followers to be the active solution to the world's problems. His encouragements in this sermon are for them to be the physical presence of the kingdom of heaven on earth. We will see this message unfold more clearly as we continue.

CHAPTER 9

Blessed Are the Merciful

"Blessed are the merciful,
for they shall obtain mercy."

Matthew 5:7

What is mercy? Is it not the extending of help to someone in some form of need? For every need there is some level of mercy that can be extended to address that need. The poor can be assisted, the hungry fed, the naked clothed, the captive liberated, the debtor forgiven, the criminal pardoned, and the sick visited. In each case, one party is in need, and the other party has something that can help that need. The question is, "Will the one in possession of the other's solution be willing to give?" There is a disparity; will the solution-possessing party choose to balance the disparity? Will they be merciful?

This is an active, not a passive beatitude. The first three beatitudes held promises of happiness to individuals that found themselves in certain conditions—poverty, sorrow, and oppression. These conditions can arise from circumstances that one has limited control over. And while Jesus promises happiness to these individuals, he does not specify that this happiness will be the result of their freeing themselves from their current circumstance. Their freedom, instead, comes from external sources—they are on the receiving end of goodwill from men or God Himself. This beatitude, however, now offers happiness to individuals who actively offer something—mercy—to others. The benefit that they ultimately receive comes from what they themselves do. Whether their acts of being merciful are from a conscientious decision to do good, or they just naturally arise from a merciful temperament is not the point. The point is that they are extending mercy to others, and in doing so, happiness and mercy shall be extended to them in return.

The Greek word for the action of being merciful is the word *eleemon.*[132] It means to be *merciful* or *compassionate.* The reward to be obtained—"mercy"—is the word "eleeo"[133] which is defined as *to obtain compassion.* Differences in interpretation stem from Greek grammar, but, as the beatitude shows, the person giving compassion will in turn be someone who receives compassion.

What is important to comprehend is that for compassion to have any meaning, two conditions must be met. First, someone needs something, and second, someone has something to give to that person in need. The need and the gift can be just about anything—material, emotional, judicial, and so forth. The compassionate person, however, sees the need of another and actively chooses to give something for the benefit of the person in need. It is also important to understand that the act of compassion has some measure of cost for the giving person—whether it be material resources, time, emotional energy, or simply acquiescence—true compassion requires action and has some form of cost to the giver.

What is interesting about this beatitude is that Jesus phrases it in an implied reciprocal structure. The person extending mercy is also a person in need of mercy—or at least that person will need mercy sometime in the future. This beatitude calls one's attention

---

[132] Strong's Word NT:1655
[133] Strong's Word NT:1653

to the fact we are all equal, in that we will all need mercy at one time or another. Mercy is a mental equalizer. We give it partly because we realize that we may need it in return. We have all found ourselves in need of mercy at one time or another, so it is not too hard to empathize with anyone in need of mercy.

Spiritually, the second part of this verse reveals that the justification for God giving someone mercy can hinge on how compassionate they have been to others. This is a consistent message of Jesus', found within this sermon and throughout the Gospels. For example, this theme brings to mind the Lord's Prayer in the Sermon on the Mount where Jesus teaches us to ask the Father to *"forgive our debts, as we forgive our debtors,"* or as many Bible translations put it, *"Forgive our trespasses as we forgive those who have trespassed against us."*[134] This is a request to God to be merciful to us, as we have been merciful to others. Jesus also teaches that we will receive back in the same proportion as we give to others.[135] And he teaches; give to the poor and you will have treasure in heaven.[136]

On one occasion, one of Jesus' disciples asked him how often he should forgive his brother. The disciple ventured a guess of seven times. Jesus, however, instructed him that he should be willing to forgive 490 times.[137] But Jesus did not stop there, he went on to give a parable about a servant who owed an exceptionally large debt, which he could not repay, to his rich king. The story is relevant to this beatitude and continues as follows:

The kingdom of heaven is like a certain king who wanted to settle accounts with his servants.

---

[134] Matthew 6:12

[135] See Luke 6:38

[136] See Matthew 19:21

[137] Matthew 18:22

And when he had begun to settle accounts, one was brought to him who owed him ten thousand talents.[138] *But as he was not able to pay, his master commanded that he be sold, with his wife and children and all that he had, and that payment be made. The servant therefore fell down before him, saying, "Master, have patience with me, and I will pay you all." Then the master of that servant was moved with compassion, released him, and forgave him the debt.*

But that servant went out and found one of his fellow servants who owed him a hundred denarii;[139] *and he laid hands on him and took him by the throat, saying, "Pay me what you owe!" So his fellow servant fell down at his feet and begged him, saying, "Have patience with me, and I will pay you all." And he would not, but went and threw him into prison till he should pay the debt.*

*When his fellow servants saw what had been done, they were very grieved, and came and told their master all that had been done. Then his master, after he had called him, said to him, "You wicked servant! I forgave you all that debt because you begged me. Should you not also have had **compassion** [our word **mercy**] on your fellow servant, just as I had **pity** [our word **mercy**] on you?" And his master was angry, and delivered him to the torturers until he should pay all that was due to him.*

---

[138] One "talent" was approximately 80 pounds of silver.

[139] One "denarius" was a day's wage. It took 6,000 "denarii" (plural of denarius) to equal one talent.

[And Jesus concluded by saying,] *So My heavenly Father also will do to you if each of you, from his heart, does not forgive his brother his trespasses* [emphasis added].[140]

The disparity of what was owed to the king versus what was owed to the "wicked servant" is immense, and that is one of the points Jesus is making. What we owe to God is immense; therefore, His forgiveness is equally immense. The debts we owe to each other are trivial by comparison, so we should be willing to be merciful and forgive each other's debts. However, the most important concern in this story is that God, who once gave mercy and forgave us, has the authority to retract that mercy and again hold us in debt for what we previously owed Him. This should be a very solemn thought—God can cancel His mercy.

With this thought in mind, it could be fitting to paraphrase Jesus' fifth beatitude to read as follows:

Blessed are the merciful, for they shall obtain **and retain** mercy.

One final thought before we move on to the next beatitude. Perhaps you have already noticed that Jesus' second and fifth beatitudes have a similar theme. In the second beatitude, *"Blessed are those who mourn, for they shall be comforted,"* the comforter is the one who is giving mercy or compassion to someone in need. So, the second and fifth beatitudes both deal with acts of mercy. The difference is that, in the second beatitude, Jesus highlights the fact that the person receiving the compassion will be *"blessed,"* while in the fifth beatitude, Jesus highlights the fact that the giver of the compassion will be *"blessed."* Once again, we see that mercy is a reciprocal

---

[140] Matthew 18:23–35

event. Both the receiver and the giver can enjoy its blessings.

Jesus' fifth beatitude has clear "equity" overtones. It can be explained in spiritual and non-spiritual terms—and both are correct in the context of Jesus' many Gospel teachings. In all cases, one's needs are being met from sources outside of themselves. If we look at a non-spiritual application, then those who address the needs of others will benefit from similar help when they themselves are in need. If we look at the text in a spiritual context, as in the mercy of being forgiven, then one's mercy toward others opens the door to obtaining (and retaining) forgiveness from God. By extension, in the latter case, one's mercy toward others is then a factor of salvation, and entrance into the kingdom of heaven.

CHAPTER 10

Blessed Are the Pure in Heart

"Blessed are the pure in heart,
for they shall see God."

Matthew 5:8

At first glance, one might look at this verse and wonder, *what could be the equity or social justice connection to this verse?* It seems rather passive, not at all active like the *merciful* verse before it, or the *peacemaker* verse which is to follow. One might even conclude that there is no connection, but they would be wrong! There is a connection, and it is an extraordinarily strong connection. It is not too hard to comprehend once you begin to trace the clues in the verse. The secrets lie in finding the meaning of the word "pure," and in tracking down precisely who are those who *"shall see God."*

Let us start our investigation by discovering what "pure in heart" means. The Greek word translated *pure* here is the word *katharos*.[141] The word means *clean*. It and its Greek variations of the same word convey the thought of washing in order to clean or make something *pure*. So, another way to read this verse is, *"Blessed are the **clean** in heart, for they shall see God."* One only needs to understand the meaning of being "pure in heart" or "clean in heart" in order to comprehend what kind of persons make up this group.

---

[141] Strong's Word NT:2513

In the Old Testament (NKJV), the phrase *"pure in heart"* occurs, but only on one occasion. It is found in Psalm 73:1. Interestingly, the Hebrew word translated "pure" in this psalm is *bar*[142] and it can also be translated as "clean." The reason for this is because the word *bar* comes from the Hebrew word *barar*,[143] which means to *clarify, brighten* or *examine. Barar* is often translated into English as *cleanse, polished, purify,* or *purge.* In short, one can think of *barar* as the action, and *bar* (pure) as the result of that action.

You might recall that earlier we discovered that Jesus lifted the phrase, *"The meek shall inherit the earth"* from Psalm 37:11, and we were able to go to that psalm and discover valuable information on the characteristics of the meek. Here, we once again have a phrase that Jesus lifted from the psalms, so we again have the opportunity to examine it for greater detail. It is as if Jesus is dropping clues in his sermon that work to tie his message, and the minds of his listeners, to the words of the Old Testament. We would be negligent in our search if we did not investigate His clues. So, let us dig deeper into who are the *pure in heart.*

Psalm 73 is a song written by one of King David's leading musicians and a choir leader—a man by the name of Asaph. However, Asaph is not just a good musician and choir director, the Bible records that he is also a *seer.*[144] A seer is a person who has visions of the future; a prophet. Therefore, when Jesus quotes the words of Asaph, he is referencing the words of a prophet. We should, therefore, expect to find some meaningful information in the psalm. Let us take a closer look. Asaph, the prophet, begins his song with the following statement:

---

[142] Strong's Word OT:1249

[143] Strong's Word OT 1305

[144] 2 Chronicles 29:30

114

*Truly God is good to Israel, to such as are **pure in heart**. But as for me, my feet had almost stumbled; my steps had nearly slipped. For I was envious of the boastful, when I saw the prosperity of the wicked* [emphasis added].[145]

Asaph's introduction is an unusual confession. He acknowledges that God is good to the "pure in heart" but then reveals he had a temporary lapse of confidence in this knowledge and he "almost stumbled"—he almost "slipped." In other words, he almost fell away from being one of God's "pure in heart." And what caused this? Asaph saw that the boastful wicked were prosperous, and he became envious of their prosperity. From verses 4 through 12, Asaph lists many traits and life conditions of these wicked—some of which may have been enticing Asaph to stumble. Here is a partial listing of those points concerning the boastful wicked:

- They are strong even to the time of death (v. 4)
- They are not troubled/plagued like others (v. 5)
- They are prideful and violent (v. 6)
- They bulge with abundance and have more than their heart could wish for (v. 7)
- They scoff at oppression (i.e., don't object to it) (v. 8)
- They speak against heaven (v. 9)
- They control resources (v. 10)
- They believe God does not know what they do (v. 11)
- They are always at ease and increasingly rich (v. 12)

Asaph ends this list of conditions by lamenting that he may have *"cleansed his heart in vain."*[146] The word he uses for

---

[145] Psalm 73:1–3
[146] Psalm 73:13

"cleansed"[147] is another Hebrew word that means *translucent, clean, innocent, pure.* So, once again, we have a reference to a "pure heart." Asaph continues his song by telling us that God gave him understanding that the wicked would eventually fall, and fall hard. He concludes the song by declaring that it is good for him to *"draw near to God"* and put his *"trust in the Lord."*[148]

Asaph's list is not concerning the things that make a pure heart. Nevertheless, this negative list does give us a good reference point of what the "pure in heart" are not like. Fortunately, the Bible does give us a positive list of what it means to be *clean* or *pure.* It is found in the first chapter of the book of the Prophet Isaiah. This chapter starts out with God criticizing His people for their sinfulness, but He then tells them what to do to become clean again. His instructions are as follows:

> *Wash yourselves, make yourselves clean* [pure]*; put away the evil of your doings from before my eyes. Cease to do evil, learn to do good; seek justice, rebuke the oppressor; defend the fatherless, plead for the widow.*[149]

Between Asaph's negative list of what the "pure in heart" are not, and Isaiah's positive list of what the pure are, I would say we now have a clear picture of the character of those who are "pure in heart." We know what they do, and do not do. Can you see a social justice and a social equity connection now? It is not too hard to see.

Before we move on to our next clue concerning those who "shall see God," I want to take a quick look at a New Testament verse that references those who are pure and clean. This verse

---

[147] Strong's Word OT:2135

[148] Psalm 73:28

[149] Isaiah 1:16–17

serves as a good bridge between our first and second clues because it describes a bride being made ready to see her bridegroom. It is found in the book of Revelation. It is a portion of the book that speaks about the redeemed of God—those who are saved and entering the kingdom of heaven. It portrays the saved as a bride, and God as the bridegroom. In other words, the passage is speaking of the redeemed coming to "see God." The passage reads as follows:

> *"Alleluia! For the Lord God Omnipotent reigns! Let us be glad and rejoice and give Him glory, for the marriage of the Lamb has come, and His wife has made herself ready." And to her it was granted to be arrayed in fine linen, clean and bright, for the fine linen is the righteous acts of the saints.*[150]

The word for *clean* in the last sentence of this quote is the same word Jesus used for *pure* in his beatitude. So, what is it that makes this fine linen *pure* and bright? It is the "righteous acts" of the saints (i.e., the believers and follows of Jesus). The Greek word for *righteous acts* is the word "*dikaioma*"[151] It means *equitable deeds, acts of charity*.

This verse in Revelation is saying that before the bride (the church or the saints) is ready to see her bridegroom, she needs to put on the fine linen wedding dress. And that dress is spun from pure and bright threads which, according to Isaiah, would be equivalent to ceasing to do evil, learning to do good, seeking justice, rebuking the oppressor, defending the fatherless and pleading on behalf of the widow. One is not ready to wear the fine linen and see the bridegroom (God) until they have engaged in actions of social justice and charity.

---

[150] Revelation 19:6–8
[151] Strong's Word NT:1345

The threads of this wedding dress are also said to be "bright." This is an interesting word because its Old Testament equivalent *taher*[152] is routinely associated with the sacrificial services and with one being forgiven of sin and made innocent because of the atoning power of the sacrifice. So, Revelation is also telling us that the bride not only needs to be socially just and charitable, but she also needs to be forgiven of sin if she is to see God—her bridegroom. She needs atonement.

I do not want to belabor this issue to the point that you become numb to it, but believe it or not, even one's atonement has social justice and charity connections. The holiest day of the Jewish year—the Holiest Sabbath—is the Day of Atonement when one stands in the presence of God. This is the day that God removes the sins of His people. It is also the day that the Year of Jubilee—a Sabbath year—starts every fiftieth year. By Jewish law this is a day when the people are to "afflict" their souls.[153] Just what that "affliction" is to consist of is not specified in the Torah, however, traditionally it has meant that one is to fast. But what kind of fast is acceptable to God? What kind of fast is appropriate for atonement?

Isaiah 58 is a portion of the Bible that addresses this topic of fasting and its relationship to atonement. In this chapter, the people of God complain that they have fasted and afflicted their souls, but they believe God has not taken notice of them. God replies by criticizing that their fast day is a day in which they pursue pleasures, exploit laborers, and do violence. He then instructs them regarding what a good fast day and a day of affliction should be. He states the following:

> *Is this not the fast that I have chosen: to loose the bonds of wickedness, to undo the heavy burdens, to*

---

[152] Strong's Word OT:2891
[153] Leviticus 16:29–34 and Leviticus 23:26–32

let the oppressed go free, and that you break every yoke? Is it not to share your bread with the hungry, and that you bring to your house the poor who are cast out; when you see the naked, that you cover him, and not hide yourself from your own flesh? Then your light shall break forth like the morning, your healing shall spring forth speedily, and your righteousness shall go before you; the glory of the Lord shall be your rear guard. Then you shall call, and the Lord will answer; you shall cry, and He will say, "Here I am."[154]

I recommend that you read the entire chapter. The chapter clearly has Day of Atonement themes because it speaks of transgression, fasting, afflicting one's soul and ends with God calling for them to honor his Sabbath—a day for fostering social justice. The point to take away from this chapter is that God is not going to resolve people's sins (give atonement) or give them guidance until they have had a change of heart and engage in acts of justice and charity. And as we have seen earlier, these Sabbath-themed requirements take faith to implement. They are sacrifices of time and wealth given in faith that God will provide for us as we make needed sacrifices. Such actions are tangible symbols that our good deeds for others are based on our belief that God has forgiven us and cares for us. We give because we have received and have confidence that God will continue to care for us. Atonement requires our faith, sacrifices and a change in how we live our lives. It is a life of faith and fine linen.

So, what about the beatitude's clue concerning *"they shall see God"*? For Jesus to have even suggested that there was a way for humans to see God is a bit provocative in itself. After

---

[154] Isaiah 58:6–9

all, Moses asked to see God's glory when he was in the mountain receiving God's commandments. God replied to Moses saying, *"You cannot see my face; for no man shall see me, and live."*[155] And yet the Bible does, in fact, tell us that the "pure in heart" do seek the face of God. This concept is found in Psalm 24, which is once again from our good friend Asaph. His words are as follows:

> *Who may ascend into the hill of the Lord? Or who may stand in His holy place? He who has **clean hands** and a **pure heart**, who has not lifted up his soul to an idol, nor sworn deceitfully. He shall receive blessing from the Lord, and righteousness from the God of his salvation. This is Jacob, the generation of those who seek Him, who seek your face* [emphasis added].[156]

We already know what it means to be *pure in heart*, and understand its justice and charity connections. What does it mean to have *clean hands*? The Hebrew word translated *clean* here is the word *naqiy*,[157] and it means to be *innocent*, *blameless*, or *guiltless*. For humans to be in such a state would mean that they have had their sins forgiven, or that their sins have been atoned for. And, as we have just seen, atonement is a Sabbath function and requires one's participation in the true Sabbath meaning of giving justice and charity—releasing and alleviating burdens. This, along with loyalty to God, and honesty, is what Asaph says it takes to seek God's face—to be pure in heart, and to one day see God.

In conclusion, based on what we have learned from Asaph

---

[155] Exodus 33:20

[156] Psalm 24:3–6

[157] Strong's Word OT:5355

and Isaiah about purity and cleanness, grant me a little liberty to reword Jesus' sixth beatitude to say what it truly implies. It goes as follows:

> Blessed are those who are not materialistic but put their trust in the Lord; those who cease to do evil, and have learned to do good; those who are honest, who seek justice, rebuke the oppressor, defend the fatherless, and plead for the widow; and those who fill their lives with deeds of charity for others; these are the ones who will ascend into the hill of the Lord, who will stand in His holy place, who seek His face; and they shall see God.

I can only imagine that is probably not what you had in mind when you first read Jesus' sixth beatitude. It certainly was not my first impression. But do you see now the equity connection in this proclamation? The *pure in heart*, the *clean*, the *innocent*, are concerned about the plight of others. They have stopped being part of society's problems and have instead entered into an active life of righting wrongs and meeting the needs of others. There really is no purity without action. Being *pure in heart* is not passive. These individuals are active, and Christ's promise to them is, *"they shall see God,"* which means their sins will have been atoned for—forgiven and removed. I will leave it to other theologians to debate the relationship of faith and works, but clearly there is not one without the other—faith and works go hand in hand into salvation.

CHAPTER 11

Blessed Are the Peacemakers

"Blessed are the peacemakers,
for they shall be called the sons of God."

Matthew 5:9

The word "peacemaker" is used only this one time in the Bible, though the concept exists throughout its entirety. It means exactly what it says: *"peace maker."* To put things simply, these are individuals who make or bring peace to people or situations that are not at peace. After all, some degree of unrest must first exist if one is to go about making peace. Peace, therefore, is the resolution of some existing problem. Even the act of maintaining peace requires some resolution of problems that threaten established peace. Whether the problem be warring nations or just a disheartened child, peacemakers serve a valuable role in society. But this beatitude indicates that their value goes beyond our society. It is clear through scripture that God Himself highly values the role of peacemaker. Take note, it is Jesus, the Son of God, who is announcing that peacemakers will be called *sons* (or children) of God. Think of it, he has elevated peacemakers to the level of close kin—placing them within his own family unit.

The concept of peacemaking implies the interaction of people. Yes, it might be possible for a person to change an attitude toward a distressing situation and thus find inner peace for themselves, but, even here, that person's newfound inner peace probably relieves someone else's distress. Though inner peace might have a place in this beatitude, Jesus' primary focus is on two classes of individuals—those who are distressed, and those who have the ability and interest to alleviate someone's distress. Any one of us can be in either of these two classes at any given time. Jesus' aim here is to help us understand that peacemakers do not view themselves as islands unaffected by the sufferings of others. They are active agents in the world, interacting with others, for the benefit of others.

Logically, the concept of peacemaking implies the concepts of equity. A peacemaker is striving to achieve some sort of balance among opposing parties or situations. I could stop here and just move on to the next beatitude, however, a brief study of the key words of this beatitude result in some amazing insights—insights too good to overlook. The keys to understanding come from focusing on the clues, *"peacemaker"* and *"sons of God."* First, we have action, then we have reward or status. Once we understand these two concepts, the interconnection between them is obvious. Let us separate these two concepts for a moment, look at each more closely, and then rejoin them together.

The concept of peace, peacemaking, and social justice or equity are intricately linked in the Bible. In short, the two are parallel concepts. Though the word "peacemaker" only appears in this beatitude, the words *"those who make peace"*—an identical concept—are mentioned in chapter three of the book of James. Here are the verses as given by the brother of Jesus. Notice all the keywords:

> *But the wisdom that is from above is first*
> *pure, then peaceable, gentle, willing to yield,*
> *full of mercy and good fruits, without partiali-*

*ty and without hypocrisy. Now the fruit of righteousness is sown in peace by **those who make peace.**[158]*

The Greek word translated "righteousness"[159] in James can also be translated as "equity." In other words, the fruit of equity (one's character or actions) are sown in peace by those who make peace. Essentially, James is saying that the works of equity sown by the peacemaker are conducted (sown) in peaceful ways for the purpose of making peace. Their actions, driven by "wisdom," are not those of a warrior subjecting one to a forced peace, but rather they exercise the diplomatic traits listed in this passage to bring about true peace. Take notice that the traits are to be put into action *"without partiality or hypocrisy."* This thought will come up again in later passages.

A relationship between righteousness and peace also appears in the book of Isaiah on several occasions. One example reads as follows:

> *The work of righteousness will be peace, and the effect of righteousness, quietness and assurance forever.*[160]

The Hebrew word translated "righteousness" here in Isaiah is once again *"tsedaqah."*[161] This word and its derivatives carry the meanings of justice, morality, equity, beneficence, and cleanness. The verse speaks for itself. The *"work of righteousness will be peace,"* because in effect, righteousness results in peace. God, through Isaiah, is plainly showing that working toward and

---

[158] James 3:17–18
[159] Strong's Word NT:1343
[160] Isaiah 32:17
[161] Strong's Word OT:6666

achieving justice and equity in a society will have positive, peaceful benefits for the whole community, leading to quietness and assurance.

Another connection between equity concepts and peace is again found in the book of Isaiah, where the prophet is lamenting the moral conditions of the people. He lists numerous problems with his contemporary society and observes the following:

> *The way of peace they have not known, and there is no justice in their ways; they have made themselves crooked paths; whoever takes that way shall not know peace.*[162]

In short, justice and peace are parallel paths. Interestingly, Isaiah earlier cites some of the problems in his society that had led to this condition. He stated the following:

> *Your iniquities have separated you from your God; and your sins have hidden His face from you, so that He will not hear. For your hands are defiled with blood, and your fingers with iniquity; your lips have spoken lies, your tongue has muttered perversity. No one calls for justice, nor does any plead for truth. They trust in empty words and speak lies; they conceive evil and bring forth iniquity . . . and the act of violence is in their hands. Their feet run to evil, and they make haste to shed innocent blood; their thoughts are thoughts of iniquity; wasting and destruction are in their paths.*"[163]

---

[162] Isaiah 59:8
[163] Isaiah 59:2–4, 6–7

This situation of the people not knowing peace had, at least in part, came about because there was no one calling for justice or pleading for the truth. Instead, the people had chosen to follow untruthful words, planned evil, and had brought forth the opposite of righteousness—that is, iniquity, a variation of the word inequity. The result was anything but quietness and assurance to the people.

I cite these verses in Isaiah 59 in order to argue an opposite point. If *"peacemakers"* had been present in that day, they would have been the ones to "call for justice" and to "plead for truth," and perhaps righteousness would have been respected, resulting in peace prevailing in society. The point to argue is that peacemakers are the ones that hold the morality of a society in check. Without strong, active peacemakers, one gets the society that Isaiah describes above. Righteousness, and all that it implies, leads to peace. Peacemakers are those who are striving for right doing, for justice and for equity, whether it is for the community at large or for its most insignificant members. Is this the type of peacemaker that Jesus had in mind when he spoke his seventh beatitude? In context with his earlier beatitudes, I would argue that it is, and this becomes apparent when we look at the phrase, *"sons of God."*

The Greek word translated *"sons"* is the word *huios*[164] in its plural form. The word can mean *sons* or merely *kinship* of varying degrees. The exact same word is frequently translated throughout the New Testament as *children*. In fact, many English translations of the Bible actually use the phrase, *"children of God"* in their translations of Jesus' seventh beatitude. To gain insight into this latter portion of this beatitude, we can therefore follow the use of this phrase—and the kinship with God that it represents—in other parts of the Bible. Does kinship with God have an equity connection? We shall soon see.

Psalm 82 is another one of Asaph's messages. Though this short psalm has an overall negative tone and ending, it gives us

---

[164] Strong's Word 5207

a key insight into what some of the important characteristics of the "children" of God should be. In this psalm, Asaph quotes God as making reference to the fact He Himself has called his people "*gods*"[165] and "*children of the Most High*" (verse 6). However, in this verse, God laments the fact that His people have not lived up to the honorary title He had given them. Because of this failure, God has chosen to judge them and bring about their downfall. And what did they do wrong, to deserve this fate? Asaph reveals their shortcomings by first revealing a probing question asked by God, and then through stating what these "*children of the Most High*" should be doing.

> *How long will you judge unjustly, and show partiality to the wicked? Defend the poor and fatherless; do justice to the afflicted and needy. Deliver the poor and needy; free them from the hand of the wicked.*[166]

From these passages we can see that God expects His *children* to be active agents in their communities, defending the needs of the less fortunate and oppressed. The expectation is high enough that God is willing to mete out judgment and punishment to His own children if they fail to represent His interests.

Jesus once asked the question, "*Who is my mother and who are my brothers?*" His answer,

> *Whoever does the will of My Father in heaven is my brother and sister and mother.*[167]

---

[165] Strong's Word OT:430 "Elohim." This word is one name of God and can also refer to judges, mighty ones, and sometimes to angels.

[166] Psalm 82:2–4

[167] Matthew 12:48–50

Here we find for the second time in the book of Matthew that Jesus demonstrates we can have close kinship with him and his Father. Being a brother or sister of Jesus, the Son of God, effectively makes us children of God as well. That status is reached by the act of doing the "*will*" of the Father in heaven. This concept closely parallels the message derived from Psalm 82. The status of "*children*" is not freely given or retained. It requires the action of doing the will of God. In the case of Psalm 82, the actions are all issues of equity—making sure that we who have positions of authority, or material goods, do not deprive those who have less.

In another passage of the Sermon on the Mount, Jesus addresses the need to do the "will of the Father"[168] (the essence of being children of God) in order to enter the kingdom of heaven. Those who are rejected from the kingdom, who did not do the will of the Father, are denounced as having "practiced lawlessness."[169] Not doing the will of the Father is therefore synonymous to practicing lawlessness. Conversely then, doing the will of the Father is the practice of the law.

But one might ask what law is Jesus referring to? The answer is given to us twice by Jesus himself in the book of Matthew. On one occasion Jesus tells us that all the "Law and Prophets" hang on two condensed commandments. First: "You shall love the Lord your God with all your heart, with all your soul, and with all your mind." And second: "You shall love your neighbor as yourself."[170] On another occasion, from the Sermon on the Mount itself, Jesus states the following:

Whatever you want men to do to you, do also to them, for this is the Law and the Prophets.[171]

---

[168] Matthew 7:21

[169] Matthew 7:23

[170] Matthew 22:37–39

[171] Matthew 7:12

This latter statement is commonly known as the "Golden Rule." Are you noticing a pattern in the above paragraphs? There is a linkage from "*Children of God*" to the actions of equity. It goes like this: Children (sons) of God are those who do the will of the Father. Those who do the will of the Father are those who practice the law. Those who practice the law are those who love God and their neighbor as themselves, and treat their fellow mankind as they themselves wish to be treated. Treating everyone fairly and justly is the essence of equity—the essence of the meanings of the word righteousness, both in Hebrew and in Greek.

Based on the verses we have looked at in this section, a side-by-side comparison chart of the characteristics of "*peacemakers*" and "*sons of God*" would look like this:

Characteristic of "*Peacemakers*"	Characteristics of "*Sons of God*"
Pure, peaceable, gentle, willing to yield, full of mercy and good fruits, impartial, non-hypocritical, bearers of fruits of equity, calling for justice, pleading for truth.	Judges justly, impartial, defends poor and fatherless, does justice to the afflicted and needy, frees others from the hand of the wicked, does the will of the Father, practices the law, loves his neighbor and treats him as he himself wishes to be treated.

It should be plain to see that the two sides of the seventh beatitude are essentially equal. Though somewhat different words have been used, the concepts these words carry are essentially the same, and they center on concepts of equity—fairness to and among mankind. Both "peacemakers" and "sons of God" are defenders of the rights and needs of everyone within their community, especially those who are being neglected or taken advantage of.

One last thing needs to be pointed out. Jesus uses the phrase *"sons of God"* in another place in the Gospels. On that occasion, found in Luke 20:36, Jesus is explaining that those who are resurrected in the coming age will no longer be subject to death, but will be like the angels and are *"sons of God."* If the future application of this phrase can be carried back to the seventh beatitude, then it can be argued that what Jesus is saying is that peacemakers will be granted the right of resurrection in the future. The argument could be valid since in the beatitude Jesus states that peacemakers ***"shall** be called sons of God."* This can be construed to imply a future title. This idea can also be supported by the fact that in Matthew 7:21 the *"sons of God"* are those who do the will of the Father and are the ones who are being granted entrances into the kingdom of heaven—a future event in the context of that passage. The event, however, can begin in one's present life.

In summary, it can be said that peacemakers are those who have the same characteristics as the sons of God. They are individuals who are doing the works of equity. They are callers for justice, pleaders for truth, defenders of the poor, the fatherless, the afflicted and the needy. They love their neighbor as themselves and treat others as they would like to be treated. They will be resurrected by God. They will enter the kingdom of heaven and be given the title *"Sons of God."*

Before we move on to the next beatitude, I would like to point out a pattern that has developed in these first seven beatitudes. Jesus' first three beatitudes dealt with people in some form of need—the materially poor, the emotionally grief-stricken, and the acquiescently oppressed. Poverty, sorrow, and oppression, these are things that can make our lives unbearable. But Jesus promises blessing to each of these groups.

Beatitudes five, six, and seven addressed individuals who actively attend to other people's needs—the merciful, the pure in heart, and the peacemaker. These are the "relievers" or the "warriors" who can address the needs of the first three groups. They are the physical manifestation of the kingdom of heaven responding to and on behalf of the poor, sorrowful, and meek. The first group of three beatitudes concerns blessings that people will receive because of the actions taken by members of the kingdom of heaven to help them. The second group of three beatitudes concerns the blessing that the people taking the action to help will receive.

Bridging between the two sets of three is the fourth beatitude, which reveals the motivation for the flow between the two groups—a hungering and thirsting for righteousness. Hungering and thirsting by either group can set into motion the actions that will fill their hunger and be a blessing. People, whether they be poor or rich, downtrodden or royal, must first want change, before change can begin to bend an unjust social paradigm of a stagnant and apathetic community. However, change does not come without opposition from those who are satisfied with the *status quo*. Those who hunger and thirst for righteousness may be filled as promised, but the meal will be bittersweet, as Jesus' next two beatitudes warn.

CHAPTER 12

Blessed Are the Persecuted

Blessed are those who are persecuted for righteousness sake, for theirs is the kingdom of heaven.

Blessed are you when they revile and persecute you, and say all kinds of evil against you falsely for my sake. Rejoice and be exceedingly glad, for great is your reward in heaven, for so they persecuted the prophets who were before you.

Matthew 5:10–12

Jesus' eighth and ninth beatitudes deal with the theme of persecution. I have chosen to address them together under one chapter because, in order to fully understand these blessings, one needs to compare them. They are, of course, different—one is more detailed than the other—and we need to ask ourselves, "Why did Jesus find it necessary to address the topic of persecution in two different pronouncements?" Before we start, however, let me ask you to carefully read the two beatitudes again and pay special attention to how they are similar and how they are different. Let us see if we come up with similar observations—shall we?

The first observation I would like to point out concerns the *heavenly* promises given to the two groups. Jesus tells the first group that the persecution they face will result in their inheriting the kingdom of heaven. He tells the second group that their persecution will result in a great heavenly reward. Notice, both groups have heavenly rewards. It would be odd for us to conclude that the blessing of the first group is not one shared by the second when both have been persecuted, and both have a part in heaven. If one has a great reward in heaven, would they not also be someone who can say that *theirs is the kingdom of heaven*? After all their reward is *"in heaven."*

I believe the answer to this riddle is uncomplicated. Both persecuted groups have the promise of *"theirs is the kingdom of heaven."* Jesus just does not repeat stating that promise in the second of these two beatitudes because it should be self-evident. What Jesus does focus on in the second of these two is the promise that the second group not only has heaven as a possession, but they will also receive a great reward in heaven as well. So, both groups receive the minimum gift of the kingdom of heaven, but those who have experienced the additional suffering of the second group—suffering for the sake of Jesus—will have additional "great" reward.

Now let us turn our attention to dissecting the eighth beatitude, and use what we learn as a platform to further understand the ninth. To start with, let us look at the Greek word Jesus used for "persecuted." It is the word *dioko*,[172] and it means being *aggressively chased* or put *to flight*. It is the picture of one being pursued and having to *flee* due to opposition. This word is used in both the eighth and ninth beatitude. Jesus is not talking merely about verbal opposition; he is meaning all kinds of oppositions even to the point of one having to fear for their safety.

The Greek word for *"righteousness"* is now a familiar one to us. It has shown up already in the fourth beatitude and several of our research texts. It is the word *dikaiosune*.[173] It means *equity*

---

[172] Strong's Word NT:1377
[173] Strong's Word NT:1343

or *equitable in character or in act.* We have seen that it is used to represent people who are socially active in defending the defenseless, or are charitable to the weaker sectors of their communities. Jesus is telling us that persecution is what one could face if they choose to enter the struggle for social equity—they will be persecuted for righteousness sake.

Up until this time, Jesus' teachings of the need for equity in society can be seen as a reasonable concept. After all, wouldn't most people agree that there are community benefits in having equitable treatment for all its members? This eighth beatitude, however, bluntly switches the utopian scene being described to a scene of reality. The pursuit of equity will be met with opposition, and even persecution.

It is human nature for any one of us to feel some level of insecurity when we are asked to surrender part of our resources. Most people are reluctant to do so if they feel their security is being threatened. Many are even ready to fight those who they perceive are threatening their security. (Jesus addresses this issue of insecurity later in the sermon.) There are even sectors of society that will not share Jesus' views, and are willing to fight to see that the needs of the less fortunate are not addressed. Greed creates a caste system, and many people do not want that system changed. Jesus does not hesitate to warn his listeners that persecution is waiting for them when they seek righteousness.

The eighth beatitude asserts that the kingdom of heaven will, inevitably, despite the opposition, be established. The fact that there will be those who possess the kingdom of heaven means that there will be a kingdom of heaven to possess. Notice also that the eighth beatitude shares this blessing with those of the first beatitude—they are both promised that *theirs is the kingdom of heaven.* It should not be too surprising that those working in defense of the weaker sectors of society— the poor—have a share in the better society they help build.

It is also easy to observe that those suffering persecution for righteousness sake are those represented by the fourth, fifth, sixth, and seventh beatitudes. These are the socially active cravers for righteousness, the merciful, the pure in heart, and the peacemakers. The kingdom of heaven is theirs as well, and they too will face opposition as they practice the actions of their characters.

So how does this eighth beatitude differ from the ninth? Recall what the ninth beatitude says:

> *Blessed are you when they revile and persecute you, and say all kinds of evil against you falsely for my sake. Rejoice and be exceedingly glad, for great is your reward in heaven, for so they persecuted the prophets who were before you.*

At first glance it would appear that Jesus is merely elaborating on the previous beatitude in this ninth blessing. It gives a reason for the opposition; it elaborates on the types of persecution; it promises an additional *great* reward, and it associates the persecuted with the heroes of the Old Testament. But a closer look reveals some interesting clues that indicate that Jesus is addressing two different classes of followers. The eighth beatitude addresses "those" who are persecuted while the ninth beatitude is addressed to "you." The eighth beatitude is a proclamation that references people in general—and specifically "those" people who are not present to hear Jesus' sermon. The "you" of the ninth beatitude is directed toward the disciples who are present to hear Jesus, and to any of the listeners who may be interested in becoming one of his disciples.

Championing the cause of social equity-righteousness is one thing, but championing the cause of a king who is building a kingdom based on that social philosophy is quite another. This is what the "you" of the ninth beatitude is addressing. The persecution this time is coming, not solely from the fact that one is fighting for *"righteousness sake,"* but that "you" are doing it for the "sake" of Jesus Christ. The word "you" in this passage reveals that the followers of this philosophy have a two-fold pursuit: they support the concepts of equity-righteousness, and they do so because they believe that the kingdom of heaven is ruled by Jesus and he has commissioned them to help usher in His kingdom. As a disciple of Jesus your motivation is not just socioeconomic, it is religiopolitical as well—you are building a kingdom which has Jesus as its king. This added layer of motivation creates additional opposition from the world, because while many may indeed be sympathetic to the plight of the poor, they may not be open to the rulership of Jesus Christ.

The opposition coming from those who reject the rulership of Jesus will be intense, according to this beatitude. Not only are his followers to be persecuted, but they will be reviled, slandered, and misrepresented. The Greek words that Jesus uses in this blessing indicate taunting, defamation of character, verbal abuses, and false accusations. The persecutions arising because of the disciples' motivation to defend equity for the sake of Jesus, provokes a level of darkness that is much greater than persecutions against those championing the causes of equity for equity's sake only.

The rewards for the disciples will, however, be greater than those that await the general public. Not only will they be rewarded with the benefits described earlier in each beatitude, but they are promised a "great" reward in heaven. And Jesus instructs his disciples to be "exceedingly glad" during this time of persecution. The Greek words convey the picture of jumping for joy in the face of their trials. The implication is, once again, that the kingdom of heaven will succeed—they are not being persecuted for a losing cause.

The distinction that there is a great reward for persecution due to "my sake" is an important one, because this is the first time in the sermon that Jesus has revealed he plays an essential role in this kingdom. He has been giving the disciples and the listening crowd directives on how to live the tenets of this kingdom. Now, he has revealed that living his words has a divine connection, and will result in great heavenly rewards. This additional reward is not obtained for the sake of righteousness. It is obtained for the sake of following Jesus' words and identifying oneself as a disciple of his. Moses and the prophets of old called repeatedly upon the people to follow the *words* that God gave them, in order to have blessing from God. The people were not to follow the *men* of God; they were to follow the *words* of God. In all these cases, the message is superior, and the messengers are subordinate. However, here, Jesus is calling on the people to follow *him* and *his words* if they are to have great heavenly blessing. This is a bold and brash statement on Jesus' part unless, of course, he is divine.

Stop and think of the implications of Jesus separating the topic of persecution into two statements: one for "those" of a general public who are seekers of righteousness, and one for "you" who are exposed to his message and have become his followers. Is Jesus saying that anyone who actively works toward a more righteous world is to have a share in the kingdom of heaven? If beatitude nine focuses on rewards to the followers of Jesus, is beatitude eight giving heavenly privileges to those who are not followers of Jesus? After all, the eighth beatitude clearly implies that the *those* are the people doing what they do for the "sake" of righteousness. Can it be that the kingdom of heaven holds a place for the non-followers of Jesus—those who do not know Christ or have not been exposed to his message, but pursue righteousness because it is right?

These are provocative questions because Christianity is severely divided on this issue. There is a full range of opinions on who will, or can, be saved and can enter the kingdom of heaven. At one extreme end of the range there is the belief that all people will be saved—after all, Jesus "takes away the sin of the world."[174] At the other extreme, there is the belief that God has predetermined from the foundation of the earth, who will be saved, and no matter what one does or does not do, God's decision is set. Between these two poles is a sea of opinions. It is therefore impossible for me to give you a definitive "right" answer. The best I can do is give you my opinion and let you evaluate it on its own merits—take it or leave it as you wish.

I take the position that Jesus is saying the kingdom of heaven is open to any person who lives a moral, honest, socially equitable and charitable life, even if (and "if" is an important distinction) they do not know Christ as their savior or king. As proof, let me give you the following thoughts.

Jesus intentionally gave us two beatitudes dealing with persecution. Why do that if heavenly blessings are only for believers? This is not a question of a degree of persecution between the two groups; according to Jesus, both are being persecuted to the point of having to flee for their safety. The second of these two beatitudes is clearly directed toward those suffering because of their devotion to Jesus. This implies that the first group is not being persecuted due to devotion to Jesus. One group is doing right because Jesus is their king, and they follow his words, but the other group is doing right because it is the right thing to do. God honors these right actions of the first group. They too will be given a blessing, even the blessing of having a share in the kingdom of heaven.

We can also rely on Jesus' own words regarding his judgments in the final days "*when the Son of Man comes in his glory*

---

[174] John 1:29

and all his holy angels with him."[175] We are told the following in this teaching of his.

> *He* [Jesus] *will sit on the throne of His glory. All the nations will be gathered before Him, and He will separate them one from another, as a shepherd divides his sheep from the goats. And He will set the sheep on His right hand, but the goats on the left. Then the King will say to those on His right hand, "Come, you blessed of My Father, inherit the kingdom prepared for you from the foundation of the world: for I was hungry and you gave Me food; I was thirsty and you gave Me drink; I was a stranger and you took Me in; I was naked and you clothed Me; I was sick and you visited Me; I was in prison and you came to Me."*
>
> *Then the righteous* [sheep] *will answer Him, saying, "Lord, when did we see You hungry and feed You, or thirsty and give You drink? When did we see You a stranger and take You in, or naked and clothe You? Or when did we see You sick, or in prison, and come to You?" And the King will answer and say to them, "Assuredly, I say to you, inasmuch as you did it to one of the least of these My brethren, you did it to Me."*[176]

Let me begin my comments here by giving you a piece of important information. The Greek word translated "*nations*" is the word *ethnos*.[177] It means *gentiles*, *non-Jews*, or *nonbelievers* in the God of the Bible, implying the *heathen* world. This

---

[175] Matthew 25:31

[176] Matthew 25:31–40

[177] Strong's Word NT:1484

story does not tell us about the judgment of Christians. This is obvious because a believer in Jesus Christ would be familiar with this story and would not have to ask Jesus the question, *"When did we see you hungry, or sick . . . ?"* Christians know that what they do for others is done *for* and *to* Christ.

It is the sheep of the gathered gentile nations that must ask Jesus, *"When did we see you . . . ?"* These are, therefore, those who have not been exposed to the teachings of Jesus. And having not been exposed to his teachings, it is highly unlikely they knowingly follow him as their Lord and savior. Nevertheless, they did follow the will of God, even though they did not know God. Jesus awards them the right to inherit the kingdom, which later in this parable is equated with having eternal life.[178]

Many Christians object to this idea, stating the Bible teaches that one can only be saved by the name of Jesus Christ. They will cite Peter's sermon on the Day of Pentecost (Acts 2:21–22) and his sermon before the Sanhedrin (Acts 4:10–12). In these sermons, Peter clearly states that *"whoever calls on the name of the Lord shall be saved,"* and that *"there is no other name under heaven given among men by which we must be saved."* I do not see a conflict between Peter's words and those of Jesus' parable of the sheep as I have presented it above.

Think of it for a moment. With the fall of mankind at the Garden of Eden, all mankind has been barred entrance into heaven. Reentry has only been made possible by the life and death, and resurrection of Jesus Christ. He has reopened the door to us—all of us—if we wish to go in. If God were to decide that a Native American living in South America in 25 BCE was of good moral character and lived a righteous life and gave him entrance into the kingdom of God, would it not be based on the fact that Jesus made his entrance possible. Even this pre-Christian individual, not knowing Jesus, would be saved because of what Jesus did for hu-

---

[178] Matthew 25:46

manity. Regardless of how "good" he may have been, he cannot enter unless Christ has opened the door. He may never have had the knowledge to call on Jesus' name, but it is still the name and life of Jesus that has saved him.

The ninth beatitude would be pointing out that our pre-Christian individual, from our earlier example, will have less of a reward than the followers of Christ who suffer for the sake of their Lord. Many Christians cannot comprehend this because they believe our pre-Christian individual has no salvation at all. I believe, however, that Jesus is teaching that he can be saved, and rewarded for his faithful life. Should that disappoint a Christian? If it does, it might call into question one's love of his neighbor, or his understanding of God's love and justice for all of His creatures.

Christians can also turn to the writings of Paul in Romans, chapter two, verses one to sixteen. Though even this is debated by Christians, Paul does appear to be saying that those who have not had an opportunity to know God's law and His will, can still be led by God. If willing, they are able to follow Him correctly and be judged accordingly.

The disciple, Peter, was also led to a similar conclusion when the Holy Spirit directed him to the home of a Gentile man named Cornelius, a sincere follower of God, though he did not know who God was. Peter preached Jesus to him and his family, and baptized them all. Later, the church in Judea questioned Peter's visit to Cornelius and his baptism of this Gentile family into the kingdom of heaven. But Peter recounted how the Holy Spirit had led him to Cornelius' home and he told the church apostles and brethren the following:

> *In truth I perceive that God shows no partiality. But in every nation whoever fears Him and works righteousness is accepted by Him.*[179]

---

[179] Acts 10:34–35; see full story in Acts 10 and 11.

Now, in this case, God sent Peter to instruct Cornelius—to reveal the name of Jesus—but what if the God-fearing man and worker of righteousness was our Native American from 25 BCE in our example above? Would God reject him because of a lack of opportunity to be told who God is and the way of salvation though Jesus Christ?

Other Christians will quickly argue that this idea violates the words of Jesus Christ in John 3:16. To those I would have to say, "Read the whole dialog of Jesus with Nicodemus". He had more to say than just John 3:16. Look at what Jesus says after that famous statement:

> *For God did not send His Son into the world to **condemn** the world, but that the world through Him might be saved. He who believes in Him is not **condemned**; but he who does not believe is **condemned** already, because he has not believed in the name of the only begotten Son of God. And this is the **condemnation**, that the light has come into the world, and men loved darkness rather than light, because their deeds were evil. For everyone practicing evil hates the light and does not come to the light, lest his deeds should be exposed. But he who does the truth comes to the light, that his deeds may be clearly seen, that they have been done in God.* (emphasis added)[180]

The issue here is one of condemnation. Those who believe are not "*condemned,*" but those who do not believe are already *condemned*. What does Jesus mean here? Two Greek words are used. The first is for the words "condemn" and "condemned," the second is for the word "condemnation." They are the words

---

[180] John 3:17–21

krino[181] and *krisis*.[182] The word *krino* means *to judge*, or *to decide, to make a decision or judgment*. This is the word the Gospel uses in the first three occurrences in the above passage. The word *krisis* means *the judgment*, or *the decision* that has been made. It is the word translated *condemnation* in the above passage. *Krino* is the act of making a decision, while *krisis* is the decision, or, in this case, the set criteria upon which the decisions are to be made.

So, with this in mind, look at what Jesus is saying here. God did not send His Son into the world to make a decision about someone's fate. Jesus was sent to save the world. How? To die for the world's sins and to be resurrected as proof that he has power over death. This was his mission as the "Lamb of God." Completing this mission reopened the doors of heaven. It made salvation possible.

Those who believe in him are automatically saved and have eternal life—there is no further decision that needs to be made in their case. They get a free pass from court, so to speak. However, those who do not believe (whether voluntarily or due to a lack of information or opportunity) are already condemned—that is, it has been prearranged that they will have to face a decision concerning their eternal life—they do not get the free pass. And, according to Jesus, what will such condemnation (*krisis*) entail, that is, upon what will "*the decision*" to condemn be based? The condemnation is based on how the individual responds to the "light." In this passage's context, light is enlightenment from God regarding "truth" and "evil." The evidence of how a person responds to the light is witnessed by one's evil or godly deeds. The set protocol for judgment (i.e., condemnation) is that those who reject the light and do evil deeds will not have eternal life, and those who accept truth and do the deeds of

---

[181] Strong's Word NT:2919
[182] Strong's Word NT:2920

143

truth will have eternal life. This sounds a lot like Jesus' parable of the sheep and the goat, does it not?

In John 12, Jesus again speaks on this theme and gives us additional confirmation as to how the process works. Note his words:

> *I have come as a light into the world, that whoever believes in Me should not abide in darkness. And if anyone hears My words and does not believe, I do not* **judge** *him; for I did not come to* **judge** *the world but to save the world. He who rejects Me, and does not receive* [i.e., obeys] *My words, has that which* **judges** *him—the* **word that I have spoken will judge him in the last day**. *For I have not spoken on My own authority; but the Father who sent Me gave Me a command, what I should say and what I should speak. And I know that His command* [Jesus' spoken words] *is everlasting life."* (emphasis added)[183]

Notice that Jesus is the standard of light and darkness. We must follow his words, given to us by the Father, to receive eternal life. If someone rejects Jesus and his words, it is the words—teachings—of Jesus that form the basis of how that person is judged in the last days. Presumably, the outcome would not be good since one who rejects Jesus would not place much value in his words of instruction. But what about those who never knew Jesus? What if they lived according to the words given by God through Jesus, even unknowingly? In the last day's judgment, would they not be found to be in compliance with the teachings of those words, and on that basis, would they not be granted entrance into the kingdom of heaven—as are the righteous sheep in Jesus' parable?

---

[183] John 12:46–50

Jesus' final points to Nicodemus in this famous dialog, are therefore that we have two categories of people; those who believe Jesus, follow his words, and are granted eternal life without need for further review, or those who do not believe (or never knew) Jesus, and have to undergo the additional step of a judicial review of their deeds. The criterion of this coming review has been predetermined and is based on how one accepts the light they have been given. My advice is, take the shortcut and believe in and obey Jesus.

I should point out that Jesus has left out one category of people in this discourse with Nicodemus. That would be the individuals who believe in Jesus but are not given entrance into the kingdom of heaven—eternal life. This category of individuals is a subject of discussion within Jesus' Sermon on the Mount. It will appear in Matthew 7 as Jesus is concluding his message. Later, in chapter 32, we will focus on this group of unsaved Christians and decipher the reason for their exclusion from the kingdom of heaven.

One final note, Jesus adds to his ninth beatitude an encouragement to his persecuted followers. It is a reminder that past prophets were also persecuted. This may not seem like much of a consolation; after all, it shows that this struggle for equity—one that has preceded the disciples—was not well received in the past. Strangely enough, however, this is of some comfort. The sufferings of champions of the past do motivate us to press on, even when the outlook for success looks grim. It can motivate one to struggle on, even in the face of death. Knowing that others have died for your cause does foster courage to face fierce opposition. Jesus' encouragement serves to associate present and future disciples with those that rank among the heroes of old. He is telling them that they are entering a dangerous, but noble, cause, and will be standing with the great and honorable leaders of the past.

CHAPTER 13

Salt of the Earth

You are the salt of the earth; but if the salt loses its flavor, how shall it be seasoned? It is then good for nothing but to be thrown out and trampled underfoot by men.

Matthew 5:13

This statement by Jesus is a bombshell! On the one hand, it is a continuation of encouragement to his followers, but on the other hand, it is immediately followed by an ominous warning that they could be discarded. Jesus' statements of blessings have concluded at this point, but contextually he is still on the same theme. He has just outlined the beneficiaries and participants of the coming kingdom; the needy and those seeking to fill those needs. His last two beatitudes focused on encouraging individuals in their struggle to create a righteous world. The last beatitude was even more specific and hones its encouragement directly toward his followers, or would-be followers, who accept and implement the tenets of his sermon. Now, Jesus proclaims that "you"—the active disciples in this kingdom—are the "salt of the earth." Once again, he is directing his words just as he did in his ninth and final beatitude.

This is an important distinction, because the following message is just as specific as well. Jesus did not say, "***Those*** are the salt of the earth," as if he was referring to the "those" of his eighth beatitude. No, he has said, "*You* are the salt of the earth," in order to make a parallel construction to the ninth beatitude, which refers to his disciples suffering for Jesus' sake. It is the "you" who are suffering to bring about a more righteous world in the name of Jesus, who are the salt of the earth.

This statement also takes a new turn. While the past two beatitudes gave the agents of righteousness and Jesus' disciples encouragement to continue in their quest by focusing on what they will gain, this statement of encouragement focuses Jesus' disciples on what their quest for righteousness can mean for others. Being "the salt of the earth" is primarily for the benefit of the world, as opposed to one's personal benefit. Jesus' statement puts into context the fact that the pursuit of righteousness for his sake reaches beyond one's immediate boundaries and will have worldwide benefits. Good done for the king has greater impact than good done for the sake of good.

The symbolism of salt is an important one because in Jesus' day salt was not cheap. In many places it was a commodity just as valuable as silver. The salt industry was a big and somewhat hostile one. Territorial battles often broke out over the control of salt deposits and trade routes. People would pay a high price for salt, not only for its ability to make a bland meal more flavorful, but also for its ability to help preserve foods in a world without refrigeration. Jesus stating that his disciples are the salt of the earth is not just a comment made solely to indicate that a little is needed to make food taste good; it is also made to indicate their value to a fallen world.

It is this intrinsic value of salt that made men in Jesus' day fight for its control that makes Jesus' "You are the salt of the earth" statement parallel his previous declaration that the disciples will be persecuted. Just as men fought for the control of salt, they will also fight for control over the "you" who follow

Jesus. The fights may be for the purpose of domination, exploitation, or silencing. "You are the salt of the earth" is a statement that is as much about warning as it is of encouragement.

The encouragement of this statement is found in the fact that salt influences the flavor of the food it is added to. Likewise, the disciples will positively influence the communities in which they work. Encouraging too, because only a small amount of salt is needed to change the taste of food from bland to savory, from tasteless to desirable. So it will be with the disciples of Christ—a small number of them can make a big difference, a good difference, a global difference, just like a small amount of salt in a recipe.

For many in this world, life's hardships are common at every turn. Those people move through life without enjoying life. They go through their daily routines, but life is bland. Jesus' proclamation is that his active disciples will add spice to those around them, and everyone in the community will find life more desirable. The essence of the kingdom of heaven, practiced in the lives of his disciples will be like the essence of salt dissolved into food. But this essence of righteousness practiced in the name of the king creates an avenue by which the king's name and tenets travel beyond the disciple's community. The recipients of the disciple's good actions will tell others of the actions, and may cite that the actions were motivated from loyalty to Christ. Christ, the king, becomes part of the story that the recipients will tell to other. In this way, Christ, too, is the salt of the earth.

But salt in Jesus' day was rarely the pure form of sea salt that we take for granted today. Salt was often dug out of the deposits of ancient lake beds, now dried up, in far-reaching deserts. The banks of the Dead Sea were one typical resource for salt in Jesus' day. This salt is a mixture of many different "salty" elements, not just pure sodium chloride. As a result, salt in Jesus' day had varying degrees of saltiness. This type of salt could also react with its environment and lose its saltiness depending on how it was stored—the type of container it is in, how long it has been stored, and the extent of its exposure to air, moisture, and dust. Salt could lose its flavoring abilities, and when it did, this valuable commodity was no longer valuable. It was just something to be thrown out into the streets and *"trampled underfoot."*

It is by this picture of salt losing its saltiness, that Jesus introduces the first of several warnings in this sermon to his disciples. Its mere mention is frightful in its own right. Can disciples, who are the salt of the earth, lose their saltiness and be discarded by the kingdom of heaven? The implication of Jesus' statement is, yes, they can. If not, why even warn of it? Why even bring the subject up?

This warning is very consistent with the teaching of God's kingdom wherever it has been found. Throughout the Old Testament, God warned His people He could reject them if they did not follow His law. On certain occasions God did reject his chosen ones—take for example, King Saul. The spirit of God left him, and his kingdom was given to David. On other occasions, God chose to only punish and then press on with a remnant of potentially faithful followers. John the Baptist, preaching the coming kingdom of heaven, used several rejection illustrations in his messages. On one occasion, John tells the Pharisees and Sadducees[184] that they need to repent and bear fruits of repentance, and not smugly think they are safe because their father is Abraham. To John, this kinship connection is of little value, because God can make children of Abraham from the stones on the ground.[185] On the same occasion, John tells the multitudes (and religious leaders) that if they are not fruit-bearing trees, they will be cut down and thrown into the fire, or be as the chaff on a threshing floor that is also discarded

---

[184] For a good, concise summary on Pharisees and Sadducees, see the following web article: https://www.newworldencyclopedia.org/entry/Pharisees

[185] Matthew 3:3–7. Also see Luke 3:7–8

and burned.[186] Immediately following John's warning to be fruitful trees, the multitude questions him regarding what they need to do (i.e., to be fruitful). John's replies are ones that follow social justice themes, as we have already seen.[187]

Jesus' "salt that has lost its saltiness" warning is no different from the warnings of John or those of numerous Old Testament passages. These are specific warnings being given to God's people. These are warnings being given to the "you" group. They are not given to the "those" group of the gentile world. Being a follower of God, of Jesus Christ, carries with it special privileges, but also special responsibilities. John told his hearers that they needed to be socially responsible to mankind in order to bear fruits and avoid being cut down and burned. Jesus, in the Sermon on the Mount, likewise tells his disciples that they need to be socially responsible to mankind in order to avoid being thrown away and trampled underfoot.

This, once again, brings up a subject that is divisive within the Christian church today—do our "works" play a role in our salvation? Many will argue that they do not. Nevertheless, the Bible is replete with warnings from Genesis to Revelation that failing to do God's works can result in the loss of reward and eternal life. James, the brother of Jesus, and Paul appear to be wrestling over this issue in the first century, as have Christian theologians ever since then. The scope of this book is not designed for an in-depth investigation of this controversy. I have a rather simple philosophy. I am focusing on the kingdom of heaven that Jesus is revealing to his disciples, and I believe that Jesus is the king of that kingdom. I simply want to uncover and understand what my king has to say about his kingdom.

In summary, this passage of Jesus' concerning, "You are the salt of the earth" is directed only to his followers, and anyone

---

[186] Matthew 3:10–12. Also see Luke 3:9
[187] Luke 3:10–14

considering being a follower. It reveals that we can have a big influence for good, even though we are few. It also continues to warn that we will be an object of contention in the world—subject to persecution. But it also goes further than this; Jesus makes it clear that to pick up the mantle and follow him is to take the responsibilities of being an active promoter of his cause. This includes the pursuit of the themes of morality, social justice, and charity; themes he has just revealed in his nine beatitudes. However, he warns that once one chooses to follow, they can potentially relax their efforts in this pursuit and become salt that has lost "its flavor." Salt that undergoes degradation like this is of no value to the kingdom of heaven, and it is discarded to be "trampled underfoot."

CHAPTER 14

Light of the World

You are the light of the world. A city that is set on a hill cannot be hidden. Nor do they light a lamp and put it under a basket, but on a lampstand, and it gives light to all who are in the house. Let your light so shine before men, that they may see your good works and glorify your Father in heaven.

Matthew 5:14–16

Many years ago, I had the privilege and honor to work as a relief and development specialist in an extremely poor East African country. For many years, my team of local men, and I, drilled water wells in needy communities. Many of those wells were in very remote locations, which could take days to reach. There were no paved roads to access many of these communities, so we hired local guides or followed tracks in the sand or dirt to familiar geographical features—such as an old termite mound, a distant mountain peak, or a wadi.[188] Travel was often cross-country through uncharted territories, with only a compass, a hunch, and a prayer.

This was a desert country, and for nine months of the year, temperatures could get hot—and I mean hot! On one such

---

[188] A *wadi* is a dry river valley.

drilling adventure, I recorded daily high temperatures of 118 degrees for twenty-one days straight. It seemed odd to me to get the same high temperature reading every day, until I realized that my thermometer had a range limit and would not show temperatures higher than 118 degrees. So, I do not know how hot it really got, but it is possible it was more than 118 degrees.

During these forays into the wilds, we would pack our convoy of vehicles with everything we needed for a month, and head out into the open desert in search of our next job at a remote village. Our routes would take us over hills and gullies, into old riverbeds, across sand dune hills and over wide-open plains that appeared to be potentially excellent farmland. I have had the opportunity to stop and stand on top of my truck and not see any life or vegetation on any of my distant horizons. Anyone might easily think they were on another planet. On some occasions, the visibility during a desert haboob[189] could be so bad, we could not see the ground outside our vehicle windows. There was nothing we could do but stop moving and wait for conditions to improve. And, when they did, the desert track we may have been following would be gone, and lingering dust would hide our landmarks. We had to pick a direction and pray that we would not get hopelessly lost. It was great fun!

On our trips to and from some of our remote drilling sites, we would often travel at night to escape the intense daytime heat. Nighttime temperatures were generally in the ninety-degree range, but the lack of intense sunlight made the nights seem much cooler by comparison.

Traveling at night was slow and often confusing, but many times, as our convoy crawled to the crest of a hill, we would see a small light flickering in the distance, just one small light against an endless dark void of night. But that one light was al-

---

[189] A haboob is a violent wind and dust storm.

ways a welcoming sign to us. We knew that that light was coming from a primitive tea shack generally located along a desert track connecting two or more points of human civilization. If we drove to that light, we could buy some refreshing tea and get confirmation about which direction we needed to proceed.

This small light was often still miles away. It could take us an hour to cross the terrain between us and the light. Dipping into a gully or following a wadi would make us lose sight of it for a while, but soon we would crest another hill, realign our direction, and eventually reach the tea shack. It would be nothing more than a small shade structure and maybe a low rock wall to serve as a windbreak. The tea stop would usually be manned by a solitary young boy or an elderly man. They, too, had seen the headlights of our trucks approaching so we were always greeted with a ready hot pot of tea.

The light we had followed would be nothing more than a small jar of dirty engine oil with a rolled-up strip of cotton rag connecting the oil to the top of the lid. The rag would slowly wick up the oil while it burned, while the flame struggled to stay alive in the desert breeze. It was this small light that had guided us for miles and brought us rest, refreshment, and a chance to confirm we were either on the right track or we needed to set a different course. It was always a light of encouragement in our dark desert world.

This is the picture that now comes to my mind every time I read Matthew 5:14. No doubt the people listening to Jesus' sermon that day also had similar experiences within the context of their primitive lives. Light at night means civilization and safety, a chance to fix one's direction, and a place to find shelter and food. Light in the darkness means life.

As if to emphasize his earlier statement of encouragement, Jesus uses this illustration to represent the compelling and far-reaching influence of his disciples on others. It is again a statement directed to "you" not to "those." This time he speaks of light. Keep in mind that during Jesus' earthly ministry, light in darkness is generated by fire—candle or lamp light. Once again, it is the disciple that is of benefit to the community, and the statement is framed in terms of something small, but very influential. There is no mention in this passage of worthless light as there was of worthless salt. All light shining into darkness has a dispelling effect. When there is light, people in darkness will benefit from it. Even a small amount of light is better than no light at all. Jesus points out that if one has light, it is senseless to cover it so that no one benefits from it. It is an irrational, unnatural behavior. If you have light, you place it in a position to benefit others.

However, Jesus does hint that light can be misused. He directs his disciples to let their light "so shine" that men will "see *your* good works and glorify *your* Father in heaven." Two things are important here. First, light, which is physical or spiritual enlightenment, is to generate good works—works that can be seen, and should be seen, by mankind. Light, in this context, is the implementation of the beatitudes that Jesus has just revealed to his listeners. If acted on, it will lead to the good deeds of sharing, giving comfort and mercy, defending the oppressed and building a righteous world, and so forth. The light and good works are linked in this proclamation. In fact, one's good works is the shining light visible to mankind. But Jesus is not just encouraging good works; he is instructing his disciples that their good works are to be done for the purpose of glorifying the Father in heaven. And this is the second important point—we have a Father in heaven to be glorified, and our good works are to be a means of directing glory to this Father—not to ourselves.

By stating to his disciples that they have an obligation to be visible (as opposed to hidden) bearers of light for the glory of the Father in heaven, he has linked the actions of his earlier beatitudes to his command. His disciples are the children of this Father, and by Father, Jesus clearly means God. As we saw earlier, those called the children of God are the world's peacemakers; those who strive for equity and justice within society. They are also those who aid the poor, comfort the distressed, and relieve the oppressed. In this "light" proclamation, the children are doing "good works" for the glory of the Father. Jesus is paralleling these "works" of the beatitudes to the "good works" that give glory to the Father—works that must be seen, works that direct glory to the Father.

There is a danger of misuse here. Although one could do good works that would be a benefit to others, their motivation could be to seek their own glory. Jesus teaches elsewhere in this Sermon on the Mount that to do so is to forfeit any future reward from the Father. (We will look at this in-depth in later chapters.) The good works Jesus is encouraging are those done, not for self-aggrandizements, but to direct men's attention to the Father of the kingdom of heaven. This is important because for the kingdom of heaven to function correctly and to grow, society must comprehend that our kingdom is ruled by a heavenly king.

The placement of this command of Jesus should not be overlooked. Jesus has just given the beatitudes that have highlighted the suffering of the poor, sad, and exploited. He has just given a call to action to help others via mercy, honesty, purity, and peacemaking. He has told his followers that those who actively pursue equity will be persecuted, but ultimately successful and rewarded. He has just told them they are valuable and need to serve their community as if they were salt—to mix with others and make life more pleasant. And now he calls them to take their new knowledge and influence their communities by good works for the glory of God. Jesus is not giving his disciples an opportunity to believe that discipleship is passive. On the contrary, good works for the glory of God are a requirement—and they are not to be hidden. Keep in mind, nevertheless, the context of the "works" Jesus is asking for can only be understood correctly by realizing the "equity" elements underlying the beatitudes he has just given, and by comprehending the good influences these elements have when put into practice in society. Works are for the benefit of others, and for the glory of the Father. Keep in mind also, that just as it takes energy to produce light—something must be consumed to produce it—so, too, the light bearers will need to sacrifice to be a light.

Perhaps one final note, the light of a candle or lamp is not generated spontaneously—someone, or something, must spark it into existence. However, once lit, the flame can be transferred from one fuel source to another. In a similar fashion, the light that we are to be to the world is not from a spontaneous source either. It is a response to the direct teachings of Jesus Christ, or the action of God's spirit on a receptive soul. Once lit, our souls have an influence on our surroundings that inevitably benefits others. And in turn, others, hopefully for the sake of the Father, are lit to become lights within their own communities—thus lighting other parts of the world and growing the kingdom of heaven.

PART III

The Sermon on the Mount
This Is the Law and the Prophets

CHAPTER 15

Get Your Thinking Sraight

Do not think that I came to destroy the Law or the Prophets. I did not come to destroy but to fulfill. For assuredly, I say to you, till heaven and earth pass away, one jot or one tittle will by no means pass from the law till all is fulfilled. Whoever therefore breaks one of the least of these commandments, and teaches men so, shall be called least in the kingdom of heaven; but whoever does and teaches them, he shall be called great in the kingdom of heaven. For I say to you, that unless your righteousness exceeds that of the scribes and Pharisees, you will by no means enter the kingdom of heaven.

Matthew 5:17–20

Jesus' sudden statement that he has not come to destroy the Law or the Prophets, but to fulfill them, appears to be an abrupt deviation from his sermon, but is it? Remember, in context, this statement is being made just after his instructional beatitudes and their implicit, as well as explicit, calls for social and moral actions. One must ask why Jesus would suddenly see the need to assure listeners that he has not come to undermine the Law or the Prophets that they know so well—or that they think they know so well. The timing of this proclamation indicates that Jesus has reason to believe that what he has just said may be confusing his listeners, and he sees the need to respond to their questions.

You might think I am reading too much into Jesus' statement by considering it a reaction to the crowd, but, if you have experience as a public speaker, you might agree with me. When you are in front of a crowd that is listening to you speak, you can see each face. You know who is engaged with your topic and who is tuning out. You can see who understands and who is confused, and you see the questioning faces and the ones who disagree with your words. I have no doubt that Jesus, as a master orator and teacher, is fully aware of his listeners' thoughts—he can see them on every face. His beatitude message is radically new to them, and many are questioning whether what he has just said is compliant with the Law or the Prophets.

Clearly, Jesus is making this abrupt statement to defend his teachings, and it is not a timid defense. What he states here, and in the discourse to come, is an authoritative—and aggressive—move that challenges the listener's comprehension of what truly is the message of the Law or the Prophets. What is their fulfillment, and who are the right teachers to guide them to an understanding of God's words? The implications made by Jesus in these few short verses are that his teachings are the fulfillment of God's word. The Law or the Prophets, as he is revealing them, will endure to the end of time, and that the teachings of the scribes and Pharisees are misrepresenting these truths and should not be followed. These are astonishing and bold claims.

But why should Jesus' listeners be confused and question what he has just taught them, especially if it is indeed the teachings of the Law or the Prophets? The answer is as follows. In the Jewish mindset of many in this time-period, success, riches and honor are viewed as blessings from God for one's piety and faithfulness to God. Status is a reward from God. The poor, the meek, the diseased or disabled, and the downtrodden are viewed as spiritual failures, and thus, by default, sinners. And yet, Jesus is promising these lowly people rewards from God—and even greater rewards await those who champion the causes of equity on this poor lot's behalf. This must indeed sound strange to the Jewish mind of that time. It is not what they have been taught, or have come to believe is the Law and the Prophets. In fact, it is the opposite. If riches and honor are a reward from God for piety and faithfulness, why would someone give that reward to persons that God has chosen not to reward? Wouldn't you be undermining a decision of God? Wouldn't you be strengthening the sinners? And wouldn't that, in itself, be a destruction of the Law or the Prophet's messages?

Part of the problem with the mindset of the Jewish people of that day stems from the fact God had made many promises in the Torah concerning how He would bless them. The people had a legal precedent to expect blessings from God. But these blessing were almost always spoken to the assembled tribes of Israel. These blessings were ones the nation would experience for its faithfulness to him. The Jews had come to see these blessing as ones conferred upon individuals and not the nation as a whole. They had missed the fact that acts of equity within the community would lead to the fulfillment of the national promises and make them a great nation. Each person would become stronger with the help of his brother. Wealth was to be for the benefit of everyone and for the nation. The law's proper implementation would elevate each individual and, in turn, the nation of Israel above all other nations. But during Jesus' time on earth, the Jewish nation was not elevated as the law had promised, so a self-centered interpretation of the Torah's blessings displaced those of national application.

Jesus is correcting the crowd by stating that the teachings he has just revealed—ones of equity to those in need—are not destroying the Law or the Prophets but, on the contrary, are actually supporting what its commands truly teach. In short, Jesus is revealing that the teachings of the Law and the Prophets are championing the causes of equity. There is no doubt that this is Jesus' stance in his interpretation of the Law and the Prophets, because he consistently upholds this concept throughout his ministry. The examples are too numerous to cover here but let me give you one from elsewhere in the Sermon on the Mount to help point you in the right direction.

In Matthew 7:12 Jesus will again reference "the Law and the Prophets." This time the context of the message is showing that God the Father is a giving God—He knows how to help others. The verses preceding this reference are meant to encourage the listeners to trust in God's care for them and thus not be afraid to be helpful to others—even if it is at a cost to you. (We will look at this in detail later.)

The Matthew 7:12 proclamation is often called the "Golden Rule." Christians routinely quote the first half—"*Whatever you want men to do to you, do also to them.*" However, they often omit the second half—"*For this is the Law and the Prophets.*" In the context of this verse, what Jesus is teaching is that being equitable to others—meeting their needs and seeing others as of equal value to yourself—is one's fulfillment of the requirements of the Law and the Prophets.

Most of Christianity teaches today that Jesus has "fulfilled" the law, and that as a result, it—the Torah—is no longer in effect. Contextually, within Matthew 5:17–20 nothing could be further from the truth. In fact, according to Jesus' statements in Matthew 5:19–20, such a teaching is detrimental, since ignoring the proper fulfillment of the Law and the Prophets will result in one finding oneself excluded from the kingdom of heaven. These statements of Jesus need to be analyzed carefully, since getting their meaning wrong can have life-threatening consequences. So, let us take a closer and more careful look.

A. I Am Come

There is no doubt that Jesus was considered a "rabbi" during the time of his ministry. The term "rabbi" is one of honor given to individuals who are renowned for their interpretations of the law. They were religious teachers. They were—and still are—well read in the law, have a firm grasp of the depths of its meaning and generally have a following of eager students to mentor. Jesus fits this model exactly and he is often called "rabbi" in the Gospels. The stories of the Gospels also have people referring to Jesus by the simple English term "teacher"—which is a function of being a rabbi.

Jesus was very much involved with the rabbinic exchange of ideas of his day. The Gospels are full of stories of Jesus having a different interpretation of God's law and how the laws were to be implemented. Some of Jesus' sayings appear to be lifted from rabbinical statements and altered to give his unique view of the issue at hand. We will see examples of this later. His life as a rabbi even seems to have started at the young age of twelve when during a Passover feast, the book of Luke records him having discussions with Jerusalem's teachers. Luke records the following:

> *Now so it was that after three days they* [his parents] *found Him in the temple, sitting in the midst of the teachers, both listening to them and asking them questions. And all who heard Him were astonished at His understanding and answers.*[190]

---

[190] Luke 2:46–48

These "teachers" may have included the famous Rabbi Shammai, Hillel the Elder, and his grandson which succeeded him, Rabbi Gamaliel, who was the teacher of Paul (or, more correctly, Saul) before he became a Christian.

During the early parts of Jesus' ministry, however, the crowds that eagerly followed to hear what he had to say, anticipated he was more than just a teacher or rabbi. They questioned whether Jesus might be Elijah returned from heaven, or the long-ago promised prophet spoken of by Moses. This expectation started during the ministry of John the Baptist.

You might recall that Jesus' cousin John began his introductory ministry before Jesus and was creating quite a stir. On one occasion, leaders of Jerusalem sent priest and Levites to ask John who he was. The short dialogue was as follows:

> *"Who are you?" He* [John]*...confessed, "I am not the Christ."*
> *"What then? Are you **Elijah**?"* [John] *said, "I am not."*
> *"Are you the Prophet?" And* [John] *answered, "No."*
> *Then they said to him, "Who are you, that we may give an answer to those who sent us? What do you say about yourself?"* [John] *said: "I am 'The voice of one crying in the wilderness: 'Make straight the way of the Lord,'"*[191]

Notice here that the priest and Levites specifically want to know if John is either "Elijah" or "the Prophet." This is due to good reason. The Old Testament has prophecies that predict the coming of these individuals, and both were to come to give the children of Israel God's words

---

[191] John 1:19–23

and instruction regarding the law and how to relate to each other. The reference to Elijah is in the last book and the last chapter of the Christian Old Testament, and it reads as follows:

> *Remember the Law of Moses, my servant, which I commanded him in Horeb for all Israel, with the statutes and judgments. Behold, I will send you **Elijah** the prophet before the coming of the great and dreadful day of the Lord. And he will turn the hearts of the fathers to the children, and the hearts of the children to their fathers, lest I come and strike the earth with a curse.*[192]

The expectation of a future appearance of Elijah was widespread among the people. The only problem was that Elijah had been taken to heaven, without seeing death, hundreds of years earlier, and no one knew what he looked like. There would be no way to identify him when he did appear, except by Malachi's vague connection of him with the "Law of Moses" and his influences on the fathers and the children. This expectation and watching was not confined to the religious leaders of Jerusalem. The Gospels record that the people were questioning this appearance of Elijah with respect to Jesus, and this even included King Herod.[193]

---

[192] Malachi 4:4–6 (emphasis added). NOTE: John replies that he is not Elijah, but this is a misunderstanding on his part. The angel that announces John's birth to his father Zacharias uses the words of Malachi's prophecy in describing John's future life's work (see Luke 1:13–17). Jesus also states that John was a fulfillment of the Malachi prophecy (see Matthew 17:11–13).

[193] See Matthew 16:13–14; Mark 6:14–15; Luke 9:7–8 and Luke 9:18–19

There was also an expectation of "the Prophet," which is a reference to a prophet promised by Moses in the Torah itself. It is found in the eighteenth chapter of Deuteronomy and reads in part as follows:

> *The Lord your God will raise up for you a Prophet like me* [Moses] *from your midst, from your brethren. Him you shall hear, according to all you desired of the Lord your God in Horeb in the day of the assembly. . . .* "I [God] *will raise up for them a Prophet like you* [Moses] *from among their brethren, and will put My words in His mouth, and He shall speak to them all that I command Him. And it shall be that whoever will not hear My words, which He speaks in My name, I will require it of him.*"[194]

This promised prophet would uphold God's words as they were revealed on the day the law was given. This passage of Deuteronomy appears to imply that the people of a future time would have questions about the law that would need clarification. The word in the text translated "desired"[195] is the Hebrew word *sha`al* or *sha`el,* which means to *inquire, ask,* or *request.* The people would have questions, and the Prophet would have God's word in his mouth to answer them. By Jesus' day the law had many differing interpretations promoted by various religious leaders. The people, no doubt, had questions about what God's law truly required of them.

The Torah had earlier warned the Children of Israel that prophets would come "working signs and wonders" and speaking words to turn them away from following God's law. Such

---

[194] See Deuteronomy 18:15–22
[195] Strong's word OT:7592

prophets were to be put to death.[196] Identifying what prophets were good and which ones were bad was a matter of great importance throughout Jewish history. With the appearance of John the Baptist and Jesus, and the great followings they were attracting, the leaders and the people were alert in evaluating these men with respect to their compliance to God's law.

When Jesus tells the crowd of listeners at his Sermon on the Mount, *"Do not think that I came to destroy the Law and the Prophets"* he is doing so to put people's fears to rest that he may be a false prophet enticing them to evil. If Jesus spoke this sermon in Hebrew, the equivalent verb for *I came* would have had the idiomatic meaning of *"my purpose is."* Thus rendering the phrase similar to, *"Do not think that my purpose is to destroy the Law and the Prophets."* In Greek or Hebrew, the message is clear: Jesus is in support of the Law and the Prophets.

B. Destroy vs. Fulfill

The book of Matthew uses the Greek word *kataluo*[197] in verse 17 which gets translated into various English versions of the Bible as "abolish" or "destroy." The word *kataluo*, however, is a compound Greek word made of the word *kata*,[198] meaning *down*, and the word *luo*,[199] meaning *loosen*. The literal translation into English is "loosen down." Now this might seem a strange word to us, but from this word, the Greek language creates the similar word *kataluma*[200] which means to *stop a journey*, *halt for the night*, and *lodge*. In En-

---

[196] See Deuteronomy 13:1–5

[197] Strong's Word NT:2647

[198] Strong's Word NT:2596

[199] Strong's Word NT:3089

[200] Strong's Word NT:2646

glish it becomes a *guest chamber* or an *inn*.

The literal picture that the word *kataluo* creates in one's mind is of individuals coming to the end of a long day's journey, loosening the straps of their burdens or those of their pack animals, and preparing to lodge for the night. It can also create the picture of a traveler, relaxing and loosening his garment and unstrapping his sandals. The Greeks would call this "loosen down"; in English we would say "loosen up."

The fact that Jesus will use the word "luo" (loosen) two verses later (verse 19), would seem to indicate that he is directing his listeners to see the *loosening* aspect of the definition of the word *kataluo*. In so doing, he is creating a word play between the *loosening of the law*, and teachers who *loosen the law*, that he will refer to shortly. This is a common Hebrew literary technique, using wordplay to help engage the minds of one's audience.

The concept of loosening the law is also a familiar one to Jesus' Jewish audience. Rabbis often debated with each other and with the students of other rabbis that held different interpretations of the Torah. You might recall that in chapter five, a reference was made about two of the prominent rabbinical schools in Jesus' day. One was the House of Hillel, and the other was the House of Shammai. Hillel's students held more lenient views, while Shammai's students were stricter. The students of these two schools often debated Torah interpretations with each other. The common people observing these debates eventually encapsulated the views of the two schools by coining the phrase:

Hillel loosens, and Shammai binds.

The term "loosens" did not represent the destruction of the law, but rather the interpretation of it to ease its burden, or interpreting it to fit the circumstances of a modern situation.[201] So, Jesus' use of the word "loosen down" can easily be seen as rabbinic terminology dealing with how one interprets the Torah and the Prophets. With this in mind, we could paraphrase Jesus' words in Matthew 5:17 to be something as follows:

Don't think I came to loosely interpret the Law or the Prophets; I come to fulfill them.

So, let us turn next to the word "fulfill." The Greek word used for "fulfill" in verse 17 is the word *pleroo*.[202] It has many meanings, and in English it can be translated as *to make replete*, *cram*, *level up*, *furnish*, *satisfy* or *execute* the duties of an office, *finish,* or *verify* (as in, a prediction coming true).

Many Christian denominations take the verse of Matthew 5:17 and make the claim that Jesus "finished" the law, and that it is no longer in effect. This seems a bit self-serving to those who want to do away with the law. After all, *pleroo* has many definitions, and the choice of any one of the alternates can destroy one's desire to do away with the law. We could just as easily define Jesus' "fulfill" as to *make it replete* (i.e., well-supplied). He might be *cramming* more into it or *leveling it out.* The word *furnish* would define Jesus as being *the source* or *the supply* of the Law and the Prophets. Valid arguments can be made for any one of these alternate words.

Even choosing the translation "finish" does not do away with the law. Take for example a carpenter building a table. He will cut the pieces, assemble it, sand it, then varnish, and polish it. Only then is it *"finished"* and ready for use. A finished table

---

[201] Keep in mind, however, that one rabbi's "loosened" interpretation of the law can be, to another rabbi, a misinterpretation or a nullifying of the law. One could make the argument that a nullified law has been destroyed in such circumstances.

[202] Strong's Word NT:4137

is just starting its life. Why can't a finished law be one that is now ready for its proper use?

So, from what we have learned about the Greek meaning of the words that we translate as "destroy" and "fulfill," it can be seen that a valid translation of Matthew 5:17 could also read as follows:

> *Do not think I came to loosely interpret the Laws or the Prophets, I did not come to loosen them up but to make them replete, well stocked and ready for use.*

Before you think that this might be a bit of a stretch in translation you would need to be aware of the context of what is to follow. Jesus is about to give six examples concerning how the people have been incorrectly instructed to follow the law.[203] In each example, Jesus plainly demonstrates that what they have been taught is something *looser* than what the law had intended. The above translation therefore fits the context of what Jesus is about to say.

So, what exactly does Jesus mean when he says he has not come to *loosen up* but to "fulfill"? Since I am presenting the concept that Jesus' Sermon on the Mount has strong social justice and equity implications, I hope you will be understanding when I say he is reinforcing these themes once again. Keep in mind that Jesus has just given his beatitudes, which integrate teachings from both the Law and the Prophets. Also notice that just before Jesus utters this abrupt, defensive statement of verse 17, he had just stated:

---

[203] These six examples are known as the "Antitheses" of the Sermon on the Mount. We will look at each one a chapter at a time.

Let your light so shine before men, that they may see your good works and glorify your Father in heaven.

What is it about good works, as defined by the beatitudes, that prompts many (not all) listeners to suspect Jesus is misinterpreting the Law or the Prophets? Why do they suspect he is *loosening* them by his command, which obligates them to help the poor and needy of society, in order to be a blessing and to be blessed by God? I would say that the issue is best explained by Jesus' linking the doing of good work to giving glory to the Father in heaven. This is what raises eyebrows.

Earlier in this chapter, I mentioned that in the Jewish mindset of many during Jesus' earthly ministry, success, riches, and honor are viewed as blessings from God for one's piety and faithfulness to God. Status is a reward from God. The poor, the meek, the diseased or disabled, and the downtrodden are viewed as spiritual failures, and thus, by default, sinners. Sinners were detestable to many pious Jews. The plight of sinners was deserved, and it would be dishonorable to God to associate with or comfort them. Jesus has just radically stated the absolute opposite concept. Aiding the poor, the meek, diseased, disabled, and downtrodden sinners is how one gives glory to the Father in heaven. This no doubt caused a flash of consternation on many faces within that crowd of listeners. So much so that Jesus sees the need to defend his position and thus utters the words of Matthew 5:17–20. And he will follow these words with six examples of how the people have been misled in their understanding of the law.

Another biblical way to demonstrate this connection between law, works, justice and equity, and fulfillment, is to cite a text from the apostle Paul's book to the Romans. The famous passage reads as follows:

> *Owe no one anything except to love one another, for he who loves another has fulfilled the law. For the commandments, "You shall not commit adultery," "You shall not murder," "You shall not steal," "You shall not bear false witness," "You shall not covet," and if there is any other commandment, are all summed up in this saying, namely, "You shall love your neighbor as yourself." Love does no harm to a neighbor; therefore love is the fulfillment of the law.*[204]

Add to this statement the fact that Jesus teaches in his parable of the Good Samaritan that anyone in need is our neighbor,[205] and you have the basis for Jesus' statement in Matthew 5:16 and his defense of that statement, which is the topic of this current chapter.

We can also look to the book of Revelation's messages to the seven churches of Asia. Within the message to the Church at Sardis, Jesus says the following:

> *I know your works . . . . Be watchful, and strengthen the things which remain, that are ready*

---

[204] Romans 13:8–10; "Fulfilled" is Strong's Word NT:4137 and "Fulfillment" is Strong's Word NT:4138, a derivative of NT:4137.

[205] Luke 10:25–37. The lawyer in this story asks Jesus, "Who is my neighbor?" After Jesus gives his story of the Samaritan helping the traveler in need who had been bypassed by others, Jesus asks the lawyer which person was neighbor to the one in need. The lawyer answers correctly, "He who showed mercy on him." Jesus' question reverses the lawyer's question. His point is that it takes two parties to have neighbors, and life is not about having good neighbors as much as it is about being a good neighbor. This story will be addressed in Chapter 20.

to die, for I have not found your works perfect [fulfilled] *before God.*[206]

The word for "works"[207] is the same one Jesus uses in Matthew 5:16 for good *works* that glorify the Father in heaven. And the word translated "perfect"[208] here in Revelation is the same word Jesus used in Matthew 5:17 to state why he came—that is, to "fulfill" the law. I invite you to read for yourself the whole message to the church of Sardis. You will notice that those in Sardis who overcome *"shall be clothed in white garments."* This sounds a lot like Revelation 19:8 where we are told the fine, white,[209] linen that clothes the church is her equitable deeds. Both Matthew and Revelation are recording Jesus' words, and on both occasions the context of the message is about works that fulfill what God wants from us in our relationship to others.

Enough said. Let me move on. You may have noticed that Matthew 5:18 also has a word that is translated as "fulfilled." This word is not the word *pleroo,* which appears in verse 17 or the Revelation quote above. The Greek word used in verse 18 is *ginomai,*[210] and it means *to come into being, to happen, to become,* or *accomplished.* It is most often used in the Gospels in reference to something being accomplished, an event happening, or a prophecy being fulfilled. So, in order for *ginomai* to be a valid choice of wording, something must have occurred, or something is to occur in the future. *Ginomai* and *pleroo* may appear to function as synonyms when translated into English, but in Greek they are distinct from each other.

---

[206] Revelation 3:1–2

[207] Strong's Word NT:2041

[208] Strong's Word NT:4137

[209] Strong's Word NT:2986

[210] Strong's Word NT:1096

As an example, our two words *pleroo* and *ginomai* appear together in the first chapter of Matthew, where we are being told of Jesus' virgin birth. The passage reads as follows:

> *"And she will bring forth a Son, and you shall call His name Jesus, for He will save His people from their sins." So all **this was done** [ginomai] that it might be **fulfilled** [pleroo] which was spoken by the Lord through the prophet, saying: "Behold, the virgin shall be with child . . . "*[211]

This is plainly a reference to a prophecy being accomplished—something predicted long ago has *come into being*. To have translated this as *"all was fulfilled that it might be fulfilled"* would have been confusing, so *ginomai* was not translated into "fulfilled" in this verse as it was in Matthew 5:18. Translators perhaps could have done something similar in Matthew 5:17 and 18 to help separate the two ideas of fulfillment. Perhaps "fulfill" in verse 17 and the word "accomplished" in verse 18 would have been a better choice of English words to represent the Greek ideas.

I say all of this because I want you to understand a particularly important point based on the context of verse 18. Jesus is stating that in order for "all" the Law (or the Prophets) to be accomplished (fulfilled) the events of heaven and earth passing away would need to occur first. One might think that Jesus is using hyperbole, because his statement is indicating that the fulfillment of the Law (or the Prophets) will be a post-earth (and possibly post-universe) event. However, the Bible predicts this very event on several occasions. Here is how one Old Testament prophecy is presented:

> *"For as the new heavens and the new earth which I will make shall remain before Me," says*

---

[211] Matthew 1:21–23

the Lord, "So shall your descendants and your name remain. And it shall come to pass that from one New Moon to another, and from one Sabbath to another, all flesh shall come to worship before Me," says the Lord.[212]

This is a prophecy that is still to be fulfilled, and it indicates that our current heaven and earth have an expiration date. A new heaven and earth are to be made. But look closely. Notice that even in this post, old-earth environment, God's followers still keep His Sabbath and feast laws. This is interesting to me, because I have been pointing out that the Sabbath laws are the ones that imbue social justice and equity. I would have to conclude that God's future world is just and equitable. It does not surprise me because Jesus teaches that these tenets are those of the kingdom of heaven. Social justice and equity are a cornerstone of God's heavenly government, and they will be preserved and lived throughout eternity.

One final note on an issue people sometimes debate. Does the single word "law" in verse 18 mean only the Torah (Law of Moses)? In verse 17, Jesus specifically mentions the words *"Law* or the *Prophets."* This would mean he is referring to the Torah and the prophetic books of the Old Testament, which include the Prophets and other prophetic writings such as are found in the psalms. In verse 18, however, Jesus mentions only the *"law."* Both verses use the same word for *law,* and when used by itself, as in verse 18, it generally means the whole of the law including the prophetic works. This must be the case here because as we have just seen the Prophet Isaiah has a prediction that is yet to be fulfilled. And there are other prophetic events that Jesus still needs to fulfill. If verse 18 were being construed to mean that only the Torah remains until the passing of heaven

---

[212] Isaiah 66:22–23. See also Isaiah 65:17 and Revelation 21:1.

and earth, Jesus would be ignoring the prophetic works—the very thing he claims he is "not" doing. It should, therefore, be concluded that the Torah and the words of the Prophets, in their entirety, must all be accomplished before heaven and earth pass away.

C. Jots and Tittles

Read Matthew 5:18 again to refresh your memory. Jesus is emphasizing the degree to which the Law and the Prophets are to remain uncorrupted well into the future, by stating that even the smallest letter and its decorative spur will not pass away. This is Jesus' reference to the "jot" and the "tittle." This is an English rendition of a Greek rendition of a familiar Hebrew expression used by Jesus. The "jot" (*iota* in Greek) is referring to the smallest letter in the Hebrew alphabet—called a *yod*. The "tittle" (*keraia* in Greek) is a reference to a small decorative mark placed on a *yod* or other Hebrew letters—called a *kotz*. In Hebrew, *kotz*, literally meanings *a thorn*. Therefore, it is used to describe the small thorn-like, or hook-like, protrusion on Hebrew letters.[213]

The *tittle* or *kotz* is, of course, even smaller than the *yod*. The point of the Hebrew expression is that careful attention is given to one's work so that not even the smallest of details is forgotten or missed. Jesus' point in Matthew 5:18 is that up until the events of heaven and earth passing away, not even the smallest mark in "all" of the Law or the Prophets will be left undone. In context, he is therefore stating that he is in full support of all of the Law and the Prophets, and has not come to destroy any of it.

Jesus once used this "heaven and earth passing away/tittle" phrase in combination with the phrase "the Law and the Proph-

---

[213] For a detailed explanation see David Bivin, *New Light on the Difficult Words of Jesus: Insights from His Jewish Context*, (Holland, MI: En-Gedi Resource Center, 2007), pages 94-96.

ets" in rebuking the Pharisees for their love of money, and their scoffing at his teaching that money should be used to benefit others. In so doing, he gave these phrases a connection to equity obligations.

The passage I am referring to is found in the book of Luke. Jesus has just given a parable to his disciples to demonstrate that one cannot serve two masters—God and money.[214] He has asked them that if one is not faithful with the unrighteous mammon (earthly wealth), who will commit to their trust the true riches (heavenly wealth)? The Pharisees have overheard this teaching, and because they are "lovers of money", they scoff at Jesus and deride him. Jesus replies with the following:

> *Now the Pharisees, who were lovers of money, also heard all these things, and they derided him. And* [Jesus] *said to them, "You are those who justify yourselves before men, but God knows your hearts. For what is highly esteemed among men is an abomination in the sight of God. The **law and the prophets** were until John. Since that time the kingdom of God has been preached, and everyone is pressing into it. **And it is easier for heaven and earth to pass away than for one tittle of the law to fail.**"* (emphasis added)[215]

Jesus is telling the Pharisees that their concept of money and of how they think the law instructs them to live is wrong— even against God. Their justified interpretation, which is an abomination to God, has been the status quo up until the time of John. Since John, however, the real message of the Law and Prophets—the message of the kingdom of heaven

---

[214] Luke 16:1–13
[215] Luke 16:14–16

(a message of equity and love for God displayed via love for neighbor)—has been preached, and people have accepted it. What the law really teaches is not passing away. It is more enduring than even heaven and earth. Jesus' implication is that the Law and the Prophets, and their equity and justice obligations—that he and John teach—cannot be altered by man's incorrect interpretations, nor by their justifications for their misinterpretations.

So, we have two examples of Jesus using the "Law and/ or the Prophets" phrase in combination with the "heaven and earth passing away/jot and tittle" phrase, in defense of his social justice and equity obligation teachings. In both cases, Jesus presents the Law and the Prophets as a central theme of the kingdom of heaven, and associates this message with social justice and the use of one's resources. And he plainly indicates that this message has an ongoing obligation far into the future. I do not think this is a coincidence. Throughout the Gospels, Jesus repeatedly teaches that keeping the law correctly, is connected to social obligations focused on the use of money or other resources to help others.

D. Breaks or Loosens?

In Matthew 5:19, Jesus states the following:

> *Whoever therefore breaks one of the least of these commandments, and teaches men so, shall be called least in the kingdom of heaven; but whoever does and teaches them, he shall be called great in the kingdom of heaven.*

The word "breaks" used in many English translations is not the best choice of word in my opinion. The Greek word used here is *luo*,[216] and it merely means *loosen*. And *loosen* is what Jesus means, given the context of this passage as a whole. This is rabbinical terminology that refers to how one interprets the law of God. And it is familiar terminology in Jesus' day. As you can recall, two verses earlier, Jesus told his listeners not to think he had come to *loosen down* the law. Now he tells them that anyone who *loosens* even the least of God's "*commandments will be called least in the kingdom of heaven.*" *Loosen down* and *loosen* are both references to how one is interpreting or misinterpreting God's law. Jesus' point is that he is not loosening (or misinterpreting) it, and neither should anyone else.

Jesus warns here that anyone who *loosely* interprets the law—that is, gives themselves room to disobey or deviate from God's true intent—"*and teaches men so,*" is in danger of being "*called least*" in the kingdom. On the other hand, whoever "*does* [the commandments] *and teaches them*" to others will be called great in the kingdom of heaven. Two points are especially important here. First, the juxtaposition of those who *loosen* the law and those who *do* the law, implies that the looseners of the law are not doing the law. Since the concept of loosening is terminology regarding interpretation of the law, Jesus is saying that one can interpret the law *too loosely*—to the point they are no longer keeping the law. Where that line is crossed is not specified, but the warning has been given.

The second point of interest is that the warning of being "*least,*" or the assurance of being "*great,*" are tied, not only to how one personally interprets the law, but to whether one teaches others to follow their interpretations. The point here concerns the high value that Jesus (and the Father) place on teaching others the law. The obligation to teach

---

[216] Strong's Word NT:3089

the law is itself a commandment found within the law.[217] God wants the law taught correctly, not a loosened version of it that borders on blatantly negating it. This statement in verse 19 once again demonstrates the value Jesus places on the law and its correct interpretation. After all, it is the law itself that serves as his credentials for being a valid teacher, prophet, and more, because the Law and the Prophets define the characteristics of a true prophet.

So, what exactly does it mean to be *"least"* in the kingdom of heaven? At this point it is not really defined. However, the next verse does give us a clue that it apparently means one's exclusion from the kingdom of heaven altogether.

E. Scribes and Pharisees' Righteousness

Another often misrepresented saying of Jesus is found in Matthew 5:20. Here, Jesus states the following:

> *For I say to you, that unless your righteousness exceeds that of the scribes and Pharisees, you will by no means enter the kingdom of heaven.*[218]

Many in Christianity today argue that in this verse Jesus is telling his listeners that one cannot enter the kingdom of heaven based on works. The logic is supposedly argued on the assumption that the scribes and Pharisees were very law abiding

---

[217] Deuteronomy 6:7

[218] The Greek word for "righteousness" only appears once in this saying of Jesus. Many translations make it appear twice. Jesus' point is that one's righteousness, i.e., *equitable deeds* (Strong's Word NT:1343) need to be better than those of the scribes and Pharisees. It is the same word Jesus uses in Matthew 6:1 that is translated as *"charitable deeds."*

and righteous, and yet this was still insufficient for them to enter the kingdom of heaven. But that is not what Jesus has said here. Think of it! He has actually said just the opposite—the scribes and Pharisees have not been law abiding and righteous enough, otherwise how could one exceed what they do. Jesus' point is that the actions of the scribes and Pharisees do not measure up to God's standards and this is keeping them out of the kingdom.

Some people will question why Jesus would make a reference to the scribes and Pharisees' *"righteousness"*, if indeed their righteousness was inaccurate or insufficient Mosaic Law keeping. With my years of experience in Arab-influenced East Africa, this phrasing is no longer a mystery to me. The Middle Eastern/African culture that I experienced was one that treaded lightly when it came to being disrespectful to anyone, especially someone with a position of honor within the community. I quickly learned that my Western ways were much harsher than that which East Africans were accustom to. If someone did poor work, it was offensive to tell them their work was "bad." You want to allow them to keep face within the community. So, a more polite response to evaluating someone's poor work would be to say something to the effect of: "It is not bad" or "It is acceptable." You might then follow it with a correction such as, "Can you do it this way and make it even better? What do you think?" This way no one gets embarrassed. They feel that their current work is appreciated and perhaps it can be made even better in the future.

I see Jesus' statement about the scribes and Pharisees as a similar cultural politeness. At this point in his ministry, he chooses to give some respect to the honored leaders of the community. Jesus' statement is a typical Middle Eastern cultural way of politely informing his listeners that their respected scribes and Pharisees are not correct. They are not bad, but they are not correct.

There can be no doubt about the fact that the scribes and Pharisees' righteousness is deficient as the following verses will give examples that target the deficiencies of the Pharisees' teachings. Jesus will present six examples of what the people have been "taught" (by the scribes and Pharisees) and then he will teach them what they really should know and do. Jesus' statement that one's righteousness needs to exceed that of the scribes and Pharisees, means just what it implies—the leaders have failed to lead correctly. There is no need to explain it away.

Jesus' run-ins with the religious leaders (particularly the Pharisees) of his day are well documented in the Gospels, and a quick review of these incidences will reinforce the position that Jesus views them as misguided leaders and teachers—their brand of righteousness is not to be followed. Here are a few examples from the book of Matthew and one from Luke:

- **Matthew 9:11** (They felt it was wrong to associate with "sinners." Jesus rebukes them for not understanding God's word.)
- **Matthew 12:2** (They felt that Jesus' view of Sabbath-keeping was wrong.)
- **Matthew 12:24** (They think that Jesus' power is from the devil.)
- **Matthew 15:6, 9** (They teach their own traditions and doctrines as   replacing the commandments of God.)
- **Matthew 16:12** (Jesus tells us to beware of their doctrines.)
- **Matthew 23:14** (They devour the houses of widows.)
- **Matthew 23:15** (They make their students sons of hell.)
- **Matthew 23:23** (They neglect justice, mercy, and faith—the weightier matters of the law.)
- **Matthew 23:28** (They are full of hypocrisy and law-

lessness.)
- **Matthew 23:31–35** (Jesus states that they are culpable for the murder of the prophets.)
- **Luke 11:52** (Luke adds to Matthew 23's list of woes the following: "Woe to you [Pharisees]! For you have taken away the key of knowledge. You did not enter in [to the kingdom] yourselves, and those who were entering in you hindered.")

That is just a glimpse of Jesus' view of the scribes and Pharisees' righteousness that he says must be exceeded. Their righteousness clearly is not the righteousness (moral character, equitable deeds, and faith) that Jesus teaches in the beatitudes and elsewhere. Jesus makes it undeniably evident to his disciples and the listening crowd that they are not to follow the teachings of these misguided leaders if they wish to enter the kingdom of heaven. Rather, one needs to "do" the righteous teachings of Jesus, as he has outlined them in His Sermon on the Mount, otherwise entrance into the kingdom will be denied.

So, even though Jesus finds the teaching of the scribes and Pharisees deficient, at this point in his ministry he is not yet ready to call them teachers of unrighteousness (as he will later in his ministry). And at this point he does not have to. As we will see in the coming six examples, nothing Jesus says the people have been taught is wrong, it is just incomplete— *loosened* to use Jesus' term. Jesus will take the scribes and Pharisees' teachings and show that the law goes further than that which the people have "heard." In short, their teachings are *too loose*. Jesus is being correct and polite in saying that the scribes and Pharisees have a degree of righteousness, but he is also right in saying that their views are incomplete and need to be exceeded. (In chapter 18, I will demonstrate that, biblically, the term *righteous* in the Old Testament can have degrees of application. That is, it can be said that a person has more, or less, righteousness than another person.)

Part of the problem of why Jesus had run-ins with the scribes and Pharisees stems from their view that the law was a set of prohibitions against doing evil, or unrighteousness. But that is the nature of the way laws are written in a society that has evil which needs to be stopped. What people usually miss is the fact that most laws have truly little to say about how much "good" you are allowed to do. In fact, laws do not put limits on good. So, laws that place prohibition on evil are, by implication, making "good" permissive.

Each one of Jesus' "But I say to you" statements within his six antitheses examples, that we will look at soon, are his way of focusing the listener's attention on the higher righteousness that the law permits—or in reality, encourages. God's law is written to combat evil, but its standards can be thought of as minimum "good" standards. The true and higher good that it seeks, the righteousness that goes beyond the written word, is the substance of the heavenly kingdom's jurisprudence. The scribes and Pharisees frequently lacked this broader perspective that the law is not just there to prevent evil, but that it is written as a springboard to achieve a higher standard of good.

Consider also that Jesus' statement in Matthew 5:20 begins with the little word *"For."* This is translated from the Greek word *gar.*[219] It is defined as a primary particle, used to *assign a reason*, or *assign an argument, explanation,* or *intensification.* In other words, Jesus' use of this word is referring his listeners back to what he has just said, to explain the logic of what he is about to say. And what has Jesus just said? He has said that the Law and the Prophets are not destroyed, and that they need to be interpreted, kept, and taught—properly. Jesus' call for equity righteousness, as

---

[219] Strong's word NT:1063

outlined in the beatitudes, is a proper teaching in agreement with the Law and the Prophets, as Jesus himself acknowledges by his declaration, he is not loosening the law but fulfilling it.

Finally, Jesus warns that a loosened or relaxed interpretation of the law, and the teaching of others to follow those loosened ideas, will result in one being called "least" in the kingdom of heaven. This verse is immediately followed by Jesus' warning to the people that they should not have the scribes and Pharisees' brand of righteousness, which we will see is an incomplete interpretation of the law. The implication is that the interpretations "taught" by the scribes and Pharisees are "loosened" teachings of the Law and Prophets. These religious leaders therefore fall into the category of being "least" in the kingdom of heaven as mentioned in verse 18. And what is more, since one cannot enter the kingdom of heaven unless their righteousness exceeds that of the scribes and Pharisees, the implication would be that the scribes and Pharisees themselves are not entering the kingdom. Therefore, contextually, when one follows the logic, "least" means the same as being excluded from the kingdom of heaven.

We are about to venture into Jesus' six antitheses that are examples of the righteousness of the scribes and Pharisees contrasted by Jesus' calls for higher righteous standards. But I want you to be aware of something. These six antitheses, as they are known, are for all practical purposes a "detour" from Jesus' main message of societal justice, equity, mercy, and faith to be merciful. If the first five of these six antitheses from Jesus' sermon are dropped from his message, you find the main theme almost uninterrupted. Jesus uses the sixth antithesis to bring his listeners back to his main topic. For example, Jesus states just prior to these antitheses that one's righteousness must exceed that of the scribes and Pharisees. Similarly, the last line of his sixth example will call for his listeners to *be perfect as your Father in heaven is perfect.* That statement is a summary of what higher righteousness is—one's sharing of the character traits of God. This will become more apparent as we move forward in our study.

Also, keep in mind that the subject matter prior to the six antitheses (Matthew 5:16–20) is a response to the listener's confusion over how "good works" is a fulfilment of the Law and Prophets, and a means of giving glory to the Father in heaven. Interestingly, immediately after Jesus' sixth antithesis, he begins a message about how to do your charitable deeds (Matthew 6:1). Jesus essentially will be returning to where he left out in Matthew 5:16. We will get there soon enough, but first, we have an interesting and informative detour.

CHAPTER 16

First, Be Reconciled to Your Brother

You have heard that it was said to those of old, "You shall not murder, and whoever murders will be in danger of the judgment." But I say to you that whoever is angry with his brother without a cause shall be in danger of the judgment. And whoever says to his brother, "Raca!" shall be in danger of the council. But whoever says, "You fool!" shall be in danger of hell fire. Therefore if you bring your gift to the altar, and there remember that your brother has something against you, leave your gift there before the altar, and go your way. First be reconciled to your brother, and then come and offer your gift. Agree with your adversary quickly, while you are on the way with him, lest your adversary deliver you to the judge, the judge hand you over to the officer, and you be thrown into prison. Assuredly, I say to you, you will by no means get out of there till you have paid the last penny.

Matthew 5:21–26

So far, we have taken a close look at the meaning of each of Jesus' beatitudes from the standpoint of what his listeners would have likely comprehended within the context of Jesus' words and familiar Old Testament teachings. The beatitudes' connections to social situations are noticeable when one traces Jesus' use of key words back into the Old Testament scriptures, as we have done. The connections to social justice, deeds of equity, and morality become very plain.

We have also explored how Jesus then focused on his disciples, and those interested in becoming disciples, telling them they are the salt and light of this world. This means that as they implement the tenets of the kingdom of heaven as outlined in the beatitudes, their lives will have a valuable and impactful influence on their communities. And furthermore, their deeds of justice and equity will be a way of giving glory to the Father in heaven.

It was this thought of glory being given to God via one's deeds of righteousness to the poor and downtrodden, that appears to have caused many within the crowd of listeners to question whether or not Jesus' views were a misinterpretation of the Law or the Prophets. After all, in the pious Jewish mindset of many, the poor, diseased, disabled and downtrodden were people God had chosen not to bless. The pious minds considered these individuals to be sinners and not people in need of social assistance for the sake of glorifying God.

Jesus rebuts this view by giving a five-pronged argument:

- He has not come to loosen up the Law or the Prophets but to fulfill them.
- Every detail of the law will remain intact to the end of time on earth.
- Teachers of the law put their lives at stake by giving loose interpretations of the law.
- Your teachers (the scribes and Pharisees) have been incomplete in their interpretations and actions.
- Your lives need to be better than those of your religious teachers and leaders if you are to enter the kingdom of heaven.

To make such bold and accusing claims without giving any proof would be a serious defamation of character on Jesus' part, so to back up his claims, Jesus now sets out to make his point by giving six examples of how the religious teachers have failed. But Jesus will not just point out the errors, he will also use each example as a teaching opportunity to demonstrate the moral principles he has outlined in the beatitudes. Each example is therefore an opportunity to further interpret the Law and the Prophets, a chance to demonstrate how his words are fulfilling them, or, as one of my theology professors used to say, "Filling them full."

Jesus will adopt a format where he gives six examples, each one being followed by corrective teachings. At the beginning of each example he says, "You have heard that it was said. . ." This alerts the crowd to "teachings" that their leaders have given them. Keep in mind for many of these listeners, they have been taught solely by what they have heard. Illiteracy is common in Jesus' day, especially among the rural crowds that are flocking to hear Jesus. The phrase, "you have heard" directs their minds back to Jesus' recent warning that teachers can give the wrong information. (Matthew 5:19–20.)

After each of these introductory lines and the identification of the issue, Jesus follows with a phrase saying, "But I say to you. . . . " Jesus then proceeds to "fulfill" the interpretation of the Law and the Prophets as his proof that his interpretation is deeper and more meaningful than that of the people's religious leaders. Each time this phrase is uttered, Jesus directs the crowd's mind back to his arguments of Matthew 5:17–20.

We are now about to look at each of these six examples carefully, but before we start, I would like to comment that I can only assume Jesus could have given many more examples if he wanted to. After all, as we have seen in the last chapter, Jesus had many other criticisms concerning the actions and teachings of the Pharisees. I am going to guess, and it is only a guess, that the six examples Jesus picked might have been areas of moral deficiencies that were widespread within the society of his day. In short, he chose to address the big issues which were familiar to his audience.

Jesus' first example deals with the issue of murder, and his "You have heard" statement goes as follows:

> *You have heard that it was said to those of old, "You shall not murder, and whoever murders will be in danger of the judgment."*[220]

"*You shall not murder*" are words that come directly from the law of God given to Moses.[221] And the danger of judgment—from God—also comes directly from the Torah, from as early as the book of Genesis.[222] Interestingly, it is not wrong to teach this to the people. The religious leaders, as well as the heads of households, are obligated by the law to teach these very things. So where is the mistake on the part of the scribes and Pharisees?

The misinterpretation, or loosening, of this law was that the leaders had limited this command to an action resulting in the loss of someone's life. Anything short of the loss of life was not considered murder—assault or injury, yes—but it was not murder. Our legal systems today share that same view.

Jesus, however, in giving his, "But I say to you" statement greatly expands (*fulfills*[223]) the meaning of murder. To Jesus, murder is more than the physical loss of life. Death can also occur at mental and emotional levels as well, and these less

---

[220] Matthew 5:21

[221] Exodus 20:13 and Deuteronomy 5:17

[222] Genesis 9:5–6

[223] Matthew 5:17

visible deaths have a serious impact on the health of a community. Jesus breaks these alternate forms of murder into three categories:

- Whoever is angry with his brother without a cause shall be in danger of   the judgment.
- Whoever says to his brother, "Raca!" shall be in danger of the council.
- And whoever says, "You fool!" shall be in danger of hell fire.

Let us briefly clarify these statements before we move on. Jesus has made a point that anger "without a cause"[224] is equivalent to murder, but is there ever a cause for some degree of anger? Perhaps. We have an example of Jesus himself being angry, and in that case his anger was generated over the fact that the Pharisees wanted to find opportunity to accuse him of breaking the Sabbath laws, thereby trying to destroy his ministry. The issue at hand dealt with whether Jesus would heal a man with a withered hand on the Sabbath day. The story, as recorded, goes as follows:

> [Jesus] *said to the man who had the withered hand, "Step forward." Then He said to* [the Pharisees], *"Is it lawful on the Sabbath to do good or to do evil, to save life or to kill?" But they kept silent. And when He had looked around at them with anger, being grieved by the hardness of their hearts, He said to the man, "Stretch out your hand."*[225]

---

[224] Matthew 5:22. The phase "without a cause" is not found in many ancient manuscripts. There are questions regarding whether or not Jesus actually made this statement.
[225] Mark 3:1–6

We also have the stories of Jesus' anger at the money changers in the temple, who were defiling God's house, the house of prayer. These "causes" were tied to blatant disregard for the word of God and active decisions to disobey it. We might call it "righteous indignation" today. If there is a cause for anger, these are our Gospel examples. References to God's anger in the Old Testament fit a similar pattern.

As for the categories of name calling, let me clarify that the word *Raca* is an Aramaic word[226] that means *empty one, worthless*. It is a term of vilification. The Greek word translated as *"You fool"* is *moros*,[227] and it means *dull* or *stupid*, or *a blockhead,* or one who is *heedless, reckless*.

Jesus' statement, "But I say to you" shows that all three of his additional definitions of murder are subject to similar penalties as physical murder. Both physical murder and anger without a cause are subject to "judgment." Calling someone "worthless" is subject to being reviewed by the council.[228] All three of these murders—physical murder, anger without a cause, and calling someone worthless— are subject to a judicial review and a determination of punishment. And finally, calling someone "dull" or "stupid" places one in danger of hell fire—that is, the possibility of God making the determination that the offense warrants the loss of one's future eternal life in God's kingdom.

The Torah gave a profound reason for why God would judge a man for shedding another's blood. It is found in the flood narrative and God's words are recorded as follows:

---

[226] Strong's Word NT:4469

[227] Strong's Word NT:3474

[228] Strong's Word NT:4892; *Sunedrion*, a word from which we get the word *Sanhedrin*. In this verse's context, however, the council is more likely a heavenly council judging one's case (see Matthew 19:28 and Revelation chapters 4 and 5).

Surely for your lifeblood I will demand a reck-oning; from the hand of every beast [that kills a man] *I will require it, and from the hand of man* [who kills a man]. *From the hand of every man's brother I will require the life of man. Whoever sheds man's blood, by man his blood shall be shed;* **for in the image of God He made man**. (emphasis added)[229]

It is the fact that God made man, and made him in His own image, that creates the high value that God places on man. De-faming, or not recognizing the significance of this divine value, carries a high price.

Note that each of these three murder subcategories that Jesus addresses deal with how an individual "thinks" about the other person. It is this thinking that leads one to devaluate God's creation, and is equated to an act of murder. Hatred of someone can lead to murder, which, of course, is obvious. But maybe not so obvious is that one's hatred (expressed as anger) for someone else will lead to a disregard of that person's welfare. If we hate someone, we will have little motivation to be just in our business dealings with them, or little interest in helping them in their time of need. Though we may not be putting an end to their life, we may be compromising their life in roundabout ways. For example, if we are angry with someone, do we have concern for him when he loses a job and begins to struggle financially? Or do we gloat and think, "It serves him right"?

What happens to an individual who gets belittled by others and called stupid and worthless? Each time, their soul dies a bit more, and they may even begin to believe the accusations and withdraw from participating in the community, or maybe rebel in anger against it. These things have an emotional cost

---

[229] Genesis 9:5–6

to everyone. The loss of harmony between brothers and sisters is seen as the death of relationships, a deterioration of the community as a whole. Jesus holds this on par with murder. Perhaps the accusations are true, but Jesus' warning is that they should not be verbalized. His beatitude of "peacemaking" would be the better course of action. The "dull" or "worthless" individual would be better served by mentorship and education, or perhaps even medical attention.

Even though Jesus sees these subcategories as "murder" his following instructions show that they can and should be corrected. Jesus states the following:

> *Therefore, if you bring your gift to the altar, and there remember that your brother has something against you, leave your gift there before the altar, and go your way. First be reconciled to your brother, and then come and offer your gift.*[230]

In the context of this passage, we find it is the worshiper before God who needs reconciling of some fault that he has created. He has done something that has caused someone to have an issue "against" him. The context suggests that it is the worshiper who is angry without a valid cause, or has called someone worthless or stupid. That individual is now mentally or emotionally injured to some degree and probably would like to avoid you. Jesus says that if we want to have a good relationship with God and worship Him with a clear mind and conscience we should stop right where we are and be reconciled to the one we have wronged. We are the ones who have done the damage; so, we are the ones who need to initiate the reconciliation. It may not be accepted by the other party, but we are to at least make the attempt to reconcile.

---

[230] Matthew 5:23–24

There is a great amount of logic in this statement of Jesus. Bringing a gift to the altar is an act of requesting forgiveness for wrongs we have done to God, or an act of praise and thanksgiving to our creator. It would be ironic to approach God in a worshipful state of mind when there are people we have offended that are made in God's image, and valued so highly by God, that he is willing to die for them. Our disharmony between each other is sure to affect our harmony with God.

Jesus' instructions address more than just the mental and emotional murders we might commit. He includes another example which also has social justice and equity implications. It reads as follows:

> *Agree with your adversary quickly, while you are on the way with him, lest your adversary deliver you to the judge, the judge hand you over to the officer, and you be thrown into prison. Assuredly, I say to you, you will by no means get out of there till you have paid the last penny.*[231]

On the surface, this does not appear to be an issue of murder, but it is plainly a case of social disharmony, which Jesus is pointing out is fertile ground for anger and name calling. His advice is to solve these problems quickly. Notice, however, who is the one at fault? The answer is "you"!

In this passage it is "you" (me included) who is to come to an agreement with your adversary before you end up in court and eventually in jail. Consider this, if the dispute is to end with you in jail, then that means the court is going to determine that you are the guilty party in the dispute. That would imply that the adversary or brother has a valid reason to have something against you. Apparently, you have wronged him in such a

---

[231] Matthew 5:25–26

way that a court will agree in your adversary or brother's favor. This clearly indicates that it is you who is the unjust party in this dispute. Keep in mind, however, that this courtroom and its judgment referred to in this "murder" example appears to be an earthly judicial body. However, since Jesus is expanding the interpretation of this law, the court could just as easily be a heavenly one, which is weighing the social justice and equity deficiencies of our lives. Jesus is therefore calling us to be peacemakers, especially when it is ourselves who have committed the injustices that need to be corrected in order to restore the peace.

CHAPTER 17

Adultery and Marriage

You have heard that it was said to those of old, "You shall not commit adultery." But I say to you that whoever looks at a woman to lust for her has already committed adultery with her in his heart. If your right eye causes you to sin, pluck it out and cast it from you; for it is more profitable for you that one of your members perish, than for your whole body to be cast into hell. And if your right hand causes you to sin, cut it off and cast it from you; for it is more profitable for you that one of your members perish, than for your whole body to be cast into hell.

Furthermore, it has been said, "Whoever divorces his wife, let him give her a certificate of divorce." But I say to you that whoever divorces his wife for any reason except sexual immorality causes her to commit adultery; and whoever marries a woman who is divorced commits adultery."

Matthew 5:27–32

Jesus' second and third examples of incorrect interpretations of the law concern issues dealing with adultery and marriage. I would again mention that I believe Jesus picked his six examples because these represented serious issues in his day. Perhaps what is more interesting is that the issues are still serious ones in our day, nearly two thousand years later. Jesus starts with the issue of adultery, by stating:

> *You have heard that it was said to those of old,*
> *"You shall not commit adultery."*[232]

Once again, this teaching has come directly from the Ten Commandments, as recorded in the Torah.[233] And once again, the scribes and Pharisees have not been wrong in teaching this to the people. Adultery was a flagrant sin punishable by death to both the man and the woman guilty of adultery. The misinterpretation, or loosening, of this law was that the religious teachers had limited this command to an action of sexual relationship with a married woman. Anything short of this was not quite adultery. Thinking or fantasizing about adultery was not a violation of the law. After all, since no one else is evolved and no harm has been done, how could one be in violation of the law? This interpretation of the law, however, ignored the fact that there was also a law against coveting a neighbor's wife. Jesus, as we will see, held that the sin of adultery begins in the mind and that one is crossing the threshold even before a physical encounter occurs.

Let me clarify a little bit here. Adultery in the Torah is, for the most part, the act of a married woman being unfaithful to her husband and having a sexual relationship with another man.[234]

---

[232] Matthew 5:27

[233] Exodus 20:14 and Deuteronomy 5:18

[234] Deuteronomy 22:22-28

That man does not have to be married for the adultery to occur; it is the woman who must be married. A married man could have a sexual relationship with an unmarried woman and not be under a death penalty—at least under certain conditions. Nevertheless, any man involved sexually with a married woman was also guilty of adultery, and the penalty of death was applicable to both parties, except in cases of rape where only the man would suffer capital punishment.

Jesus makes a correction to the Pharisees' limited—or should we say "loose"—interpretation of the law by expanding it to include sins of the mind, as he did with the law concerning murder. Jesus' statement, "but I say to you" instructs as follows:

> *But I say to you that whoever looks at a woman to lust for her has already committed adultery with her in his heart.*[235]

The Greek word used for "woman" in this verse is *gune*.[236] It means a *woman* and more specifically a *wife*, therefore a married woman. The Gospels could have used the Greek word *parthenos*.[237] This would have changed the female subject to a *maiden*, implying an *unmarried daughter* or a *virgin*. So, in this statement Jesus is still in keeping with the Old Testament precedent that adultery is an act committed with a married woman.

I find this distinction particularly important because what Jesus is defending here is the solemnity of the marriage relationship, and by extension, the family unit that a marriage is intended to create. Jesus' expansion of this law to include lust for a married woman is warning men outside of a family unit

---

[235] Matthew 5:28

[236] Strong's Word NT:1135

[237] Strong's Word NT:3933

not to interfere with the relationship of a man and his wife. And he is demonstrating that that interference does not need to be sexual. The word "lust" used here is from the Greek word *epithumeo,*[238] and it means *to set the heart upon,* or *to long for* (rightly or wrongly). It gets translated into English as *to covet, desire,* and yes, *to lust after.* But the Gospel could have used two other similar Greek words that speak of stronger sexual desires.[239]

The fact that Jesus chose to use a word with a broader meaning is significant. It shows that a violation of the adultery law does not need to be solely driven by a strong sexual desire for another man's wife. Just coveting her is enough for a violation to occur. A wish that she was your wife rather than his, is a form of adultery under Jesus' broadened definition of this Ten Commandment law. And consider this; Jesus has reduced the sin of adultery from one involving two parties to a sin involving only one party. That one party is to stay out of another man or woman's marriage relationship.

Under Jesus' expanded definition, even a one-party violator of the adultery law would still be subject to a death penalty. This becomes obvious in Jesus' next statement, as follows:

> *If your right eye causes you to sin, pluck it out and cast it from you; for it is more profitable for you that one of your members perish, than for your whole body to be cast into hell. And if your right hand causes you to sin, cut it off and cast it from you; for it is more profitable for you that one of your members perish, than for your whole body to be cast*

---

[238] Strong's Word NT:1937

[239] Strong's Word NT:1938; *epithumetes,* a craver, a strong lusting and NT:1939: *epithumia* a strong longing for what is forbidden, concupiscence.

into hell.[240]

Contextually, the "sin" being spoken of in these two verses is the sin of adultery being committed by the "one" party, and in both examples, the result is the loss of one's eternal life in the kingdom of heaven. It is highly unlikely that Jesus expects someone to pluck out their eye or literally cut off their hand. He is using hyperbole here. After all, even a person with one eye or one hand could still commit the type of sin Jesus has outlined. Jesus' point is that the sin is so serious and so life-threatening that if it took putting out an eye or cutting off a hand to stop it, you would be better off maimed than to lose your eternal life in the kingdom of heaven. That should tell us something about how serious God is that we do not interfere in another person's marriage relationship, and what degree of devotion God expects from us.

It is also important to understand that Jesus' reference to what the eye sees and what the hand does is an expansion of the sin of adultery, as well as the act of lusting. The act of the eye would include voyeurism, pornography, and stalking. The act of the hand would include any molestation or inappropriate touching of a married person that a violator may wish to do.

Up to this point I have focused on Jesus' expanded interpretation of the adultery law being a man, married or single, lusting after a married woman. But the tables can just as easily be reversed to include a woman, married or not, lusting after a married man. The principle of not interfering in the solemnity of a couple's marriage relationship and family unit still holds true.

The same logic being used by Jesus in this example could be applied to one mentally lusting for any number of sexual taboos listed in the law. For example, in chapter 18 of the

---

[240] Matthew 5:29–30

book of Leviticus, we find a list of numerous sexual sins that are not necessarily committed with a married person. These include various forms of incest, fornication, and other sexual abominations.

In addition, if one is single and lusting after a single man or woman, they are still not off the hook. Recall that the Gospel's word for "lust" is the least specific option of the various verbs available in Greek, and its meaning includes coveting. Coveting is still a sin. The ninth commandment reads as follows:

> *You shall not covet your neighbor's house; you shall not covet your neighbor's wife, nor his male servant, nor his female servant, nor his ox, nor his donkey, nor anything that is your neighbor's.*[241]

"Anything that is your neighbor's" includes his daughter or son. The principle of not interfering in the solemnity of a man's family unit again holds true. Coveting a man's single daughter or son could be a sin considered adultery, especially if the coveting or lusting is solely for one's sexual gratification.

Jesus' third example of a misinterpreted law deals with the subject of marriage and divorce. To refresh your memory, here is what he said:

> *Furthermore, it has been said, "Whoever divorces his wife, let him give her a certificate of divorce." But I say to you that whoever divorces his wife for any reason except sexual immorality causes her to commit adultery; and whoever marries a woman who is divorced commits adultery.*[242]

---

[241] Exodus 20:17
[242] Matthew 5:31–32

In Jesus' day the topic of when did a man have the right to divorce his wife was a polarizing dispute among the various rabbinic schools. We will get to that issue in a moment, but first, let me give you some background and clarification on Jesus' statement.

The certificate of divorce that Jesus references is from the Torah and is found in the book of Deuteronomy, chapter 24. Here, Moses makes a statement that a man might give his wife a certificate of divorce if it "happens that she finds no favor in his eyes because he has found some uncleanness in her."[243] Needless to say, this is a rather vague set of circumstances. What exactly is "no favor" and what exactly is "uncleanness"?

These two conditions were topics of much debate. There are only two Old Testament examples of the use of the certificate of divorce. One is in the book of Isaiah, where God uses symbolic language to state that a mother (symbolic of a nation) is given a certificate of divorce due to her children's transgressions.[244] The second example is from the book of Jeremiah, where symbolic language referring to the nation of Israel, states that the certificate of divorce is given due to adultery.[245] The adultery in this case includes the worship of idols, an infidelity in terms of loyalty to God.

This idea of infidelity being **idolatry** as well as marital unfaithfulness fits within Jesus' "but I say to you" teaching. The Greek word used to translate the term *"sexual immorality"* in Matthew 5:32 is the word *porneia*.[246] The word relates to *harlotry, adultery*, and figuratively, *idolatry*. It is not limited to sexual immorality.

---

[243] Deuteronomy 24:1

[244] Isaiah 50:1

[245] Jeremiah 3:6–9

[246] Strong's Word NT:4202

Jesus' position is quite clear. A divorce for any reason that does not involve the wife's infidelity to the marriage relationship (or possibly religious apostasy) would be an invalid divorce. A man divorcing his wife for any other reason, would cause her to commit adultery if she were to marry another man. Her new husband would also be committing adultery. How can this be? The answer is a matter of perspective. In the eyes of God, the first divorce would not be justified so the original couple is still married. The wife leaving and having a sexual relationship with another man (her new husband), would be the same as being unfaithful to her first husband. Keep in mind, Jesus is holding the first husband at fault because he is causing the sin of adultery to occur.

Jesus' position is not a new revelation to his listeners; it is in fact a statement plainly showing that he disagrees with the Pharisees position on divorce. It therefore ties back to Jesus' statement that one's righteousness needs to exceed that of the scribes and Pharisees. In Jesus' day there were two polarized opinions on when a man could divorce his wife. One opinion came from Hillel the Elder, and the other came from Rabbi Shammai.

Hillel interpreted the terms in Deuteronomy of "no favor" and "uncleanness" very liberally, and felt that divorce was a man's prerogative for something as mundane as his wife burning his meal. Rabbi Shammai, on the other hand, felt that these terms only applied to a woman's infidelity. These positions date back to the first century BCE.

The Pharisees taught, and practiced, that a wife could be divorced for just about any reason, thus siding with Hillel's opinion. Jesus, on the other hand, sided with Rabbi Shammai and limited divorce to infidelity. What Jesus adds to this rabbinical debate is the fact that the man at fault for initiating an invalid divorce is potentially causing further sin within the community.

Matthew records a later exchange between Jesus and the Pharisees on this topic. It is found in chapter 19. The Pharisees appear to be trying to prove Jesus wrong on his Sermon on the Mount position by asking him a question they think will trap him. They ask, *"Is it lawful for a man to divorce his wife for just any reason?"*[247] This is clearly a question seeking an evaluation on a Hillelian position, since it was Hillel the Elder who supported divorce for any reason.

Jesus replies that it is not lawful, and he cites the creation account in the Torah to show that God made husband and wife one flesh. He concludes that man should not separate what God has put together. To this the Pharisees reply:

> *Why then did Moses command to give a cer-*
> *tificate of divorce, and to put her away?*[248]

The Pharisees think they now have Jesus trapped, because Moses in the Torah allowed a certificate of divorce. In their minds, Moses—a man, and leader—had allowed something that Jesus says a man should not do. So, the fact that Moses exercised authority to do something Jesus thinks should not be done is proof to them that Jesus is wrong in his thinking on divorce. The Pharisees are concluding that Moses, with his God-given leadership authority can separate what God has put together. Likewise, a man, who is the leader of his household would have authority to divorce his wife for *"just any reason."* In short, in the Pharisees' opinion, a man has Godlike authority over his wife. It is not the tightest of arguments, but it is worth a try in the minds of the Pharisees.

---

[247] Matthew 19:3
[248] Matthew 19:7

Jesus' reply tells us something about the social justice and equity position of his statement given in the Sermon on the Mount. Jesus tells them:

> *Moses, because of the hardness of your hearts, permitted you to divorce your wives, but from the beginning it was not so. And I say to you, whoever divorces his wife, except for sexual immorality, and marries another, commits adultery; and whoever marries her who is divorced commits adultery.*[249]

Jesus almost repeats, verbatim, the position he gave on the Sermon on the Mount. In doing so, he is telling the Pharisees that his position has not changed. But note the reason why he says that Moses permitted divorce. It was due to the "hardiness" of the people's hearts. Stop and think what this implies. You have a situation where a man is at odds with his wife. The reason is not important. What is important is that there is a love loss, and the respect he has for her (or maybe it is her loss of love for him) is making the home life miserable. There is stress, there is anger, there are retaliations—passive or aggressive—for offensive actions. The condition may be deteriorating to dangerous domestic violence. We have a situation where both parties are in pain and are causing severe discord within their families and their community. There is a need here for mercy, for comforting of those who mourn, for making peace, for judging justly and implementing a moral solution. However, as Jesus points out, due to the hardness of hearts—that is, their refusal to reconcile and give mercy or make peace—Moses grants permission to divorce. In other words, it is better for all the individuals involved, and for the community, to let the

---

[249] Matthew 19:8–9

husband and wife separate, than to let anger and violence continue to brew. However, as Jesus says, this was never God's original intention. The certificate of divorce is the lesser of two evils in a fallen world.

CHAPTER 18

"Yes" Be "Yes," "No" Be "No"

Again, you have heard that it was said to those of old, "You shall not swear falsely, but shall perform your oaths to the Lord." But I say to you, do not swear at all: neither by heaven, for it is God's throne; nor by the earth, for it is His footstool; nor by Jerusalem, for it is the city of the great King. Nor shall you swear by your head, because you cannot make one hair white or black. But let your "Yes" be "Yes," and your "No," "No." For whatever is more than these is from the evil one.

Matthew 5:33–37

In this next example of the law being misrepresented, or loosened, by the religious teachers of the day, Jesus has again cited a teaching that is not wrong, and again comes from the Torah itself. Jesus' statement is a combination of two separate commands. However, before I quote the first one, I will also give you the verse before it and the verse after it. It is important to see the context of how God presented this command, because in that context lies a strong social justice theme. The first of the two commands is recorded as follows:

You shall not steal, nor deal falsely, nor lie to one another. And **you shall not swear by My name falsely**, *nor shall you profane the name of your God: I am the Lord. You shall not cheat your neighbor, nor rob him. The wages of him who is hired shall not remain with you all night until morning.* (emphasis added)[250]

The second command in its context reads as follows:

When you make a vow to the Lord your God, you shall not delay to pay it; for the Lord your God will surely require it of you, and it would be sin to you. But if you abstain from vowing, it shall not be sin to you. **That which has gone from your lips you shall keep and perform,** *for you voluntarily vowed to the Lord your God what you have promised with your mouth.* (emphasis added)[251]

You will notice from these two commands in the Torah that God does not have a prohibition on making vows. Vow-making in the name of God, or a vow to God is allowed. However, it should not be a false vow, or oath, and it is to be taken very seriously and carried out promptly. By the way, the Hebrew words translated as "swear" and "vow" carry the same understandings as the Gospel's Greek words translated "swear" and "*oath*."[252] Regardless of which language is used, all are references to solemn statements or solemn promises to carry out some kind of action.

---

[250] Leviticus 19:11–13

[251] Deuteronomy 23:21–23

[252] Strong's Word OT:7650, OT:5087, NT:1964/1965 "false oath", "perjury" and NT:3727. (Also NT:3660 used in Matthew 5:34.)

The scribes and Pharisees were experts in the law and understood these commands perfectly. They understood that an oath in the name of God was binding and could not be broken. However, being law experts, they also noticed a loophole in the Torah. These commands did not say that a person could not make an oath invoking the reverences or authority of some person, place, or thing.[253] And if one did so, would those oaths be binding? Maybe they would, but surely not as binding as an oath made in the name of God.

In first-century Judea, the use of this loophole had become widespread. Our text above from the Sermon on the Mount and others in the Gospels, as well as ancient rabbinical writings, affirm this. Making an oath by swearing on created things was an ordinary practice and was meant to increase the trustworthiness of one's word in business or personal interactions. The *safety* of using this type of oath—for the oath maker— was that if he could not keep it, he was not sinning against God. The *problem* was that its use and abuse had become so commonplace that oath making had become meaningless and flippant. The word of an individual, with or without an oath, was suspect. A person could only trust someone he knew well. Someone outside the community could only be trusted based on a recommendation or by testing their honesty. Not a whole lot has changed, has it?

Jesus, however, teaches the people that this type of loophole is wrong because if one thinks about it carefully, it does not really exist. And Jesus begins by giving four examples to support his argument. The first three are based on information found in the Old Testament. They are as follows:

- Do not swear by heaven, for it is God's throne.

---

[253] Jesus has harsher words to the Pharisees on this issue late in his ministry (see Matthew 23:16–22).

- Do not swear by earth, for it is God's footstool.
- And do not swear by Jerusalem, for it is the city of a great king (i.e., God).

The book of Isaiah identifies the first two and asks a question regarding the third. It reads as follows:

> *Thus says the Lord: "Heaven is my throne, And earth is my footstool. Where is the house that you will build me? And where is the place of my rest?"*[254]

The book of Psalms identifies God's earthly city of residence as Jerusalem. It reads as follows:

> *Great is the Lord, and greatly to be praised in the city of our God, in His holy mountain. Beautiful in elevation, the joy of the whole earth, is Mount Zion* [Jerusalem] *on the sides of the north, the city of the great King.*[255]

Jesus' fourth argument as to why one should not swear is derived from these first three. It is as follows:

- Do not swear by your head, because you cannot make one hair white or black.

Jesus' points are quite simple: heaven, earth and Jerusalem are all God's. He is the one that created them. Even mankind is a product of God the creator. Therefore, if one invokes an oath based on anything God possesses or creat-

---

[254] Isaiah 66:1
[255] Psalm 48:1–2

ed, that person is making an oath in the name of God. That oath is just as binding as any made. If we do not carry out any of our oaths which invoke God or his creation, we have sinned against God. The Torah does not have a loophole for oath makers.

Jesus prefaced his four supporting arguments with the advice, "I say to you, do not swear at all." This is good advice given the seriousness of any oath one makes. It also highlights God's statement in the Torah that not making an oath is not a sin—oaths are optional, not required.

Jesus' final words for this loosened law example indicate that one's *word*, without an oath, should be all that one needs. He puts it as follows:

> Let your "Yes" be "Yes," and your "No," "No." For whatever is more than these is from the evil one.[256]

An individual should have enough moral integrity and self-respect that they would always honor their word. If they say "Yes," you can count on them to perform what they have agreed to do. And if they say "No," you can rest assured that you have asked them to do something that is outside their ability or comfort zone, and they will not change. If everyone were trustworthy and lived and died by Jesus' advice, oaths would be obsolete.

This misinterpreted or loosened law example given by Jesus fits very well with his social justice and equity theme of the beatitudes. Recall that Jesus is giving these examples of loosened law-keeping in defense of his teaching that his beatitudes are the works that glorify the Father in heaven. When I opened this chapter, I made it a point to give you the context of the command on making oaths in the Torah. Here it is again:

---

[256] Matthew 5:37

*You shall not steal, nor deal falsely, nor lie to one another. And **you shall not swear by My name falsely**, nor shall you profane the name of your God: I am the Lord. You shall not cheat your neighbor, nor rob him. The wages of him who is hired shall not remain with you all night until morning.* (emphasis added)[257]

Notice that the context of God's command is based on not stealing, or dealing falsely, or lying to someone else. It includes not cheating your neighbor, or robbing him, and not withholding wages from employees. This command implies that oaths are being used to do these things, therefore God commands that we do not swear falsely, but keep our word. No doubt, the "loophole" that the Pharisees thought they had found in the law was being used to make oaths that could be "acceptably" broken, resulting in theft, false deals, lies, cheating, robbery, and missing wages. All these things are social injustices.

How much of the world's social injustices and inequities have been initiated by false oaths—oaths that one or more parties never intended to keep? False oaths are always given with the intent to deceive and ultimately rob someone of something. Social injustices and inequities are frequently driven by deception clothed in honesty. It is often preceded by the promise of justice and equity, but its fulfillment was never possible or even intended. Our personal relationships, our communities, our society, our governments, nations, and the world hold a catalog of false oaths and broken promises. There are too few individuals, or government bodies, that honor their words as binding. Worse yet, meaningless words and deceptions are a way of life, and are too often used to intentionally mislead and

---

[257] Leviticus 19:11–13

manipulate others. Unfortunately, today, we even flippantly expect our leader to give us false promises.

"Let your 'Yes' be 'Yes,' and your 'No,' 'No.'
For whatever is more than these is from the evil
one."[258]

Jesus could not have been more right. What a better world this would be if we all lived by this simple axiom.

The use of these supposedly nonbinding oaths on the part of the scribes and Pharisees is a good example of their inferior righteousness. It brings to my mind a story found much earlier in the Bible that illustrates the value that early societies placed on the solemnity of one's word. The story also highlights the fact that the word *righteousness*, as used before Christianity, can be a term that represents the degree or quality of one's actions, rather than the possession of the perfect character of God. The story is found in Genesis 38 and deals with Judah and his daughter-in-law, Tamar. If you are not familiar with it, take time to read it in its entirety. Following is an abridged summary.

Tamar was given as a wife to Judah's firstborn son, Er, but Er died before having any offspring. As was the custom in those days, Tamar was then given to Judah's next eldest son, Onan. It was Onan's duty to have children with Tamar, and these children would serve as Er's children and receive his inheritance. Onan, however, abused this duty, and the Bible records that God took his life as punishment for his sin. Custom then required that Tamar be given to Judah's next son, Shelah, but this son was still a young boy. Judah instructed Tamar to return to her father's house and remain a widow until Shelah was old enough to marry and give her offspring on behalf of Er. Tamar took Judah at his word and returned to her father's house.

---

[258] Matthew 5:37

Years passed by, and Shelah was eventually old enough to take Tamar for a wife, but Judah did not honor his word, and Tamar remained a widow. The story records that one day Tamar got word that Judah would be in her region of the countryside checking on his sheep, and she hatched a deceptive plan to take matters into her own hands. She dressed as a harlot and veiled her face and waited by the road that Judah would take. Judah saw her and solicited her services. As payment, he promised to give her one of his young goats later in the day. She asked to have his signet ring and staff as a pledge to hold until he delivers the young goat. Judah agreed and gave her the items, had sexual relations with her, and then proceeded on his way.

Later, one of Judah's servants was sent to give the harlot a young goat and to retrieve the pledged items, but the servant found that the harlot had left. Months later, Judah received word that Tamar, his daughter-in-law, was pregnant. Angry at her infidelity, he ordered that she be put to death. However, she produced the signet ring and staff, and stated that she was pregnant by the man who owned those items. Judah acknowledged that the items were his, and she was not put to death. In doing so, Judah made the following relevant statement:

She has been more righteous than I, because I did not give her to Shelah my son.[259]

This is a curious story, and you might ask, "What does this have to do with Jesus' example of the Pharisees righteousness?" Here is the answer. Neither Judah nor Tamar were righteous in their actions. Judah displayed poor judgment, lack of self-control, lust, and failure to keep his promise. Tamar practiced

---

[259] Genesis 38:26 (see other examples of being "more righteous" in 1 Samuel 24:17; 1 Kings 2:32; Jeremiah 3:11, Ezekiel 16:52, and Habakkuk 1:13).

deception and harlotry to solve her legal case on not being given to Shelah to produce heirs for her late husband, Er. Nevertheless, Judah conceded that Tamar had been more righteous than himself. Why? It is because of the value that Judah, and his society at that time, placed on one's word. A promise was to be kept. A "Yes" was to be a "Yes." Failing to keep one's word was a sin graver than harlotry, infidelity, and deception. Judah's failure to keep his word was an act of unrighteousness that surpassed the unrighteous actions of his daughter-in-law, Tamar. However, Judah, following the cultural norms of his day, stated his conclusion more positively and in the reverse; Tamar was said to be more righteous than he.

When Jesus states that one's righteousness needed to exceed the righteousness of the scribes and Pharisees, he is doing the same thing as Judah, as was the custom of the day. The scribes and Pharisees were deficient in their righteousness, therefore Jesus states that his followers need be more righteous than they are. Jesus' statement is not giving the scribes and Pharisees any kudos; it is doing just the opposite—but it is nevertheless polite, which helps them save face within the community.

I should make one final point. Jesus' saying that we should "not swear at all" need not be construed to mean that oaths in a court of law are prohibited. An oath administered in court is done for the purpose of connecting a witness to the potential penalty of perjury, should that witness not tell the truth. One takes the oath with the knowledge that if they give a false statement, they are subject to the punishment of perjury by the court. One takes an oath to verify that they are going to be trustworthy, which is what an oath was always supposed to be—a pledge of honesty.

CHAPTER 19

Nonviolence

You have heard that it was said, "An eye for an eye and a tooth for a tooth." But I tell you not to resist an evil person. But whoever slaps you on your right cheek, turn the other to him also. If anyone wants to sue you and take away your tunic, let him have your cloak also. And whoever compels you to go one mile, go with him two. Give to him who asks you, and from him who wants to borrow from you do not turn away.

Matthew 5:38–42

Jesus begins his fifth example of misinterpreted law, or incomplete righteousness, with another true statement from the law. This statement, "An eye for an eye and a tooth for a tooth" is only a part of a much more comprehensive set of laws in the Torah.[260] It includes other forms of harm including a life for a life. People today often view this law as a barbaric relic of the past, and cringe that such a thing would ever be suggested, much less permitted. But this law is not so much about *what is to be permitted* as it is about *what is to be prohibited*. This statute was quite commonplace in the ancient Orient and Near East and would have been

---

[260] Exodus 21:24; Leviticus 24:20; Deuteronomy 19:21

understood by Jesus' listeners. It is stating that a penalty is not to exceed the crime. It calls for restraint and limits one's vengeance. In other words, if someone damages our mailbox, we are not at liberty to burn down their house.

While this statute limits how much revenge or compensation one can seek for a wrongdoing, it does not prohibit the offended party from accepting less, or even forgiving the person in the wrong. Justice asks for equal compensation, but God's higher righteousness can accept loss in an attempt to reconcile a relationship between an offender and the offended. And this concept serves as the basis for Jesus' teachings in the three examples that follow this statement, but first let us look at what Jesus means by saying, *"But I tell you not to resist an evil person."*

The New King James Version of the Bible has added the word "person" to the text of Matthew 5:39; the Greek text only has Jesus saying, *"not to resist evil."* As a result, some Christians teach that Jesus is saying it is wrong for Christians to resist evil of any kind. In their minds, getting involved in a social cause to right a wrong would be an act of unsanctioned resistance. So, by extension, asking for a wage increase from a greedy employer would be wrong. Such ideas are unfounded. After all, if "evil" is not to be resisted, what would be the purpose of the great commission command to go into all the world and teach everyone everything Jesus commanded us? Defending the fatherless and widows, relieving burdens, and all the other social corrections encouraged by the beatitudes, would be pointless. All the above are evil situations or conditions, and we are explicitly commanded to correct them.

The key to the inclusion of the word "person" in Matthew 5:39 can be seen, in part, by the fact that Jesus again uses this word "evil"[261] in his next example. In this context, the word plainly

---

[261] Strong's Word NT: 4190, "poneros" meaning *hurtful, evil.*

refers to an evil person.[262] Also, we have the preceding verse that speaks of injury being met with equal punishment. These injuries are implied to have been delivered by a person—an evil person. You would not seek compensation from a tree if you broke your arm while falling out of it. So, an "eye for an eye" is guiding the social limits between personal relationships. Therefore, the insertion of the word "person" into Matthew 5:39 is a reasonable translation approach for capturing the full meaning of this verse. Jesus' point is that we are not to resist an evil person, and his following examples plainly demonstrate that we are not returning violence with equal violence in return.

The word "resist" also gives us a clue to what Jesus is saying. This is translated from the Greek word *anthistemi*,[263] and it means *to stand against* or *oppose*. In short, Jesus is saying we should not engage in a fight against an evil person. We are not to seek to even the score or engage in a game of tit-for-tat. The offender's violence is not to be met with equal or even lesser violence from the offended Christian. Jesus' approach to dealing with an evil person is to react, but in a nonviolent manner.

To support this strategy, Jesus gives three scenarios, summarized as follows:

- If someone slaps your right cheek, offer your left as well.
- If someone wants to sue you for something, give him more than he asks.
- If someone in authority orders you to do something, do even more for him.

All three of these examples have a common theme of a person being oppressed by another person. These people

---

[262] Matthew 5:45

[263] Strong's Word NT:436

think they have a level of control over us; they see us as inferior to themselves. When we do not "resist" but instead return kindness to them, it will create confusion in their minds, and partially disarm their anger or call into question their belief that they have control over us. It might even stop a reoccurring cycle of violence to the benefit of a community, or hopefully plant the seed of reconciliation or friendship. This is a higher righteousness than the law requests, and its ultimate goal is the creation of a more just and equitable society—that which the law is truly trying to achieve.

Jesus' final advice within this section is:

> *Give to him who asks you, and from him who wants to borrow from you do not turn away.*[264]

This advice is probably separate from his advice on how to deal with an evil person, though it could easily include evil persons as well. Luke records a similar line in his record of Jesus' sermon that replaces Matthew's word "borrow" with the word "take."[265] Luke's version instructs us to not seek to get the items back. In either case, both versions indicate that there are people in need that may approach us seeking our help in meeting a need, and we are not to turn them away if the need is real. (Jesus gives an example later of when not to give.) This teaching also has a social justice and equity theme. It fits in with Jesus' teaching of peacemaking, even at our own expense, and it has an overall lifting effect on a community.

I like to use the example of a poorer neighbor coming to my house to borrow a shovel so he can dig and prepare a garden. I follow Jesus' advice and give him my shovel, letting him know

---

[264] Matthew 5:42
[265] Luke 6:30

he does not need to return it. Later, when I need a shovel, I buy a new one to replace the one I gave away. We both now have shovels to meet our needs. In addition, we now can work in the garden together to do twice as much if needed. The gift of the shovel advances the quality of his life—health, finances, food, security, hopefully friendship, and so on. While the giving of the shovel enriches my life.

Jesus lived these teachings of his. He resisted evil persons and evil ways in a nonviolent manner in an attempt to make the world a more peaceful, equitable, and just place to live. It is his higher righteousness—the ways of the kingdom of heaven— and he asks us to live this way too.

CHAPTER 20

Love Your Enemy and Be Perfect

You have heard that it was said, "You shall love your neighbor and hate your enemy." But I say to you, love your enemies, bless those who curse you, do good to those who hate you, and pray for those who spitefully use you and persecute you, that you may be sons of your Father in heaven; for He makes His sun rise on the evil and on the good, and sends rain on the just and on the unjust. For if you love those who love you, what reward have you? Do not even the tax collectors do the same? And if you greet your brethren only, what do you do more than others? Do not even the tax collectors do so? Therefore, you shall be perfect, just as your Father in heaven is perfect.

Matthew 5:43–48

Jesus begins his sixth example of misinterpreted law, or incomplete righteousness, with a statement that is a bit different from those of his earlier examples. The other examples began with statements that could be found in the Torah. This statement, however, is made up of two parts, the first being, *"You shall love your neighbor,"* which is also found in the Torah, and the second being, *"and hate your enemy,"* which is not found in the Torah.

In fact, it is not found anywhere in the Old or New Testaments. Search as you wish, and you will find a variety of disparaging statements and wishes concerning one's enemies, but you will not find a statement telling you to hate him. This false teaching of *"hate your enemy"* had been given an appearance of legitimacy by tacking it onto the tail end of a true command of God. It is an old trick, but it does not turn a false statement into a true one. So, for the first time, Jesus has cited a teaching of the Pharisees that was commonly known to the people but was not in the Bible.

It is not hard to comprehend that a statement instructing the people to *"hate your enemy"* existed in Jesus' day. Many of the Pharisees, especially those of the House of Shammai, strongly opposed Roman occupation. Foreigners were viewed as unclean, and anyone who collaborated with them—tax collectors, government leaders, or commoners—were considered traitors of the Jewish people and subject to being despised. The Jewish people were encouraged to cultivate hatred of their enemies throughout the many sectors of their society. It was not just the Pharisees who were at fault; a movement or party known as the Zealots were especially bent on the removal of the hated Roman occupiers, and they led many violent attacks against the Romans and the Jews who collaborated with them.

The full wording of the first part of Jesus' opening statement, when quoted from the Torah is, "You shall love your neighbor as yourself."[266] Even this statement from God was one that the rabbis and Pharisees found open for debate. They would ask among themselves, "Just who is one's neighbor?" The range of acceptable classifications was wide. Some of the schools of the sages taught that fellow students of the law were neighbors, so it was limited to scribes and Pharisees.

Some schools of the scribes and Pharisees taught that it was wider than that. They taught that the neighbor was every blood

---

[266] Leviticus 19:18

relative, every friend, or person living in their locality, i.e., in their community. Still other schools taught that it was much broader yet. They taught that every Jew was a neighbor, but Jews only! No person could be a neighbor if they were not a Jew. . . . Some schools were much more liberal. They taught that gentile proselytes who had joined the Jewish faith were neighbors as well. The most common teaching, however, was that only good Jews were considered neighbors. Publicans, harlots, or any public sinner—even if Jewish—was positively excluded.[267]

These classifications are understandable, but should never have been so exclusive. The Torah itself called Egyptian households neighbors, even on the night of Passover.[268] God also extended His care or healing powers to non-Jews in the Old Testament[269] and at times gave foreign kings prophetic insights.[270] God as creator sees all of mankind as His creation and His responsibility. Being just one part of that creation, the Jews could have extended the definition of neighbor to include all created humanity. Jesus, himself, later in his ministry would define a "neighbor" as anyone helping someone in need regardless of their cultural origin, religion, or status.[271] We will look at this definition in detail later in this chapter.

Jesus counters this opening statement of mixed truth and falsehood with his typical, *"But I say to you,"* teaching pattern, by telling his listeners frankly, *"love your enemies."* Notice Jesus did not say make friends with your enemies. Friendships are two-way relationships; you are a friend to

---

[267] https://www.bereanbiblechurch.org/transcripts/matthew/som/5_43-48.htm

[268] Exodus 3:22; 11:2

[269] For example: 1 Kings 17 and 2 Kings 5

[270] For example: Daniel, chapters 2 and 4

[271] Matthew 22:34-40; Mark 12:28-34; Luke 10:25-37

someone, and that other person sees you as a friend. Love, on the other hand, can be a one-way relationship. Of course, we all hope to get love in return from those we love, but that is not necessary for us to love someone. Jesus is asking us to "love our enemies" even if it remains a one-way relationship and there is no love in return.

Jesus' whole sermon up to this point, in the minds of his listeners, has centered on the obligation to love one's neighbor. Now, however, he teaches them to "love [their] enemies" as well as their neighbors. Essentially, anyone they meet is a candidate for love. But Jesus takes this social command a step further. While one's true neighbor is likely to be cordial and easy to love, enemies will pose additional challenges. Jesus' next statements serve as a good definition of who the enemy may be—and it does not have to be a foreigner. An enemy in Jesus' context is anyone who curses, hates, spitefully uses, or persecutes a person.

The recommendation for dealing with these challenging individuals follows the same nonviolent teaching of Jesus' fifth antithesis. But now, Jesus directs our actions to an even higher level of commitment: for curses, give blessings; for hatred, do good to them; and pray for the spiteful and the persecutors. Is Jesus joking? No, he is not! In fact, what he has to say is biblical. The Torah itself, teaches that if you were to find your enemy's ox or donkey wondering astray, you should get it and bring it back to your enemy.[272] In short, you should be concerned for your enemy's welfare and his ability to feed himself and his family. That is social justice that goes beyond one's biases and hatred. It is an intentional acceptance of the dignity of others and a purposeful action to not let one's inner animosities degrade oneself to a state of indifference.

---

[272] Exodus 23:4-5

King Solomon, in his proverbs, tells us neither to rejoice nor be glad when our enemy falls or stumbles,[273] and his sage advice to us regarding treatment of our enemies is an echo of Jesus' instructions:

> *If your enemy is hungry, give him bread to eat;*
> *and if he is thirsty, give him water to drink; for*
> *so you will heap coals of fire on his head, and the*
> *Lord will reward you.*[274]

King Solomon's motivation for doing good to our enemies is for the purpose of disarming their dislike of us. When we are willing to feed and give drink to someone who has wronged us, they are forced to recalculate why they are opposed to us. It may not change their attitude toward us completely, but it does start to erode their paradigm of who we are. We are playing with their minds, so to speak. But Solomon is not presenting it as a mind game; he sees the actions as ones that the Lord would approve of and for which we will be rewarded.

There is a "mind game" aspect, however, to both Jesus and Solomon's instructions. The *mind* being altered is ours. Think of it! What happens to our mind when we actively seek to *bless*, *do good* and *pray* for those who oppose us? For one, we begin to see our oppressors as individuals who may have the potential to be redeemable. We begin to hope that perhaps the bad we experience is temporary and reversible. It sets us on the path of de-escalation of potential violence, and directs us toward reconciliation. Our mind becomes the mind of a peacemaker. Prayer is essential because this level of love comes from God.

Jesus, too, reveals that doing good for enemies elevates us in the eyes of God. Those who treat enemies in a non-vengeful,

---

[273] Proverbs 24:17-18

[274] Proverbs 25:21-22

non-violent, *good* manner can be "*sons of your Father in heaven.*" Jesus presents this honorable status as something that is reached by doing *good* to our enemies. This echoes the reward mentioned in Jesus' beatitude for the peacemakers, who "*shall be called the sons of God.*"[275] This should come as no surprise because peacemakers, while trying to achieve peace, routinely must work with individuals that are hostile. People who love their enemies will make effective peacemakers.

Jesus' reasons for being good to enemies, however, focuses less on the rewards God will give to us, and more on the fact that doing so aligns our character with the character of God Himself. Our good treatment of those who are evil to us reflects God's good treatment of those who are evil to God. Our Father in heaven does not get treated very well by all His creation. He, too, has to contend with those who are *evil* as well as the *good*—the *just* as well as the *unjust*. How does He handle the situation? He causes His blessings of sunshine and rain to fall on both equally. The bare essentials of life are not withheld from either class. He remains a generous God.

Here lies an important point. We have two information-packed statements that relate to Jesus' call for us to love our enemies. The first is "*that you may be sons of your Father in heaven.*" Immediately following this statement is the English word "for," which is translated from the Greek word *hoti*.[276] *Hoti* is a conjunction that joins two thoughts, and it merely means *because* or *why*. When this Greek word is used in New Testament manuscripts, it signals us that the "*because*" or "*why*" of the first statement is about to follow in the second. So why is it that by loving our enemies we "*may be sons of our Father in heaven?*" The answer is **because** "He" [our Father in heaven] makes His sun rise on the evil and the good,

---

[275] Matthew 5:9
[276] Strong's Word NT:3754

and sends rain on the just and the unjust. In short, the God of heaven is generous and does not withhold His life-giving sunshine and rain to anyone, not even to those who oppose Him. If we do the same, we are acting in character with the God of heaven and are viewed as His children.

Following this statement about God's generous nature, Jesus gives us two examples to demonstrate that being generous like God is indeed a much higher calling than what is expected from the normal person. Jesus points out that everyone loves those who love them in return. Even tax collectors [sinners in the listener's eyes] will do this. If we do the same, why should there be any reward? Jesus repeats this same argument with a second example. If we only greet those who are our friends, we have done nothing different than sinners greeting their circle of friends. Jesus' two examples reveal that being *"sons of our Father in heaven"* will require greater interaction with people outside our comfort zone.

Jesus ends this antithesis with a statement that is now well-known and often agonized over, *"Therefore you shall be perfect, even as your Father in heaven is perfect."*[277] I say "agonized over," because many Christian theologians argue that Jesus is intentionally setting the bar of righteousness so high, it would be impossible for any human to attain it. "Who can possibly be *perfect* like God the Father?" they ask. So, these theologians argue that we are therefore forced to rely solely on the righteousness of Christ for our salvation and ignore Christ's plain statement that we are *"therefore"* to be perfect as our Father in heaven is. In their minds, Christ is asking us to do something we cannot do.

Personally, I would have to ask them, "Why do you think this? Why would Jesus ask or command us to do something that is not

---

[277] Matthew 5:48

possible? Is that honest of him? Is Jesus doing this to make a sar-castic point or to frustrate us? Is it supposed to be a facetious joke? Or could it be that maybe what Jesus asks is actually possible?"

I feel that such theologians are missing Jesus' point. The Greek word used to get our English word for "perfect" is *teleios*.[278] It means *complete*, such as *labor completed, growth completed*, with the thought of being *mature*, or having complete *mental or moral character*. Jesus is saying we need to be mature in our thinking toward others. We need to grow up and conduct our relationships in a godly fashion.

Besides these specific Greek definitions, Jesus has—within this passage itself—defined what he means by the Father's "perfect-ness." It is easier for us to understand if we temporarily overlook Jesus' explanation of who our enemies are, and the two examples that immediately follow his statement about God's generosity. These examples, given so we better understand how we limit our generosity to those we know or like, temporarily deviate us from his explanation of God's character. So, let us accept our shortcom-ings for the time being and reword Jesus' statement to focus only on what he has to say about his Father's character. If we do so, we get the following:

> *But I say to you, love your enemies. . . . that you may be sons of your Father in heaven; for He makes His sun rise on the evil and on the good, and sends rain on the just and on the unjust. . . . There-fore, you shall be perfect, just as your Father in heaven is perfect.*

Does this help? Does it not show us that Jesus is merely saying that when we love our enemies and do good to them, we are being generous like his Father? Jesus is stating, by his

---

[278] Strong's Word NT:5046

conclusion, that unbiased generosity is a *perfect* act of God and we should do likewise. All the other information in the passage, which we removed above, is telling us who our enemies are, and that if we do not exercise godly generosity, we are no better than anyone else. This higher righteousness is not far beyond our reach. We are not being asked to be God; we are being asked to be generous like God. It is a choice we can make and follow if we want to accept Jesus as the king of this heavenly kingdom.

The book of Luke also records this portion of the Sermon on the Mount, and in Luke's version of the sermon, Jesus says:

> *But love your enemies, do good, and lend, hoping for nothing in return; and your reward will be great, and you will be sons of the Most High. For He is kind to the unthankful and evil.* **Therefore, be merciful, just as your Father also is merciful.** (emphasis added)[279]

When comparing the two versions of the sermon, we see that Luke equates Matthew's concept of "perfect" with God's "mercy." In Luke's wording, we can easily see the social justice and equity themes of the sermon—doing good, creating equity, being merciful, and not limiting our actions to only those who like us. These themes are in Matthew's version as well, but are a bit harder to recognize at face value.

Within Matthew's version of the Sermon on the Mount, Jesus had earlier made a command that his listeners should respect their enemies. Recall that before Jesus made his statement to *love your enemies,* he had told his listeners that "*whoever compels you to go one mile, go with him two.*"[280] This

---

[279] Luke 6:35-36
[280] Matthew 5:43

was a reference to Roman soldiers—enemies—asking Jews to carry their gear for them, which was a right the soldiers had and one the Jews despised. Jesus, however, taught that these enemies should be treated better than they requested. Then several sentences later, as Jesus builds the logic of his sixth antithesis, he refers to God giving rain to the "unjust." The Greek word[281] translated "unjust" here implies the *wicked* and specifically the *heathen*. Clearly, God allows rain to fall on all nations of the earth, so Jesus' argument can easily be used to show God's mercy being extended to everyone—even those the Jews considered to be enemies.

Jesus has now completed his six antitheses, which have shown the people how the scribes and Pharisees have held and taught a narrow view of the law. Jesus' introductory choice of words created a picture that these teachings have been a "loosen-up" form of the law. They have been a minimum standard of righteousness, which Jesus claims is insufficient for entering into the kingdom of heaven. This "loose" righteousness of the scribes and Pharisees must be exceeded if one wants to be part of the kingdom. Jesus' six areas of "corrected" or "fulfilled" interpretations of the law present higher standards that should be met in order to enter the kingdom of heaven. These higher standards fulfill the aspirations of the law. They focus one's mind, not on what God is trying to prevent in society, but on what He is trying to achieve in a heavenly kingdom on earth.

Before I move on to the next chapter, let me point out to you that Jesus frequently focused on the need for his Jewish listeners to be more loving and concerned for the welfare of non-Jews. This was a truly radical position to take in Jesus' day. While it is true that Jesus himself stated that his ministry

---

[281] Strong's Word NT:94 "*adikos*"

was confined to the lost sheep of the house of Israel,[282] it is also true that he often extended his mercy beyond that stated mandate. Healing was given to non-Jews who approached him in faith.[283] When Jesus first peached in his hometown, he cited two stories of non-Jews in the Old Testament as examples of God's mercy being extended to others outside the house of Israel—in preference over God's own people.[284] Jesus rarely hesitated to speak with foreigners or anyone the Jews might consider to be sinners or enemies. By his actions and teachings, Jesus demonstrated that anyone can be a neighbor, which we should love as ourselves. This is perhaps best seen in Jesus' parable of the good Samaritan—a fitting parable for today's divided society.

A. The Parable of the Good Samaritan

Jesus' parable of the Good Samaritan answers the question, "Who is my neighbor?" This is a profoundly important question, because both the law and Jesus state that we are to love our neighbor, and that this love is a factor in inheriting eternal life. The answer to this question is important.

The story begins when a Jewish lawyer, seeking to test Jesus, asks him, *"Teacher, what shall I do to inherit eternal life?"*[285] Jesus does not answer the question directly. Instead, he asks the lawyer what the law says and what his interpretation of it is. To this, the lawyer correctly repeats the law and statements that Jesus himself has made

---

[282] Matthew 15:24

[283] Matthew 8:5-13, 15:21-28

[284] Luke 4:25-27

[285] Luke 10:25

in the past—*love God completely and love your neighbor as yourself.*[286] Both of these points are well known by any self-respecting Jewish lawyer, and to answer one's own question is not much of a test.

So, what is the test that this lawyer genuinely wants to administer to Jesus? Of course, what he wants to know is Jesus' position on who is our neighbor, so his first question was just a way to engage Jesus and set him up for his second question. The lawyer is scheming that Jesus' answer to that question will cubby-hole Jesus into siding with a particular opinion of one of the many Jewish schools of thought. Forcing Jesus to give a public opinion on this matter will create opportunities to alienate him from various groups and undermine his public support. Notice, the lawyer cunningly parrots the law to Jesus but refrains from giving his own interpretation of it as Jesus had asked him to do. His reply to Jesus is only as follows:

> *You shall love the Lord your God with all your heart, with all your soul, with all your strength, and with all your mind,' and 'your neighbor as yourself.'*[287]

Jesus tells the lawyer he has answered correctly and that he should, "Do this and you will live."[288] The lawyer then asks his test question, "And who is my neighbor?"[289]

Jesus answers this question by telling the lawyer a parable about a Jewish man on his way to the city of Jericho. This man is met by thieves, robbed, stripped, beaten, severely injured and left for dead. While lying naked on the road, a Jewish

---

[286] Luke 10:27 See also Mark 12:28-34
[287] Luke 10:27
[288] Luke 10:28
[289] Luke 10:29

priest sees him but passes by without giving any aid. Likewise, a Levite soon follows and sees the man. He, too, passes by without giving aid. Then a third man comes upon the scene. He is a Samaritan, and unlike the other two Jews, he takes pity on the wounded traveler and binds his wounds, treats them with his own oil and wine, and transports the man to an inn, where he further cares for him during the evening. The next day the Samaritan leaves, but not until he has instructed the innkeeper to continue caring for the man, and pledges to cover all the cost he might incur.[290]

The irony of this story is that most Jews would not expect to get this level of attention from a Samaritan. Samaritans and Jews did not see eye to eye. Jews, especially, looked down on Samaritans. The reason for this is recorded in the Old Testament and in Jewish traditions. Let me explain, as this history can be seen as paralleling events within our own society.

The Samaritans were a substantial group of people that lived in the land during Jesus' time. Their origin traces back to the fall of the ten tribes of Israel at the hand of the Assyrian nation under the rule of King Sargon II in the eight century BCE. Most of the children of Israel were taken captive, leaving only a remnant to work the land. However, as was the Assyrian practice, King Sargon II repopulated the land with people from other conquered territories. They were brought to the Israelite cities of the region of Samaria to work the land, produce incomes, and pay tributes to the king in order to increase his wealth.

Sargon's repopulation plan had problems from the start. The Bible records that the relocated people were met with a plague of lions that terrorized the land. This problem was attributed to a belief that the newly relocated people were not

---

[290] Luke 10:30-35

familiar with the rituals of the local "god" and that he was offended by their lack of respect for him. To remedy the situation, King Sargon sent back to the land one of the Israelite priests to instruct the people on how to worship the Israelite God.[291]

During the following centuries, these relocated people intermarried with the remaining Israelites and adopted a hybridized form of Judaism based on their understanding of the Torah. By the time of Jesus, Jews viewed Samaritans as half-breeds that followed a corrupted version of the Jewish religion, while the Samaritans felt that their worship of God was purer than that of the Jews. The two groups were divided on points of race, religion, culture and even where the God of Israel should be worshiped. The Samaritans were, however, a minority, and were generally at the mercy of the more powerful Jewish majority. The Jews recognized the Samaritans as residents in their region but not as neighbors. To many Jews, Samaritans were worse than foreign gentiles. A parable of a good Samaritan saving the life of a wounded Jewish man would be a story that did not resonate well with a Jewish audience, let alone a Jewish lawyer.

Jesus ends his parable by asking the lawyer a question, *"So which of these three do you think was neighbor to him who fell among the thieves?"*[292] This is actually a brilliant question on Jesus' part, because it does not directly answer the lawyer's original question of "Who is my neighbor?" Instead, Jesus is asking him, "Who was the neighbor?" Jesus is tactfully demonstrating that a neighbor is not just a relationship that you have toward another person. It is also a relationship that another person has toward you. Neighborliness is a two-way street. You cannot be a neighbor by yourself. The lawyer is forced to concede that the relationship of neighbors took place

---

[291] 2 Kings 17:27-28
[292] Luke 10:36

between the Samaritan and the Jew, not between the Jew and his own people. He answers Jesus' question with the reply, *"He who showed mercy on him."*[293]

In conclusion, Jesus states succinctly to the lawyer, *"Go and do likewise."* Four words packed with so much meaning, the lawyer has nothing more to say. The implications of this dialogue are obvious to the lawyer. If you want to inherit eternal life, you need to see the Samaritans as your neighbors. You need to take action to care for them when they are in need. You need to bind their wounds and contribute your resources—oil and wine. You need to find a safe place for them and pledge your wealth to see that their recovery is complete. Jesus has essentially told the lawyer to go and return the favor.

While Jesus structured his story to illustrate a neighborly relationship between two unlikely companions, it should not be concluded that Jesus was only commanding the lawyer to be neighborly to Samaritans. The broader application is that we should see a neighbor whenever we look at anyone in need of help, and see a neighbor in anyone willing to help us. Broader still is the goal of seeing anyone different from ourselves as a neighbor. And ultimately, we are to love those neighbors as ourselves—history, race, religion, culture, or politics are not to be factors of consideration.

I mentioned earlier that I see parallels in this story with our modern-day societies. The history of African Americans has many similarities to that of the Samaritans. African Americans suffered conquest in Africa and were relocated to a new region to work the land and build-up the wealth of those who controlled the land. In the new world, Central and North American and the Caribbean, Africans have slowly integrated genetically, culturally, and in terms of religion.

---

[293] Luke 10:37

Like the Samaritans, African Americans have taken on a new identity that is different from their past but is not fully integrated with those of the majority of its present homeland. African Americans now have a hybridized existence that places them at odds with their ancestral motherlands and their current homeland. Jesus' instruction to this situation would be the same as that which he illustrated in his *Good Samaritan* parable; each party needs to see the other as his neighbor and love them accordingly.

This same scenario has repeated itself throughout history and throughout the world as one culture, either by force or integration, begins to dominate another group, or begins to divide itself based on any number of social markers. The result is the same; the parties separate and begin to see each other as enemies. Jesus' parable of the good Samaritan teaches us that this is a wrong attitude and that we need to view others as neighbors and be willing to be neighbors ourselves. Our eternal lives may depend upon it. After all, the parable was given within the context of what one needs to do to inherit eternal life.

B. A New Commandment

Jesus' command to "*love your enemies*" as recorded in Matthew 5:44, was indeed new to his listeners and quite surprising. But this would not be the last time Jesus would give such a command to his disciples. In Jesus' "great commission," shortly before his ascension to heaven, he made it clear to his disciples that his teachings were to be extended to non-Jews who were to be invited to become his disciples.[294] But even before this, the book of John records Jesus' last conversation with his disciples shortly before his crucifixion. During that conversa-

---

[294] Matthew 28:18–20; Mark 16:15; Luke 24:36–49; Acts 1:8; Acts 10:1—11:18

tion Jesus states a "new commandment" for them to keep. It goes as follows:

> A **new commandment** I give to you, that you love one another; as I have loved you, that you also love one another. By this all will know that you are My disciples, if you have love for one another. (emphasis added)[295]

I have often wondered how this command is "new"? Is it new because of *who we are to love*, or new because of *how we are to love*? I have come to conclude that the answer is both, and the support for the two comes from an out-of-this-world perspective. Let me focus on the "who" first.

Jesus' command to love "one another" was not new to the disciples. The Torah had long ago instructed them to love their neighbor as themselves, and Jesus had spent much of his ministry instructing his disciples to do just that. Loving one another is the emphasis of Jesus' social justice and equity themes throughout his ministry. Our love and kindness are not to be confined to a small circle of reciprocating loved ones. So, what is "new"? The answer might be found in the Greek word used to give us the English words "*one another.*"

The words "*one another*" are translated from the Greek word, *allelon*.[296] This word is the plural form of a word meaning *else* or, in context, someone who is *different*.[297] It can be argued that Jesus is commanding his disciples to love "*the others.*" Those who are outside your circle. The *else* that is not part of your community. Those who are *different* from you. By implication non-Jews, foreigners, and those who might be considered enemies. Asking for love to be extended to these "others" would be consistent with

---

[295] John 13:34–35

[296] Strong's Word NT:240

[297] Strong's Word NT:243

what Jesus has been teaching all along. He has taught that this is part of the perfect character of the Father and has stated that we should be perfect just as the Father is perfect. If Jesus is giving this new commandment with the implication that love is to be extended to everyone, Jew and non-Jew, then his command is a new one for the disciples. He is codifying his teaching into a law that is on par with Mosaic commands. Such love, when exhibited, is to be a visible indication and characteristic of one's discipleship to Christ.

This concept that Jesus' new command is for us to love those who are different from those within our typical and comfortable circle of neighbors, is supported by Jesus' statement telling us *how we are to love* this group of people. The key to understanding *how* is found in the context of the command to love the *others*. When these words were given, Jesus and his disciples had just finished the last supper and were on their way to the Garden of Gethsemane. Jesus knew his mission of earth was almost complete and he would soon be returning to his Father in heaven. Let us look at what Jesus says prior to, and after, this new command. He states the following:

> *Little children, I shall be with you a little while longer. You will seek Me; and as I said to the Jews,* ***"Where I am going, you cannot come,"*** *so now I say to you. A new commandment I give to you, that you love one another; as I have loved you, that you also love one another. By this all will know that you are My disciples, if you have love for one another.*[298] *…In My Father's house are many mansions; if it were not so, I would have told you.* ***I go to prepare a place for you***…*that where I am, there you may be also.* (emphasis added)[299]

---

[298] John 13:33—35
[299] John 14:2—3

Notice that the *new commandment* is sandwiched between two references concerning Jesus' heavenly origins. It is in the context of Jesus reminding his disciples he has come from heaven and is returning to heaven, that he tells his disciples to love others "as I have loved you." Is it a far stretch of the imagination to conclude that as Jesus ponders his origins and destiny, he sees himself as someone who has successfully loved the others? Think of it! Jesus left the serenity and security of a stable heavenly society to live in a foreign, turbulent culture. And yet, he did so willingly, even knowing it meant he would die, for the purpose of revealing God's love to fallen man and to direct them to higher standards of life. And he demonstrated that he loved the people he came to serve. So much so, he wants them to be with him always.

This is what Jesus meant when he said, "a new commandment I give to you, that you love one another [the others], as I have loved you." He is commanding that his tribal-minded disciples move beyond their love for only their community of Jews, and instead accept the whole of humanity as neighbors to be loved. Christ followers must now see themselves as servants to the world, as Jesus saw himself—even if it means the possible loss of one's life while serving "the others." [300]

This brings us back to the theme of this chapter and Jesus' command to "love your enemies." Jesus' declaration in Matthew 5:44 to "love your enemies" was a truly foreign concept to Jesus' Jewish listeners, but it was one Jesus was already living. The command to love one's enemies—or one's perceived enemies—is truly a divine, or out-of-this-world, concept. Love

---

[300] John 15:12–17 Here, Jesus once again commands his disciples to "love one another." The same Greek wording is used as that found in John 13:34. However, in the context of this command to love the "else" or "others," Jesus is making it clear that his love for others [his disciples] requires the loss of his life. The implication is that the disciples' love of others may require the same level of devotion.

for others was being modeled by the divine being, Jesus, and we are to follow that model and love others as he loved us.

Before we move on to the next chapter, remember I mentioned earlier that Jesus' six antitheses, which we have now covered, were a detour from the direction the Sermon on the Mount was moving in until that point. Jesus recognized that listeners in the crowd were reacting questioningly to his statement that "good works" to those in need glorify the Father in heaven. To defend this statement, he detoured to point out the shortcomings of the scribes and Pharisees' teachings of the law, and their related righteousness deficiencies. But now the detour is complete, Jesus begins to pick up where he left off. The ending of the sixth antithesis gives the command to return to a superior "righteousness." It is a righteousness that exceeds that of the Pharisees—*"be perfect just as your heavenly Father is perfect"* by being willing to do good to the evil and the unjust. Next, Jesus begins a new topic, which is once again about "good works"—how to do your *righteousness* and how to give your *charitable gifts*. Jesus has come full circle; the sermon is now back on its original justice and equity track.

PART IV

The Sermon on the Mount
Justice, Mercy, and Faith

CHAPTER 21

Charitable Deeds vs. Rewards

Take heed that you do not do your charitable deeds before men, to be seen by them. Otherwise you have no reward from your Father in heaven. Therefore, when you do a charitable deed, do not sound a trumpet before you as the hypocrites do in the synagogues and in the streets, that they may have glory from men. Assuredly, I say to you, they have their reward. But when you do a charitable deed, do not let your left hand know what your right hand is doing, that your charitable deed may be in secret; and your Father who sees in secret will Himself reward you openly.

Matthew 6:1–4

Jesus has now completed his six antitheses, where he has given examples of misinterpretations or loosening of the law, followed by what he says the law is teaching. In nearly every case, the scribes and the Pharisees have not been wrong in quoting the law and teaching people what they should not do. However, in every case, Jesus has done the opposite and focused not on what the law *prohibits*, but on what the law is trying to *achieve*. The people have been taught that they should not kill, but Jesus has seen a fuller application of the law and instructed them to have honorable and respectful relationships with each other. The people have been taught not to commit adultery, but Jesus has seen a fuller application of the law and instructed the people to respect society's marriages and family unions as sacred and untouchable.

Although, from this point onward, Jesus no longer gives examples of incomplete teachings from the scribes and Pharisees, he does continue to teach the disciples and listening crowds about misconceptions of conduct in one's spiritual life. As we have seen in the beatitudes, Jesus has revealed that being a part of the kingdom of heaven requires social action on the part of its citizens. Members of the kingdom of heaven are to be sensitive to the suffering and needs of others. They are to be mindful of the poor, the oppressed and the disadvantaged. Weaker individuals within society are to be protected from injustice and extended mercy. Righteousness—justice and equity—is something we should all long for, even as we long for food to survive. From this point onward, in Jesus' Sermon on the Mount, this theme does not change. He will begin to refocus our attention to our service to others and do so with increasing detail. However, as Jesus progresses in this sermon, he will also begin to weave into it a theme of "faith"—faith to be equitable and to be just; to not be fearful in paying the personal cost of helping others.

Jesus now returns to his social justice and equity themes with a new series of three teachings that address areas of incorrect spiritual behavior in his society. These are the areas of how one does charitable deeds, how one prays, and how one fasts. In each of these three areas, Jesus will specifically instruct his disciples and the listening crowd to do these things in "secret" rather than openly and for attention. And this is our clue to what Jesus saw as the problem of his day.

It is especially interesting that Jesus picks these three topics—charity, prayer and fasting—to address next. Interesting, but not surprising. You will need a little bit of background to see what Jesus is doing here. So, let us take a closer look.

In the Jewish religion, as well as Christianity and most other religions, there is a perception that one will be under condemnation from their god(s) if they fail to do what their god(s) requires of them. In short, there is a consequence for disobedience or even neglect of one's duties. Most religions do not view the consequence as an injustice on the part of their deity; rather, it is an act of justice that must be carried out to maintain a just society. Of course, no one wants to suffer the consequence of their sins or shortcomings and most religions have provisions for asking for forgiveness and averting penalties that one's deity might perform. In the case of Judaism, there are three human acts capable of averting a negative divine decree: charity to others, prayer, and repentance.

Nowhere is this seen perhaps more clearly than in the Jewish traditions of Rosh Hashanah and Yom Kippur. Rosh Hashanah is the biblical equivalent of the Feast of Trumpets, and Yom Kippur is the equivalent of the holiest day of the year, the Day of Atonement. The two holy Sabbaths are separated by ten days, which have become known as the "Days of Awe." The Day of Atonement is seen as a day when God judges the people of Israel, both individually and corporately. Tradition teaches that one's fate for the coming year will be set by God's judgment on that day. And God is judging each person based on their conduct during the past year. The ten Days of Awe are a time to right one's wrongs of the past year, seek people's forgiveness, be charitable, offer special prayers, and repent. The Day of Atonement is also a day of fasting—a physical representation of one's cessation of wrongdoing—or repentance.

While charity, prayer and fasting (repentance) may be essential during the Days of Awe, any of these three can be pursued at any time of the year, to foster goodwill between oneself and God. So, Jesus' choosing to address the three areas of charity, prayer and fasting is intentionally focusing on what the Jewish people would do to improve their standing in the eyes of God. And Jesus does not make any indication that doing this is wrong. After all, in each of his three teachings he will conclude that one will be openly rewarded by the Father in heaven for the correct application of these three actions. However, Jesus does point out that each of these actions can be done incorrectly, and that the results one wishes to obtain—favor in God's eyes—will be lost. At the heart of the matter, is one's attitude or motivation in doing these actions in the first place—do you want a reward from man, or from God? We will look at each of these—charity, prayer, and fasting—one chapter at a time.

Jesus starts this section of his sermon with a caution to his listeners. Matthew 6:1 begins with the words "Take heed." This is the Greek word *Prosecho*,[301] which is a warning to someone, meaning *keep this in mind*, *pay attention*, or *beware*! What Jesus has to say following this is important, and he wants his listeners to wake up and get it right. His focus that follows is on one's performance of "charitable deeds."

Now, I need to make an interesting clarification here. In our Matthew passage for this chapter, the New King James Version of the Bible uses the words *"charitable deed(s)"* on four occasions. From an English perspective, we would assume that the same Greek word was used all four times. However, the Greek text uses two different words in this passage, not one. The first Greek word for *"charitable* deed(s)" appears in verse 1 and is the word *dikaiosune*,[302]

---

[301] Strong's Word NT:4337
[302] Strong's Word NT:1343

and it means *equity of act or character*. The next three times we see the words "*charitable deed*(s)," it is a translation from the Greek word *eleemosune*,[303] which means *compassion* toward the poor, *beneficence*. Interestingly, the *Complete Jewish Bible* substitutes one word in all four references, and that word is the Hebrew word *tzedakah*.[304] *Tzedakah* has broader meanings and includes *rightness* of behavior and is associated with *justice*. It has come to mean the giving of charitable contributions to others in need—not as a spontaneous gesture of goodwill, but as a systematic obligation to benefit others; a requirement to do good.

It is not hard to see here that Jesus is speaking about our actions to help people in need, not just with money or materials, but with moral support and social clout as well. He is clearly returning to the equity and social justice themes imbedded in the beatitudes. And Jesus is encouraging his listeners to practice *tzedakah*, but not to do it openly.

From Jesus' statements we get a clear picture of what he does not want the members of the kingdom of heaven to do. They are not to make a show of their giving of charitable gifts or deeds. No sounding of trumpets, no fanfare, and no public gatherings of approving onlookers is to be allowed. That is, if one genuinely wants to be in right standing with God. Apparently, however, we do have a choice; we can be open about our charity and get our reward from men here on earth, or we can be secret about our charity and let God reward us as He chooses. Jesus' advice is that we do our works in secret and let God give the appropriate reward.

Jesus calls those who wish to be public about their charity, "*hypocrites.*"[305] This is a word that means being an *actor* under an assumed character, like on a stage. It is a good choice of wording. Think of it. Recall that in Jewish thought, giving

---

[303] Strong's Word NT:1654

[304] Strong's Word OT:6666

[305] Strong's Word NT:5273

charity is believed to be one way to improve one's standing with God. It is a way to get a reward, especially if that reward is some much-needed forgiveness or an escape from a negative consequence. Jesus has stated that doing charity secretly is something God will reward, while public giving does not get a reward from God. So here we are with someone being an "actor." They are publicly assuming the role of an individual rewarded by God, when behind the acting mask is an individual who is not rewarded by God—they were only acting the part. And like an actor, the only praise they will get is the applause from people watching the play.

Jesus' instruction differentiates one's true attitude for giving. The actor gives to get the praise of men, and is therefore insincere about his standing before God. He appears to be concerned about how God sees him, but in reality, he is more concerned about how his community views him. And God will leave it to his community to be the one to reward him or not. On the other hand, there are those who genuinely want to have a right relationship with God and that relationship is a personal one between them and God. There is no desire to put public applause into that relationship. These individuals are sincere, and I would doubt that they are even motivated by the possible reward that the Father may give them—the relationship is enough of a reward for them.

Jesus' opening caution, of *"Take heed,"* at the beginning of this passage, ties directly to the fact that doing one's righteousness publicly has no reward from the Father in heaven. The caution therefore implies that the reward from the Father is of far greater value than the reward of glory from men. This passage is both an appeal to do things for the right spiritual reasons—glorifying God, not oneself—and a call to seek the far better reward that the Father will give. Many of those rewards have already been mentioned in the beatitudes.

Perhaps you have already noticed that these verses have a lot in common with Jesus' earlier statement about doing good works. Recall Jesus said:

> *Let your light so shine before men, that they may see your good works and glorify your Father in heaven.*[306]

Jesus has returned to this theme of doing good, and here he has made it plain that the purpose of doing good is to "glorify the Father." He has now clarified the fact that doing good for the purpose of public adoration (glory from men) is not going to be acceptable to the Father. There appears to be a contradiction here; in one case Jesus asks us to be public, and in the second case he asks us to be secret. Which is correct? How can one do both?

I will have to confess that I found these statements contradictory to start with. It was not until I realized that Jesus is speaking about two different types of *good* that I began to see the sense of what he is saying. In the pursuit of doing right and helping those in need, there are times when one's actions are needed immediately, and cannot be hidden from the public. For example, someone is lost and is clearly distressed and needs directions, or someone is being bullied and needs to be rescued. These are times to spring into action and be the salt and light that God wants of us. The problem is in the public domain already, and corrective action will be open for all to see. These are public "good works" and cannot be done in secret. We are to act, but we are to deflect any praise we might get, to the fact that we are members of the kingdom of heaven, doing what our king asks of us, and the praise goes to our Father in heaven.

---

[306] Matthew 5:16

When I lived and worked in East Africa, I discovered that the locals have a saying they will often recite when someone thanks you for helping them. It translates roughly to, "No need to thank me for doing what God expects of me." The West, unfortunately, lacks such a convenient statement and the cultural understanding that the good we do for others is for God's glory.

On the other hand, there is also much good needed, that can be done without the public knowing we are involved. For example, a food bank needs money to buy more food to help its clients, or someone is behind in paying their electric bill. We can intervene in these cases and never make a public show of our involvement. These are acts of charity or alms giving, and they are to be kept secret in order to avoid the praise of men, and to prevent us from being too proud of ourselves for doing so.

I love Jesus' clarifying statement of *"do not let your left hand know what your right hand is doing."* I have had to think hard on what he might have meant with this. I now think of this in terms of having a *right-hand man,* someone I seek for advice and help in time of need. This would be opposed to all those on my left, who though they might be friends and family, are not my *go to people* of first resort. I have often planned to do something charitable for a targeted individual but found that I do not have the knowledge or full resources to accomplish the task. As a result, I have sought the help of others to get the plan executed. This is when I turn to my right-hand men to give me help, and together, we get done what I could not do alone. This is an acceptable charitable practice, as long as my right-hand men and I don't let the left-hand people in on the secret. I feel that this is what Jesus is telling us.

In closing, I would like to comment that there are times when charity or alms giving may not be able to be done in secret. That fact alone should not deter us from being charitable, if we have the means and willingness to do so. Jesus did say to be secret about charity in order to receive a reward from the Father, but he did not say we are prevented from any public charity altogether. The situation of a particular need may call for a public response. In such a case, we can respond, and we are still free to direct praise to the Father. When necessary, give publicly and give glory to God. The fact that God has given you the ability to respond to someone's need is reward enough.

CHAPTER 22

Prayer:

Justice, Mercy, and Faith

And when you pray, you shall not be like the hypocrites. For they love to pray standing in the synagogues and on the corners of the streets, that they may be seen by men. Assuredly, I say to you, they have their reward. But you, when you pray, go into your room, and when you have shut your door, pray to your Father who is in the secret place; and your Father who sees in secret will reward you openly. And when you pray, do not use vain repetitions as the heathen do. For they think that they will be heard for their many words. Therefore, do not be like them. For your Father knows the things you have need of before you ask Him.

Matthew 6:5–8

From the topic of charity, Jesus moves to the next action, which the Jewish people believe can influence God and cause Him to look favorably on them, and possibly reverse a negative decree He might have against them. That topic is the one of prayer. Prayer, communication to one's God, has always been important in every religion known to man. This communication to God has taken many forms and is often accompanied with incense, music, sacrifices, and songs or meditation. As a result of these additional things needed to speak to God, the places of prayer have become equally important and have resulted in the building of gardens, grottoes, shrines, mosques, temples, and churches. Some of these places of prayer are the grandest buildings on earth.

There are many precedents concerning God responding to prayer in the Bible so the concept of praying to God for any need is not wrong by any means. Nor was it wrong for the Jewish people to believe that their prayers might change God's willingness to respond favorably to the one praying. Christians often quote 2 Chronicles 7:13–15, which states the following:

> *When I shut up heaven and there is no rain, or command the locusts to devour the land, or send pestilence among my people,* **if my people who are called by my name will humble themselves, and pray and seek my face, and turn from their wicked ways, then I will hear from heaven, and will forgive their sin and heal their land.** *Now my eyes will be open and my ears attentive to prayer made in this place.* (emphasis added)[307]

This is God's statement to King Solomon after the dedication of the first Jewish temple in Jerusalem—a house of prayer. God is plainly saying that prayer with the right attitude and correct motive will be heard, and He will respond in good favor—even stopping plagues He may have sent in judgment upon the land.

Once again, Jesus does not argue the fact that prayer, like charity, is of no value to one's standing with God. As with charity, genuine and sincere prayers will also be acceptable to God, and the Father is willing to reward those who pray in good faith.

---

[307] 2 Chronicles 7:13–16

Once again, the personal attitude and motivation of the person doing the praying is what is questioned. If someone wishes to make an appeal to God the Father for anything, it should be a matter between him and God. It is not an opportunity to be a pious actor on a stage, seeking the applause of men.

Yes, Jesus has once again used the word picture of an actor (hypocrite) as a way in which one should not pray. Standing in the synagogue or on a street corner to be seen, and maybe heard, by men may be just an act of piety rather than sincerity. Jesus again reveals that such actions, if one wants to pray that way, are good only for the rewards of men. God, Himself, is not interested in listening.

Jesus instructs his listeners that the proper way to approach God in prayer is to do it in secret, as with the case of being charitable. One should go to their room to pray before God without the public viewing their communication to God. Such prayer will be more sincere and honest with God, and Jesus states that the one offering the prayer will be rewarded "*openly*" by the Father.[308]

This type of prayer also has a much greater advantage to the one doing the praying. Prayer is as much about being heard by God as it is about hearing from God. We pray to God to praise Him and to receive answers to our petitions. Being an actor in a synagogue, or on a street corner, does not afford a good opportunity to listen to God's voice. Being silent in one's room behind closed doors is a much better place to hear what God wants to tell you. The Bible plainly teaches us that God has a powerful voice,[309] but He speaks to us in a more subdued manner[310] and even with a still small

---

[308] Many early manuscripts of the Gospels omit the word "openly" as a reward for charity, prayer, and fasting. They just say that you will be rewarded by the Father.

[309] Psalm 29

[310] John 10:27

voice.[311] It is our responsibility as faithful Christians to listen for that voice.

Jesus also advises his listeners to not be like the heathens (we can also add Christians now) who pray with vain repetitions. The Greek word used here is *battologeo,*[312] and it means to *continue tediously on a subject*, or to be *repetitious.* Jesus teaches that this is not necessary since God already knows what we need before we even start praying.[313] In fact, God knows what we need, even when we ourselves do not know what we need, and should be asking for.

To help us better understand the structure and process of prayer, Jesus gives us an example of prayer that is very brief and has limited scope, but it is remarkably profound and deep. His model prayer, believe it or not, summarizes the law and at the same time summarizes his Sermon on the Mount. I will show you how, but first the model prayer is as follows: Jesus said, "In this manner, therefore, pray:

> *'Our Father in heaven, hallowed be your name. Your kingdom come. Your will be done. On earth as it is in heaven. Give us this day our daily bread. And forgive us our debts, as we forgive our debtors. And do not lead us into temptation, but deliver us from the evil one. For yours is the kingdom and the power and the glory forever. Amen.'"*

Matthew 6:9–13

A lot has been written about the meaning of this prayer, and you can Google and research it for yourself at any time. I

---

[311] 1 Kings 19:12

[312] Strong's Word NT:945

[313] Matthew 6:8

would like, however, to show you an interesting interpretation I discovered, and let you evaluate it for what it is worth. It is an insight you may not find on Google or hear from the pulpits.

One day, while studying the Gospels, I was reading the passages of Matthew 23 where Jesus laments the shortcomings of the Pharisees. In one passage, he criticizes them for giving too much attention to small legal details, thereby missing the "weightier matters" of God's law. The passage reads as follows:

> *Woe to you, scribes and Pharisees, hypocrites!*
> *For you pay tithe of mint and anise and cummin,*
> *[but] have neglected the weightier matters of the*
> *law: **justice** and **mercy** and **faith**. These you ought*
> *to have done, without leaving the others undone."*
> (emphasis added)[314]

In wondering what Jesus meant by summarizing the important parts of the law being justice, mercy, and faith, I recalled a similar Old Testament saying from the Prophet Micah. It reads as follows:

> *He has shown you, O man, what is good; And*
> *what does the Lord require of you, but to **do just-***
> ***ly**, to **love mercy**, and to **walk humbly with your***
> ***God**?* (emphasis added)[315]

Jesus in his rebuke to the scribes and Pharisees has reworded this simple theme and reduced one's *humble walk with God* to an act of "faith"—faith in seeing God's law as something beneficial to follow.[316]

---

[314] Matthew 23:23

[315] Micah 6:8. Also see Zechariah 7:9 and 8:16

[316] Psalm 119: 35, and 45. Also see Psalm 119:1–7 and the whole of Proverbs, chapter 3

With these things fresh in my mind, I realized one day, while reading the Lord's Prayer, that Jesus has incorporated these three elements into his model prayer. Each point within the prayer is either a matter of justice, mercy, or faith—the weightier matters of the law. Let me break it down for you by taking each part separately. Jesus begins the prayer with a statement of faith. It goes as follows:

"Our Father in heaven, hallowed be your name. Your kingdom come. Your will be done. On earth as it is in heaven."[317]

How is this above verse a statement of *"faith?"* Think of it! To pray this way, one must first believe that we have a Father who resides in heaven. We must believe in His great superiority that requires us to hallow His name. We must have faith that He has a kingdom in heaven, and that His kingdom—the embodiment of His will—would be of great benefit to us if it were here on earth, too. Turning to the Father in prayer is itself an act of faith; after all, why pray to God for any reason if you do not believe He exists.

Next, Jesus directs our minds to issues of justice.

Give us this day our daily bread.[318]

How is the above verse a statement of *justice*—social justice? Think of it! It is a statement in which we acknowledge that God's equitable ways are good. He has created a world that of itself can provide for all of us, and as His law has directed, we are to share that provision and not hoard its resources for ourselves. Notice that

---

(especially verse 23).

[317] Matthew 6:9–10

[318] Matthew 6:11

we are to ask that God give "us" . . . "our" . . . "daily" . . . "bread." We are not to be concerning only for "our" own needs but for the needs of "us"—the community as a whole. We are to pray that God will justly furnish the needs of every individual who is in need of something—some may need more and some less, but we ask that God give us and them what is needed today.

Notice, too, that we are not to seek for our weekly or yearly bread, which would be a case of hoarding and might result in a disparity for others. We are only to take what we need for this day so that everyone will have something to eat. I believe bread represents our basic needs for survival, and a person's daily "survival" needs might be more than just food. It may be shelter, or clothing, friendship, medical care or legal representation to defend against an oppressor. We ask God that those needs will be met this day—for us and for others. This is also an act of faith in that we trust God will remain with us and care for us tomorrow by filling that day's request as well.

Notice this statement brings the minds of Jesus' Jewish audience back to the exodus story of the manna being given in the wilderness, in order to preserve their lives. Recall also that the exodus story creates one of the earliest foundations of the Sabbath laws—laws of social justice—for the Jewish people. With this experience, God began teaching the people to use only the resources they need for the time being, and to trust Him to supply their needs in the future.

Next, Jesus directs our minds to issues of mercy.

And forgive us our debts, as we forgive our debtors.[319]

The above verse is a statement that asks for mercy from God based on our participation in giving mercy to those who need

---

[319] Matthew 6:12

it from us. Jesus again speaks in plural language, and again, it is we ourselves as well as our communities that need to extend mercy to all those in need of it. This, too, is based on the sabbatical laws that we have touched on in earlier chapters. Mercy is willingness to give others rest and to relieve them of their burdens. Mercy also gives back to others and it does not count the cost of what is incurred in being merciful—forgiving debts. Mercy is the aiding of the poor, the comforting of the mourners, the hungering and thirsting for righteousness and putting that longing into action. It is the epitome of the pure in heart and the peacemakers.

As Jesus begins to close his model prayer, he redirects our minds back to issues of faith.

> *And do not lead us into temptation, but deliver us from the evil one. For yours is the kingdom and the power and the glory forever. Amen.*[320]

How is this a statement of faith? Think of it! This is an expression of faith in God's leading—faith in the goodness of His law. It acknowledges that evil exists, and we can be led astray and become a captive of the evil one. Not leading us into temptation is the same as leading us away from temptation and toward good, which is the purpose of God's law. And being delivered from the evil one leaves us in God's presence. As the psalmist says:

> *Lord, who may abide in your tabernacle? Who may dwell in your holy hill? He who walks uprightly, and works righteousness, and speaks the truth in his heart; he who does not backbite with his tongue, nor does evil to his neighbor, nor does*

---

[320] Matthew 6:13

he take up a reproach against his friend; in whose eyes a vile person is despised, but he honors those who fear the Lord; he who swears to his own hurt and does not change; he who does not put out his money at usury, nor does he take a bribe against the innocent. He who does these things shall never be moved.[321]

As mentioned earlier, prayer is not so much about being heard by God as it is listening to God and, of course, doing what we have heard from God. This is a statement of faith; faith in God's wisdom in leading us by His laws and instructions to walk uprightly and do works of right doing—justice and mercy.

At the conclusion of this prayer—the "Lord's Prayer" as it is known—Jesus chooses to make one clarification or elaboration on the themes he has just presented. His subject reverts to his theme of forgiveness (mercy), and he adds the following encouragement and warning:

For if you forgive men their trespasses, your heavenly Father will also forgive you. But if you do not forgive men their trespasses, neither will your Father forgive your trespasses.

Matthew 6:14–15

In the prayer itself, Jesus has used the words "debts" and "debtors," but in his elaboration, he has used the word "trespasses." These first two words come from Greek words that have similar but slightly different meanings. The words translated as debts/debtors are the Greek words *opheilema*[322] and

---

[321] Psalm 15:1–5
[322] Strong's Word NT:3783

opheiletes.[323] These words refer primarily to financial and/or material possessions owed to someone else, but they can also refer to moral obligations. The word translated "trespasses" in Jesus' additional comments comes from the Greek word *paraptoma*.[324] This word means a *sideslip*, a *deviation* from a path, an *error*, either unintentional or willful.

Within the Lord's Prayer, a person could understand "debts" to mean financial obligations only. We should forgive these as the sabbatical laws require and perhaps expect that God might also forgive us of money we owe to Him—such as unpaid tithes or offerings or pledges.[325] However, Jesus' elaboration of his prayer using the additional word "trespasses" makes it plain that what he means by his statement within the prayer is *any shortcoming*, whether it be financial or moral, and whether it be between individuals or between man and God. This line in the prayer, and in Jesus' clarifying statement, is a parallel to the fifth beatitude—blessed are the merciful—and all that it implies as we explored in chapter nine. Jesus is clear, how God relates to us can be affected by how we treat others. Jesus' teaching, therefore, adds legitimacy to the Jewish concept that our standing with God can be influenced by our behavior to our fellow man. This is a driving theme throughout the Sermon on the Mount and throughout the Gospels.

---

[323] Strong's Word NT:3781

[324] Strong's Word NT:3900

[325] Malachi 3:8–10

CHAPTER 23

Fasting

Moreover, when you fast, do not be like the hypocrites, with a sad countenance. For they disfigure their faces that they may appear to men to be fasting. Assuredly, I say to you, they have their reward. But you, when you fast, anoint your head and wash your face, so that you do not appear to men to be fasting, but to your Father who is in the secret place; and your Father who sees in secret will reward you openly.

Matthew 6:16–19

From the topic of charity and prayer, Jesus moves to the next action that the Jewish people believe can influence God and cause Him to look favorably on them, and possibly reverse a negative decree He might have against them. This topic is the one of fasting. Again, the Jewish people have a precedent to believe that fasting is a way to approach God. As we mentioned earlier the most sacred day of the Jewish year—Yom Kippur, or the Day of Atonement—is a day that calls for fasting and prayer, as God decides one's fate for the coming year.

Fasting is associated with the acts of repentance or an urgent plea to God for intervention regarding a serious problem. The

Prophet Daniel is recorded as fasting when he prayed his prayer of repentance on behalf to the Israelite captives in Babylon.[326] On another occasion, the Prophet Joel records the words of the Lord calling for the people to repent saying:

> *Turn to me with all your heart, with fasting, with weeping, and with mourning."* And Joel advises the people regarding this command by saying, *"So rend your heart, and not your garments; return to the Lord your God, for He is gracious and merciful, slow to anger, and of great kindness; and He relents from doing harm. Who knows if He will turn and relent, and leave a blessing behind Him?*[327]

Perhaps there is no better example of fasting and repentance to be found in the Bible than in the story of Jonah, when a heathen city heeded Jonah's call for repentance in order to be spared destruction by God. The book of Jonah records Nineveh's reaction as follows:

> *So the people of Nineveh believed God, proclaimed a fast, and put on sackcloth, from the greatest to the least of them. Then word came to the king of Nineveh; and he arose from his throne and laid aside his robe, covered himself with sackcloth and sat in ashes. And he caused it to be proclaimed and published throughout Nineveh by the decree of the king and his nobles, saying,*
>
> *"Let neither man nor beast, herd nor flock, taste anything; do not let them eat, or*

---

[326] Daniel 9:3

[327] Joel 2:12–14

drink water. But let man and beast be cov-
ered with sackcloth, and cry mightily to God;
yes, let everyone turn from his evil way and
from the violence that is in his hands. Who
can tell if God will turn and relent, and turn
away from His fierce anger, so that we may
not perish?"

Then God saw their works, that they turned
from their evil way; and God relented from the
disaster that He had said He would bring upon
them, and He did not do it.[328]

While the king of Nineveh ordered a complete fast, even restricting water, it is important to point out that, within the cultures of the East, fasting generally does not have to be the act of abstaining from all food, though it could be. Many of the various religions I met in Africa and the Middle East practiced fasting that did not require abstaining from all food. In the minds of the East, a fast can be the act of going without something—food or other necessity or luxury—for a prescribed period of time. Many individuals practice this form of limited fasting for years on end.

A fast of any kind is an internal hardship, and we naturally want others to empathize with us as we make our sacrifice. We enjoy the encouragement and praise that others can give us. Keeping our fast a secret, as Jesus recommends, is not second nature to most of us.

The Muslim cultures I associated with during my years in Africa practiced the Ramadan fast each year. This month-long religious festival requires the faithful to abstain from eating and drinking during daylight hours. Feasting, however, is allowed

---

[328] Jonah 3:5–10

in the night. Many of the Muslims I worked with took great pride in displaying how much they were suffering during their fast. Witnessing this firsthand was an opportunity to see a living example of Jesus' words in Matthew 6:16.

For example, often, I would need to go to a government office during Ramadan in order to secure a permit or negotiate some issue. Getting help during Ramadan was nearly impossible. I would go from desk to desk and be met with the same expressions—a weary face, drooping eyes, ruffled hair, and apathy. It was not unusual to find officials asleep at their desks, or behind their desks. When asking them for help, their reply was usually a mournful, "Don't bother me, I'm fasting." I have seen the sad countenances and the disfigured faces of many fasters.

Jesus reminds us once again that seeking the accolades of others can be insincere and hypocritical—it is akin to preforming as actors on a stage. For Jesus, fasting is something between oneself and the Father in heaven. It should be done in secret. He again tells us that the rewards we will get for our open display of piety, will only be the rewards that this earth can give. It is better to live one's normal routine while fasting, and let your fast be before God alone, who will give you a heavenly reward—now or in the future, as He chooses.

There is a social justice component to fasting in the Bible. The Prophet Isaiah records God giving the children of Israel instructions for the type of fast that was acceptable to Him. It is recorded in Isaiah 58. The chapter starts out with the people lamenting that they have been fasting, but God has not been responding to their fast. God points out to them that while they have been fasting, they have also been fighting with each other, engaged in strife and debates, and exploiting their laborers. God asks them, sarcastically, "You call this a fast?"[329]

---

[329] My own paraphrase of Isaiah 58:5.

God then outlines what He is looking for when a person conducts a true fast or an affliction of one's soul. He says:

Is this not the fast that I have chosen: to loose the bonds of wickedness, to undo the heavy burdens, to let the oppressed go free, and that you break every yoke? Is it not to share your bread with the hungry, and that you bring to your house the poor who are cast out; when you see the naked, that you cover him, and not hide yourself from your own flesh? Then your light shall break forth like the morning, your healing shall spring forth speedily, and your righteousness shall go before you; the glory of the Lord shall be your rear guard. Then you shall call, and the Lord will answer; you shall cry, and He will say, "Here I am."[330]

This true and acceptable fast brings us back to Jesus' statement of letting our lights shine that men see our good works and glorify our Father in heaven.[331] It brings us back to secret acts of charity. And it brings us back to the model prayer; one that focuses not just on speaking to God but also on listening to Him, and doing what we have heard He wants—justice, mercy, and faith. The fasting that God rewards is equated to actions of justice and equity in our communities.

---

[330] Isaiah 58:6–9
[331] Matthew 5:16

CHAPTER 24

Treasure in Heaven

Do not lay up for yourselves treasures on earth, where moth and rust destroy and where thieves break in and steal; but lay up for yourselves treasures in heaven, where neither moth nor rust destroys and where thieves do not break in and steal. For where your treasure is, there your heart will be also.

Matthew 6:19–21

At first glance it might appear to us that Jesus is changing his subject matter and beginning to speak about a new topic. But he is not changing his subject at all; he is just recapping in summary his last three points. Keep in mind that with each of his previous topics—charity, prayer, and fasting—Jesus points out that an individual has the option of being rewarded by men for their open displays of acted piety, or being rewarded by God for their secret acts of sincerity. Jesus has merely changed the word "reward" to "treasures," but the topic is still the same; do you want rewards or treasures here on earth, or would it be better to have rewards or treasures in heaven?

Jesus' above summary is this: as you carry out your acts of charity, prayer, and fasting, you will be laying up treasures. However, charity, prayer, and fasting done in the acting style of the hypocrites lays up an earthly reward or treasure. The disadvantage to hypocrisy is that earthly treasures are easily destroyed by the smallest of earthly things and are subject to being taken away unexpectedly. How true this is in our day and age. A moment of fame is often followed by months of humiliation and disgrace. And wealth can vanish in a moment.

Within each of Jesus' three earlier topics of charity, prayer, and fasting, he had advised his listeners to seek rewards from the heavenly Father. His advice now within this summary is that we should lay up treasures in heaven. This is done by pursuing the will of God the Father with a sincere heart, not trying to win the adoration of men, but, in faith, walking humbly with our God. As we have seen within the last three topics, these actions are not passive ones or ones that we do in isolation. Charity is for the benefit of others; prayer is faith in action as we give forgiveness and mercy as a prerequisite of receiving forgiveness and mercy. It also involves our recognition that there is a requirement to have everyone's daily needs met. Fasting, true fasting, is working toward a just and equitable society, starting with our own actions first.

But there is something more to what Jesus is saying here, and it lies in the structure of his sermon. I personally find it quite fascinating and brilliant. Jesus has just given three teachings that deal with concepts of how the Jewish faith thinks it can influence God's relationship with themselves—charity, prayer, and fasting. And Jesus does not deny that God will respond to these actions if done in sincerity. However, to help align our minds correctly, Jesus is about to revisit each of these topics from a slightly different angle. He will give three additional teachings that parallel each of these three earlier concepts. However, this time the teaching focuses less on the actions being done, and more on the spiritual relationship that should serve as the motivation for the actions. We will look at each of these in more detail in this and the coming two chapters, but briefly here are the parallel structures we will explore.

Charity—(Chapter 24) How do we lay up treasures in heaven? (Matthew 6:19–21)

Prayer—(Chapter 25) Are our thoughts in alignment with God's thoughts? (Matthew 6:22–23)

Fasting—(Chapter 26) Who are we serving? Are we feeding our egos, or are we being good stewards in the service of God? (Matthew 6:24)

Let us begin our detailed look at the first of these three parallels. Jesus' use of the word "treasure" is clearly an equity issue, because, as we will learn, he sees charity as the way to accumulate treasure in heaven. The word "treasure" is translated from the Greek word *thesaurus,*[332] which means a *deposit,* or *wealth*. And this deposit or wealth is something we can have now on earth or we can store it in heaven. This will not be Jesus' only use of this word during his ministry. This theme of laying up treasure on earth or heaven is repeated, and is often in the context of how we use our earthly resources or wealth for the benefit of others.

We have already reviewed one such story in chapter five of this book. Recall the parable of the farmer who had a bumper crop of grain, so much so that his old barn could not hold it. His solution was to demolish the old barn and build new and better ones to store his wealth for use long into the future. Jesus states that God reprimands him and cuts his life short. Jesus' concluding words are:

So is he who lays up treasure for himself and is not rich toward God.[333]

Jesus' point is that the farmer chose to hoard his wealth for his own pleasure rather than make it available to those who could also

---

[332] Strong's Word NT:2344
[333] Luke 12:21

benefit from it. He chose the earthly reward, and it was stolen from him. He should have chosen the heavenly reward.

Jesus also made a very straightforward statement about how earthly wealth can be used to lay up treasures in heaven, when he instructed the rich, young ruler to go sell all his possessions and give the money to the poor and then come follow Jesus. The ruler had come to Jesus believing he was living a good and lawful life and wanted to know what more he needed to do to have eternal life. Jesus' well-known reply was as follows:

Jesus said to him, "If you want to be perfect, go, sell what you have and give to the poor, and you will have treasure in heaven; and come, follow Me."[334]

You might recall that within Jesus' Sermon on the Mount, being "perfect" was defined as being generous to the evil and the good, the just and the unjust, as God the Father Himself is. Jesus was asking this man to give his wealth to the poor without prejudice. Many pastors make a point that Jesus was not asking the ruler to perform works to get his salvation, and this may be true, however, the verse plainly indicates that giving to the poor would result in treasures in heaven, and that this would happen before he followed Jesus. Otherwise, Jesus should have said, "give to the poor, and come follow me, and you will have treasures in heaven." My point is that Jesus' statement is consistent with other uses of the word *treasure* and that following Jesus involves social actions. Giving to the poor is an act of loving God and loving one's neighbor as oneself—the two principles on which all the Law and the Prophets hang.

It should be noted that this ruler was also being asked to exercise faith in Jesus. Jesus had given him two commands

---

[334] Matthew 19:21

that would lead to his having eternal life. He was being asked to accept what Jesus was teaching and he needed to acknowledge that Jesus was the king of the kingdom he was seeking to enter.

Lastly, there is also Jesus' short parable about the treasure hidden in the field. The entire story goes as follows:

> *The kingdom of heaven is like treasure hidden in a field, which a man found and hid; and for joy over it he goes and sells all that he has and buys that field.*[335]

This parable has been spiritually interpreted to mean a host of different things, but at face value it is quite straightforward and consistent with Jesus' equity teachings. The kingdom of heaven is the treasure! Getting that treasure required the liquidation of all of this man's possessions to give to someone else so that he could have the treasure. That is essentially the same instruction that Jesus gave to the rich, young ruler. The only part left out of this particular parable is the command to "follow me."

In both these illustrations, the true thoughts of the heart are revealed in the respective characters. How seriously did each one want the treasure of heaven? The rich young ruler departed, keeping his earthly wealth. The other man sold all his goods, bought the field (and its treasure) and went on to get his reward. The degree of earthly or heavenly treasure we possess is just an indication of where our hearts are.

---

[335] Matthew 13:44

CHAPTER 25

Good Eye Versus Evil Eye

The lamp of the body is the eye. If therefore your eye is good, your whole body will be full of light. But if your eye is bad, your whole body will be full of darkness. If therefore the light that is in you is darkness, how great is that darkness!

Matthew 6:22–23

As I mentioned in the last chapter, I see Jesus expanding on his three previous topics of charity, prayer, and fasting. We have just looked at the parallel to charity. This chapter will reveal Jesus' parallel teaching concerning the topic of prayer. As previously mentioned, each one of these new statements focuses on one's mental perceptions that are required to carry out the actions of charity, prayer, and fasting in the right spiritual frame of mind. So, how does the above statement qualify and add to Jesus' previous teaching on prayer? The answer is that when we enter into communication with God, it is we who must align our minds to His way of thinking, not God who has to align Himself to ours.

Jesus makes the statement that *"the lamp of the body is the eye."* This is a literal statement as well as a symbolic one. It is through our eyes that we are able to see light. Without our eyes and their ability to process the light entering them, we will be severely limited in our understanding of the world around us. We can still function, but we will never be able to fully appreciate the wonder and beauty of God's mind as revealed in His creations.

Both light and lamps in the word of God are symbols of correct knowledge and truth. God's word, His ways for us, is called a lamp unto our feet to guide us in our paths; His commandments are our lamp.[336] Of course, God's word and commandments do not generate a literal light on our paths. This metaphoric light is one that illuminates our minds and directs us toward good. Likewise, Jesus is also making a reference to our "mind's eye" and how it processes the light from God. Similar metaphors are used in all cultures throughout the world to try to capture how one understands information. We often say to someone, *"Do you see what I mean?"* We are rarely referring to what they physically see, rather we are asking if they have an understanding *in their mind* of the things we are trying to communicate.

Jesus' reference to having a "good eye" and being *"full of light"* is concerning one's attitude toward life, and especially toward life as God would have us live it. If our thoughts and actions are aligned with His—our ways are His ways—then we are full of His light and are on a safe path in life.

However, a person can have a different view of the world than the one God would want us to have. One's life model can be based on a different knowledge or belief system. This is what Jesus terms as the "eye is bad." Some translations of the Bible use the term "evil eye"[337] For such a person, their inner being is considered darkness—the goodness of God's ways is

---

[336] Psalm 119:104–105; Proverbs 6:22–23

[337] The word "bad" is translated from the Greek word *poneerós* (Strong's Word NT:4190). An equally valid translation is "evil", and many Bible translations use the word "evil" instead of "bad". The Complete Jewish Bible translates the phases as one having an "evil eye".

not appreciated or realized. Jesus concludes that, for such a person, their "light," which is really darkness compared to God's knowledge and truth, is a very grave place to be. If one has a concept of the world that is diametrically opposite to God's knowledge and truth, they can be self-deceived into thinking that their ways are superior to God's ways. In such a state it can become impossible for them to perceive that God's ways are light. To such an individual, their dark frame of mind is a trap that keeps them blinded from God's light. Their "light" (their understanding of morality and life) is therefore, in reality, a great darkness.

But what does this all mean? Keep in mind, I have proposed that this statement of Jesus' runs parallel to his teaching about prayer. This statement of light and darkness concerns how our mind needs to be aligned with the mind of God, if we are going to have any meaningful communication with God. Keep in mind also that I have suggested that prayer is not so much about God hearing from us, as it is about us hearing from God, and doing what we have heard Him tell us to do. And finally, keep in mind that Jesus has distilled his model prayer down to three key elements—justice, mercy, and faith.

If I am even remotely correct about this statement of Jesus' paralleling his teaching on prayer, then I expect Jesus is telling us to share the mind of God as reflected in that prayer. As we have seen, Jesus' prayer taught us to have faith in his Father and the tenets of His kingdom. He has directed us to ask that His kingdom's ways be done here on earth. He has taught us to depend on God for only our daily needs, and to see that everyone else has their daily needs met. And finally, the forgiveness and mercy extended to us should be according to the forgiveness and mercy we extend toward others. My "good eye" should therefore be one that has faith in the Father and shares His concerns for others' material and social needs, as well as a willingness to be merciful. And, by implication, a "bad, or evil eye" would therefore be one that is suspicious of God's ways, is not merciful to others, and is not concerned with material equity or the basic needs of others. A "good eye" is one that belongs to a follower of God. A "bad, or evil eye" is one that belongs to someone who rejects God and does not see the value of His way of life.

The "evil eye" paradigm is dealt with in one other place in the gospel story, and it does shed light on Jesus' teaching here in the Sermon on the Mount. It is found in one of Jesus' parables given near the end of his ministry. The context of this parable is quite striking. Let me set the stage and lead you through a series of events. First, a rich young ruler comes to Jesus to ask what he needs to do to have eternal life. Jesus tells him to keep the commandments, which the ruler believes he has done. Then, Jesus tells him to sell what he has and give to the poor without prejudice and come follow him. The ruler declines and Jesus comments to his disciples that, *"it is hard for a rich man to enter the kingdom of heaven."*[338]

The disciples are shocked by this statement since they are still considering the rich to be people who have been blessed by God, and therefore closer to the kingdom of heaven than ordinary people. They ask Jesus, *"Who then can be saved?"* Jesus replies, *"With men this is impossible, but with God all things are possible."*[339] Peter then comments that he and the disciples have given up everything to follow Jesus and he wonders what they will get from it. Jesus assures him that their reward is great.

At this point, Jesus gives the disciples a parable to illustrate what the kingdom of heaven is like. The parable, in short, goes as follows:

[338] Matthew 19:23
[339] Matthew 19:26

The kingdom of heaven is like a landowner who went out early in the morning to hire laborers for his vineyard. Now when he had agreed with the laborers for a denarius a day, he sent them into his vineyard. And he went out about the third hour and saw others standing idle in the marketplace, and said to them, "You also go into the vineyard, and whatever is right I will give you." So they went. Again he went out about the sixth and the ninth hour, and did likewise. And about the eleventh hour he went out and found others standing . . . , and He said to them, "You also go into the vineyard, and whatever is right you will receive."

*So when evening had come, the owner of the vineyard said to his steward, "Call the laborers and give them their wages . . . and when those came who were hired about the eleventh hour, they each received a denarius. But when the first came, they supposed that they would receive more; and they likewise received each a denarius. And when they had received it, they complained against the landowner. . . . But he answered one of them and said, "Friend, I am doing you no wrong. Did you not agree with me for a denarius? Take what is yours and go your way. I wish to give to this last man the same as to you. Is it not lawful for me to do what I wish with my own things? Or **is your eye evil** because I am good?" So the last will be first, and the first last.* (emphasis added)[340]

---

[340] Matthew 20:1–16

This parable has been interpreted in many ways by theologians, but I wish to limit our review of it to how it gives us clues to Jesus' use of the phrase "eye evil" in his Sermon on the Mount. There are a few things you need to know, to start with. First, the phrase in Matthew 6:23, and here in Matthew 20:15, is identical in Greek. They are based on the Greek words for "eye," "thine," and "evil" (*opthalmós sou poneerós*).[341] So, once we understand what the parable is saying, we can see how it fits into Jesus' meaning in Matthew 6.

Second, the landowner in this parable is referring to an ancient superstition within the Mediterranean and Near East regions during Jesus' time. The superstition is one that appears to date back to early classical Greek history. It has since spread to other continents and is still alive and well today. It is the superstition of the "Evil Eye." This is a belief that people can cause harm to others by a mere envious glance at coveted objects of their owners. It is the concept that some people have powers to destroy, or jinx someone's good fortune, by just giving an envious look at something. Superstitions can be powerful to those who believe in them. Jesus is not endorsing this "evil eye" superstition, but the landowner in his story is addressing a potential belief in it among his disgruntled laborers.

The story's situation is easy for all of us to understand—if we worked harder and longer, we should get paid more. Nevertheless, the landowner chose to pay everyone the same. This was very generous to those who came to the field later in the day, but it does seem unfair to those who started in the early morning. However, the landowner has a good point; he kept his word and agreement with the first labors and is free to give any amount of his own money to anyone he chooses to give to, and for any reason.

We do not have details about the landowner's motives but let me conjecture a bit about his day. Our good-hearted land-

---

[341] Strong's Word NT:3788, NT:4675 and NT:4190, respectively.

owner needed laborers to complete what appears to be an urgent task—hence his repeated trips to the market to find workers. It could be possible that each time he returns to the market he finds new laborers who have arrived late to the market. Perhaps they are late because they had difficulties getting to the market earlier. Maybe they had to travel further than the others, or had to finish a small job. Maybe a family member was sick and needed care. Maybe they were older and too stiff in the morning. Regardless of the individual situations, the landowner chooses not to penalize them for showing up late; instead, he sees an opportunity to provide for all the various families represented by these laborers by giving them each a day's wage. Everyone represented went home that night with a day's wage and no one in the community went hungry due to any extenuating circumstances that prevented a full day's work.

People with a "good eye" will see the mercy and justice in this landowner's actions and be grateful for his kindness. He has cared for many within his community. People with an "evil eye" will feel that they should have materially benefited more than others and will be blind to the mercy and justice of the landowner's actions. Their desire for more will make them envious of the landowner's wealth, and they will covet it as something that should belong to them. Ironically, the wealth being in the hands of this generous landowner was of better help to the community than if it had been concentrated in the hands of those few with the evil eyes. It is not likely that the disgruntled laborers would be as generous if the tables were turned. Wealth, therefore, in the correct hands, is a blessing to a community. Society benefits when there are wealthy landowners with "good eyes".

It can be argued that at least one of Jesus' points in this parable is that the kingdom of heaven is like this landowner, in that he is willing to give to each equally, regardless of whatever obstacles or limitations they may be facing. Those who showed up late were still in need of work—they still need to eat and care for their families. Those not in need did not come to the market that day. Hence, wealth, in the right hands, is a tool to help everyone in need within the community, not just a reward for those who work harder. The landowner's giving equal pay to those who worked a limited time was an act of charity. Their showing up for work merely allowed him the basis to give to each laborer without shaming them for taking a handout. He was being careful to preserve their dignity—an important gesture in this culture.

There is an important lesson here. In the kingdom of heaven's "good eye" world, social justice does not have to begin when the poor or oppressed rising up to demand fair treatment. It occurs, preemptively, because those with wealth and power see the plight of the poor and the oppressed, and respond willingly with their wealth and power to address the inequities within their societies. Their actions of equity have a personal cost, but they willingly sacrifice for the benefit of their neighbors. "Good eye" social justice comes from the top-down. "Evil eyes" are in darkness and will not perceive the benefit to society that the "good eyes" are trying to achieve.

Now let us take this back to the Sermon on the Mount. Jesus has been teaching the value of action within our communities to help the poor, comfort those in sorrow, and defend the underprivileged and oppressed. He has asked us to seek the right, be pure in heart and be peacemakers. He has warned us there are those who will persecute us for doing so. Nevertheless, following such actions is the essence of what the Law and the Prophets is trying to create—a society that is just, merciful, and operating on faith in the heavenly father. This is the true light that the Word of God imparts to the minds of those who can see the pattern of God's fairness and lordship. He is the owner of everything, and He wants all His creation to have its daily needs met, and we have a part in ensuring that His will is done on earth. This is the paradigm of the "good eye."

Not everyone in the world, however, shares this mindset. Many have the paradigm of the "evil eye." It is selfishness; it is greed. Those who have it are interested in accumulating wealth, even if it means others may not have their basic needs met. Justice and mercy are good when it is given to them, but they do not feel the need to ensure others have it as well, especially if it is given at cost to themselves. This is what Jesus terms a great darkness, for it has a degrading effect on the community as a whole. It keeps people in bondage and never lets them experience the sabbatical rest. And ultimately, as we will see, it will exclude the holder of the dark paradigm from entrance into the kingdom of heaven.

CHAPTER 26

God or Money? You Choose!

No one can serve two masters; for either he will hate the one and love the other, or else he will be loyal to the one and despise the other. You cannot serve God and mammon.

Matthew 6:24

This is Jesus' third statement that adds more detail to his earlier topics of charity, prayer, and fasting—ways in which man can influence God's view of a person's life. And by "influence" I simply mean that if God is proposing a negative decree against someone, that person can make changes in their life that could reverse or delay God's judgment. This was a Jewish belief in Jesus' day, and I would say that this concept still exists in Christianity today. Right or wrong, we often feel we have offended God, and we attempt to make amends by compensating with good.

Before I outline the parallel I see with Jesus' teaching on fasting, let us understand a few details first. The picture Jesus is presenting in this statement is one of a servant serving a master. The word "*serve*" is from the Greek word "*douleuo,*"[342] and it means *to be slave to*, or *in bondage to*. This is fulltime service to a master, either voluntarily or involuntarily. Jesus is

---

[342] Strong's Word NT:1398

not talking about holding two jobs at the same time and having weekends free. This is a position that requires you to be available when needed, to do whatever is asked of you. Therefore, Jesus' first statement, *"No one can serve two masters,"* is a practical reality of his day, and it will be reinforced by his last statement in this passage, *"You cannot serve God and mammon."*

Even though *"douleuo"* is fulltime service, Jesus does offer the hypothetical situation where a person would be in fulltime service to two masters. How would such a person react to the demands of such a workload and the required responsibilities? Jesus states that one of the masters will ultimately be preferred over the other. The person in servitude will eventually find life with one of the two masters unbearable in comparison to the other master. His loyalty will grow for one, while his dissatisfaction will grow for the other.

I should point out that the Greek word for *"he will hate"*[343] used in this passage can mean *to hate,* but it can also mean to love one of two objects or persons *"less"* than the other. This is only natural. Even a person who has two jobs they enjoy will generally view one as more enjoyable.

Jesus' illustration, however, is not meant to be one that gives a commentary on earthly employment. The illustration was given to help us better understand his main point—we cannot serve God and mammon. "Mammon"[344] is an Aramaic word that means *wealth* or *avarice.* It is a word that is used to personify or deify wealth, as in one making the accumulation or pursuit of wealth their god or object of worship. It is not the possession of wealth that is bad, *per se,* as much as it is the devotion to obtaining and retaining it. *Avarice*—the extreme greed for wealth or material gain—is probably the better English definition of the word "mammon."

---

[343] Strong's Word NT:3404 *"miseo"*
[344] Strong's Word NT:3126

When avarice is understood as the meaning of mammon, it is not hard to understand why Jesus would say that "*You cannot serve God and mammon.*" The two are diametrically opposed to each other. The Sermon on the Mount, which is calling for us to be members of God's way of government, is teaching a lifetime of sharing our resources with others. This inevitably has a cost in time, energy and most probably our wealth, or at least our potential to accumulate it. It is a life of sacrifice for the good of others. Mammon has no such motivation to serve. To mammon, service is a waste of time, unless it leads to the accumulation of more material wealth. Any action that diminishes this accumulation is a step taken in the wrong direction from one's goal of being wealthy.

Followers of mammon are tied to their wealth. Their wealth is what defines them and gives their lives meaning and direction. The wealthier they are, the more imprisoned they may become by their need for wealth. The possession of more things requires more maintenance, more cost, more protection of wealth, and more worry. Mammon can easily become a slave master to those who love wealth, and being a loving servant of mammon will lead one to love God less, and possibly even despise Him.

Being a servant of God, on the other hand, intuitively works the opposite way. The servant sees himself as a steward of God's wealth that has been entrusted to him for the service of others. As John the Baptist told his crowd of listeners, if you have two coats, give one away to someone who does not have a coat and do likewise with your food. If one sees their *coat wealth* as ultimately God's property, sharing that wealth with those in need, as God has asked, is not a hardship. It is rather a responsibility of being a servant of God. And being a loving servant of God, we would share His world view. Living with this kind of mindset would make the accumulation of wealth for one's personal benefit, a mark of failure to one's goal of serving God. As long as others have basic needs within our community, or world, such an accumulation of wealth would be considered an act of oppressing those in need in the eyes of the God. True stewards of God's resources would find the neglect of others offensive.

This is a teaching of Jesus on many occasions throughout the Gospels. The Sermon on the Mount is only one such case. The books of Matthew and Luke also deal with this subject in the parable of the faithful and evil servant, which we looked at in chapter five. In that chapter, I quoted Matthew's version of the story, but Luke's version gives additional details that concern us now. Here is the story for your review.

Who then is that faithful and wise steward, whom his master will make ruler over his household, to give them their portion of food in due season? Blessed is that servant whom his master will find so doing when he comes. Truly, I say to you that he will make him ruler over all that he has. But if that servant says in his heart, "My master is delaying his coming," and begins to beat the male and female servants, and to eat and drink and be drunk, the master of that servant will come on a day when he is not looking for him, and at an hour when he is not aware, and will cut him in two and appoint him his portion with the unbelievers.

And that servant who knew his master's will, and did not prepare himself or do according to his will, shall be beaten with many stripes. But he who did not know, yet committed things deserving of stripes, shall be beaten with few. For everyone to whom much is given, from him much will be re-

*quired; and to whom much has been committed, of
him they will ask the more.*[345]

In the first part of this passage, as was the case in chapter five, we have a servant that has been entrusted with the duty of controlling the master's food resources and making sure they are distributed to the household as needed. If that servant does his job, everything is well and good. But if that servant becomes evil and begins to abuse the household by not giving them their food as assigned—and using the resources for his own pleasure—the master will punish him.

At face value we can interpret this to mean that God—the master—will entrust to us some of His resources for the purpose of distribution to others in His household. This is the way the kingdom of heaven works—God owns everything, and we are His stewards to manage His wealth as instructed. Failure to see the resources as belonging to the master, or using them in ways He did not instruct, is grounds for punishment.

The second part of this passage is what is not recorded in the book of Matthew, and it gives us some surprising details. Ignorance of God's will is still an offense, but the penalty is less severe than knowing God's will and failing to do it. But it is the last line that I find most interesting, *"For everyone to whom much is given, from him much will be required."* Could this mean that if a Christian finds himself wealthy, he is in a better position to help others? Could it mean he may have a larger burden to bear in meeting the basic needs of others?

This may perhaps answer a question I asked earlier in this book. Do you remember what John the Baptist told the people when they asked what they needed to do to avoid

---

[345] Luke 12:42–48

being punished by God? His first reply was that if you have two coats, give one to someone who has none.[346] I asked, what then should be a believer's response if he owns three coats, or maybe four, or five? Let us face it. If one has more *coat wealth*, the responsibility to give is greater. John's admonition was to give away one of your two coats. If you had three coats and gave one away, you would still have two coats and still be in a position to respond by giving one more coat away to someone who had none. Greater wealth opens the door for greater response to others' needs. The rich have a proportionally higher cost in meeting God's equity and mercy standards. Perhaps that is why Jesus said it is hard for a rich man to enter the kingdom of heaven[347]—they may feel they have too much to lose, or just fail to respond to all that God might ask.

And herein lies where I see Matthew 6:24 having a parallel connection to Jesus' teaching on fasting. Fasting is sacrifice. It requires denying yourself of something, and that something could be "mammon." Recall that in chapter 23, we quoted the Prophet Isaiah on what God said is a fast acceptable to Him. Here is the quote once more:

> *Is this not the fast that I have chosen: to loose the bonds of wickedness, to undo the heavy burdens, to let the oppressed go free, and that you break every yoke? Is it not to share your bread with the hungry, and that you bring to your house the poor who are cast out; when you see the naked, that you cover him, and not hide yourself from your own flesh? Then your light shall break forth like the morning, your healing shall spring forth*

---

[346] Luke 3:10–11
[347] Matthew 19:23

speedily, and your righteousness shall go before you; the glory of the Lord shall be your rear guard. Then you shall call, and the Lord will answer; you shall cry, and He will say, "Here I am."[348]

God's words, presents by the Prophet Isaiah, show that God is asking us to not choose the ways of mammon. Our wealth is not to be held onto and accumulated. It is not to control our lives. Instead, we are to see our wealth as something we have for the benefit of other who are in need. Giving to those needs is a true fast in God's eyes. Giving is the denying of ourselves of property that could be held to benefit ourselves. It is a sacrifice. It is a fast acceptable to God. It is the exercise of sharing a characteristic of God—generosity.

True fasting is the act of putting mammon to rest. It is actively pursuing justice and equity in one's society. It lifts peoples' burdens, defends the oppressed, feeds the hungry, and clothes the naked. This will require one's personal time, energy, and financial resources. This is true service to God and the principles of the kingdom of heaven lived out on this earth. It is denying oneself the benefits of excessive earthly gains so that those in need can have resources they need to survive and grow. Your wealth is God's resources entrusted to you for redistribution to those in need in due season. There is room for wealth in a Christian's life, but not for mammon—the extreme greed for wealth and material accumulation. Mammon and God are separate masters with opposing goals. There truly is no way to serve both. We must choose one or the other. Fast and starve mammon, while growing your relationship with God and your fellow man.

---

[348] Isaiah 58:6–9

CHAPTER 27

Do Not Worry, Have Faith!

Therefore, I say to you, do not worry about your life, what you will eat or what you will drink; nor about your body, what you will put on. Is not life more than food and the body more than clothing? Look at the birds of the air, for they neither sow nor reap nor gather into barns; yet your heavenly Father feeds them. Are you not of more value than they? Which of you by worrying can add one cubit to his stature? So why do you worry about clothing? Consider the lilies of the field, how they grow: they neither toil nor spin; and yet I say to you that even Solomon in all his glory was not arrayed like one of these. Now if God so clothes the grass of the field, which today is, and tomorrow is thrown into the oven, will He not much more clothe you, O you of little faith? Therefore do not worry, saying, "What shall we eat?" or "What shall we drink?" or "What shall we wear?" For after all these things the Gentiles seek. For your heavenly Father knows that you need all these things. But seek first the kingdom of God and His righteousness, and all these things shall be added to you. Therefore, do not worry about to-

morrow, for tomorrow will worry about its own things. Sufficient for the day is its own trouble.

Matthew 6:25–34

This remarkable section of Jesus' sermon starts with the word "Therefore." This draws our attention back to what he has just stated. After all, whenever we have a *therefore* we must look at what has come *before*. It is in this context that we move forward into the reasoning of what is to follow. And what is it Jesus has just said? "No one can serve two masters. . . . you cannot serve God and mammon."

Considering this statement and everything Jesus has taught in the Sermon on the Mount up to this point, it is clear that Jesus is directing us to share our personal resources with others—be they material, emotional, or physical. He is saying that you cannot serve God (who asks you to care for the poor, hungry, widowed, orphaned, and oppressed), and also serve mammon (the extreme greed for material accumulation or a lust for power and control). The two cannot go together, and Jesus is asking us to choose the unselfish path of following God. This cannot be done freely.

Jesus' message has been an equity message. The kingdom of heaven is about service to our neighbors in need. So naturally the person whose wish is to become rich and powerful for the benefit of themselves—serving mammon—will find himself at odds with the kingdom of heaven. But on the other hand, the one who wishes to serve God will realize there is a cost he is obligating himself to. The natural extension of embarking on this course will be to ask oneself, "How much is this going to cost me? If I give away my material wealth, how am I going to feed and clothe myself and my family?" Jesus is about to address these unspoken, but very substantial, questions brewing in the minds of his listeners.

Such worry is valid, and it can be enough to make one hesitate in making a commitment to the kingdom of heaven. But here, Jesus directly addresses this fear head-on with a simple argument. The Father in heaven supplies the needs of even the lowliest creatures of earth; why should you think he will not do the same for you? Jesus gives his audience two examples of God's care. The birds of the field do not plan for the future, but they still find food and live because of the provisions of God. The flowers of the field do not provide their own clothing, yet what they have was designed and given to them by God, and their glory exceeds the beauty of the attire of a great king.

In both illustrations, Jesus argues that anxiety over these things is pointless, and demonstrates a lack of faith in the care that God can give. It demonstrates a lack of knowledge in what God can offer to those who follow His self-sacrificing way of life. We are more valuable in God's eyes than the creatures of the field. Worry is a mental phenomenon that cannot add to one's provision or physical growth. Jesus, however, implies that it can stunt one's spiritual growth in that it paralyzes a person from experiencing life in its most rewarding way. Anxiety over whether one will have enough provisions for life if they follow God is symptomatic of a lack of faith in God, and lack of faith is the disease that stunts one's spiritual growth and ultimately robs one of his divine reward—both here on earth and in heaven.

These arguments from Jesus are a challenge to us, to live as he is living—to live the equity of the kingdom of heaven's message and to have full faith that God will sustain you. It is a call to live for justice, to be merciful, to champion the needs of others and have faith to live this way. And it is a challenge to experience the miraculous provision of God's care for His children, and the joy and excitement that comes with this course of life. It is a challenge to have faith to give your second coat to the person who has none and to learn that God will care for you if that kindness puts you into a position of need in the future. It is a challenge to learn that God is a better master than mammon is.

The crowd listening to this sermon plainly understands that Jesus wants them to follow God, not mammon. No doubt they are questioning the consequences of making such a commitment. But Jesus immediately tells them that there is no reason to be worried or anxious about making the decision to follow God. And most specifically, the anxieties that Jesus targets are concerning one's life, food, drink, and clothing. This indicates that Jesus is aware his appeal to the crowd to follow God as he instructs, leads one to wonder how they would survive if they lived as Jesus is asking them to live. Clearly, Jesus' message creates the impression one is not to accumulate material wealth but instead be prepared to give it to others in need.

Keep in mind that Jesus is not asking for an occasional donation to your favorite charity. He is asking for a life-long, selfless, total commitment to the principles of the kingdom of heaven. This is a commitment that could make a follower wonder where his next meal, or next glass of water, is coming from. This implies that a deep sacrifice can be requested of a follower at any time. The very fact Jesus isolates the possible anxieties to the most basic of human needs—food, drink, and shelter—is indicative of the depth of the possible sacrifices the kingdom of heaven can impose on its followers. And yet, even though such sacrifices could put our own lives into jeopardy—at least in terms of our view of a given situation—we are to have faith and know that God will not let us be deprived of the basic needs of life. Our life will be preserved, we will have food and drink, and we will have clothing.

There is an irony here in the teachings of Jesus. He is asking us to give to others the very necessities of life that we ourselves might worry about. If we find a hungry person, we are to feed them, even if we fear it might mean we will go hungry. If we find someone with no coat, we should give him one of ours, even if we might have need of it in the future. To those in need, we represent the role of God in meeting their basic provisions in life. We have acted within the character of God by being the provider to the one in need. That action has made us somewhat poorer, and now we, in turn, wait upon the provision of God to meet any need we might have because of our sacrifice. There is a displacement of burdens in the chain of need. In essence, the very poorest among us is helped by God when we give help to them. We become a link in a divine chain of compassion that is binding us together while we pass the provisions of God from one end to the other.

Jesus instructs his listeners to not ask these questions of what they will eat, drink, or wear, saying that these are the common concerns of the "gentiles." In saying this, Jesus is again making an appeal to one's faith. After all, the Jewish people believed their God was superior to the gods of the gentiles. So, if the gentiles are asking their gods for these basic needs, why wouldn't the superior God of the Jews already be aware of their needs? And that is precisely Jesus' point; God (your heavenly Father) already knows what you need and is making provision for those needs to be met.

Many translations for this passage use the English word "seek" two times—one regarding the provisions the gentiles "seek" and one for what the followers of God are to "seek." The same English word appears twice in the text, but the two come from two different words in Greek. The "seek" for the gentiles comes from the Greek word *epizeteo*,[349] and it means *to search, to demand* or *to crave*. The Greek word used for "seek" for God's followers is missing the *epi* prefix and is simply the word "*zeteo*,"[350] It also means *to search*

---

[349] Strong's Word NT:1934
[350] Strong's Word NT:2212

or *seek,* but, to a Jewish mind to "seek," when used in reference to God, conjures up images of worshiping God. It is an instruction *to seek the will of God,* or *to strive to follow His ways.* Jesus is making a comparison designed to present the gentiles as craving for mammon, while the true followers of God will be those acting from a position of worship and faith.

This leads us to Jesus' well-known instruction to his followers to seek God and His righteousness above everything else, and all other things will be provided. His famous passage is often taken out of context and misused, so we need to take a closer look. The passage reads as follows:

> *But seek first the kingdom of God and His righteousness, and all these things shall be added to you.*[351]

The word *zeteo* is the one that is behind the word *seek* here, and we now understand that it means being in compliance with the will of God. Jesus is telling us that this should be our "first" priority. He is directing us to be in compliance with the tenets of the kingdom he is promoting in his sermon. But we are also being told to seek "*His righteousness.*"

The word used here for "righteousness" is one that we have looked at earlier in this book. It is the Greek word *dikaiosune.*[352] As you might recall, it has two meanings. The first is the common one used in Jesus' time meaning "equity" *in actions* and *in character, doing what is right.* The second meaning evolved later in Christian history to represent "justification" in Christ, or the imputation of Christ's righteousness in place of our sinfulness.

I have heard many sermons on Matthew 6:33 where preachers have used the meaning of Christ's imputed righteousness

---

[351] Matthew 6:33
[352] Strong's Word NT:1343

as the righteousness we are to seek. While this is good advice, it does not acknowledge the historical setting or context of Jesus' words. It also ignores the most likely understanding that Jesus' listeners would have comprehended. Jesus' message up to this point has been one of service to others as a way of being in service to God and His kingdom. It has associated this service with acts of right doing in caring for the poor, the needy, and the oppressed. It has been overflowing with themes of social justice, mercy, and forgiveness, and Jesus has just asked his listeners to not fear a lack of their basic needs when they choose to follow God. *"His righteousness"* can mean nothing more than the right actions of character that are becoming of the citizen of the kingdom of God. In short, it is *"His"* Father's brand of righteousness that he is teaching to them.

If the term *"His righteousness"* was to be confined to a post-Christ meaning of the word, why would it impose on your supply of food, drink, and clothing? Would that kind of righteousness make one worry about the "things" of life, or worry that one will go destitute of life's most basic necessities if they follow as Jesus is directing? How would *justification* relate to serving God rather than material wealth, which is the context of Jesus' subject matter? No, this righteousness is the commonly expected meaning of its day—equity of action and character. It involves faith to live the tenet of the kingdom of heaven here on earth. Faith to implement its love to others regardless of the price it may cost you.

In the Sermon on the Mount, Jesus is teaching the weightier matters of the law—justice, mercy, and faith. The faith here is not faith in an imputed righteousness that will cover your sins and allow you to enter the kingdom of heaven. It is, instead, faith to live the righteous requirements of that kingdom. Faith to be merciful, faith to be a peacemaker, faith to do the works that will cause men to glorify their Father in heaven. It is not an issue of faith versus works. It is an issue of having faith to work—because the works that Jesus wants from you will be costly. One cannot enter the kingdom free of duty or obligation to his neighbor in need. His needs must be met with our resources—be it money, intellect, skills, or time. We will have to give, and in so doing, depend on God to meet any need that our sacrifice will impose on our survival. This is the righteousness that Jesus is calling for us to seek.

Preachers of a prosperity gospel will often use this verse in Matthew to argue that if we seek the kingdom of God and His righteousness, we will become rich and have everything our heart has ever desired. I would argue that this teaching is out of context. Jesus has specifically limited his list of worries to our most basic needs in life—food, drink, and clothing. So, when Jesus promises "all these things will be added to you," he is meaning that your basic needs will be met, and you will not be left destitute. He is not guaranteeing that you will have a luxurious life here on earth—treasures are to be laid up in heaven, not on earth.

One day, while I was commuting to work, I was following a very expensive European luxury car when I noticed that the license plate frame had written on it "Matthew 6:33." I had to shake my head in disbelief, and I admit I consider the statement the driver is making to be a corruption of Jesus' instructions. Nevertheless, I will give the unknown owner the benefit of the doubt. Perhaps he is a billionaire and gives away ninety-nine percent of his wealth. Who am I to criticize his choice of vehicles if that is the case? On the other hand, I have experienced Jesus' promise on a far smaller, but meaningful, way in my life and on many occasions. I have stepped out in faith, made sacrifices, and had my life preserved as promised. Let me give you one example.

Years ago, I had the opportunity to go to Africa as a volunteer during a famine relief effort. To pursue this opportunity, I had to risk losing a well-paying job. I was also told by those recruiting me that where I was going was a remote and harsh place, and that I should bring everything I would need in order to survive with me. It was suggested that I prepare as if I was going on an extended camping trip. As a result, I arrived in that remote African country with a bulky backpack filled with equipment and various rations and survival gear.

On my first trip out of the safety of the capital city into the famine, I hauled all my treasured security paraphernalia, feeling quite insecure that it could all be stolen or lost—then what would I do? It did prove to be a remote and very harsh part of the world, as I had been warned, but what my advisors had not known was that among all that poverty and need were people who had incredibly open hearts. I was welcomed as someone who was concerned about their situation. The people shared the little food they had, shared their last pots of tea, and found cots for me to sleep on. They knew I was there to help and wanted to aid me in any way they could. I rarely opened my backpack except to give something away that I then realized I never needed.

On my second trip out of the safety of the capital city, I took my passport and wallet and a small bag with a change of clothing and a toothbrush. I knew God would supply everything else I needed. I never returned to my good job back home. Instead, I embarked on a seven-year adventure serving some of the poorest people on earth—an experience that most people fear, or only dream about. I never got rich, I owned almost nothing, but God supplied all my basic needs and enriched my life beyond all my wildest expectations—no luxury car was needed.

CHAPTER 28

Judge Not?

Judge not, that you be not judged. For with what judgment you judge, you will be judged; and with the measure you use, it will be measured back to you. And why do you look at the speck in your brother's eye, but do not consider the plank in your own eye? Or how can you say to your brother, "Let me remove the speck from your eye"; and look, a plank is in your own eye? Hypocrite! First remove the plank from your own eye, and then you will see clearly to remove the speck from your brother's eye. Do not give what is holy to the dogs; nor cast your pearls before swine, lest they trample them under their feet, and turn and tear you in pieces.

Matthew 7:1–6

The opening line of the above passage, *"Judge not, that you be not judged"* is perhaps the most abused verse in the Bible. It is often used as a way to silence opposition to one's wrongdoing, or as a way to justify conduct that one does not wish to have questioned. This is easy to do when one wishes to ignore both the explication of the original Greek, and the context of what Jesus is saying, as well as Jesus' teachings in other parts of the Gospel. We will look at this issue in more detail shortly, but first I want to point you to the context of Jesus' words, since it is the context that makes this statement meaningful in its correct light.

What is that context? In the preceding verses (covered in the previous chapter), Jesus dealt with the issue of individuals worrying about what they might have to eat or drink, or what clothing or shelter they might lack if they follow Jesus' social justice teachings. These worries stemmed from one's consideration of whether they should serve God or mammon—being abundantly generous or accumulating material wealth. In the context of the Sermon on the Mount, Jesus has appealed to his listeners to be self-sacrificing in their service to others, especially to those who are poor, needy, and oppressed. Jesus has made it clear that doing this will put you at odds with society, and will result in persecution, as well as require the sacrifice of your material wealth. The natural questions to follow would be, *How am I going to live if I do what you are asking of me?* or *What am I going to eat, or drink? What am I going to do when my clothes wear out?* Jesus answers those questions with his classic assurance that God will care for you if you seek first the kingdom of God and His right way of doing things—pursuing justice and mercy, with faith in God.

Put yourself in the place of Jesus' disciples, and all those considering becoming disciples, who are listening to this sermon on that hillside. Has Jesus convinced you to jump into the world of service? Are you now ready to seek justice for the oppressed and to begin giving of your means to those in greater need than yourself? Are you willing to throw yourself onto the mercy of God's care? Or do you still have questions? Are you still hesitating to join the service of God? I ask you, what might be the next most logical line of questions that someone who is hesitating might have for

Jesus? Would not their thoughts be turning from, *How am I going to survive?* to *Why should I help someone who has probably ruined their own life because of their mistakes? Haven't they proven to be incapable, and won't they just waste my help if I tried?* Are these not judgment calls that are being made to rationalize away the principles of the kingdom of heaven?

On the other hand, for those who have decided to be of service, a next logical question is, *Who do I help?* And that question can open the proverbial "can of worms." We want the help that we give to someone else to be—well, let us face it—helpful. As a result, we begin to look for individuals to help whom we believe will benefit greatly by what we can do for them. This creates a long chain of judgment calls regarding another's circumstances, history, and future potential. We start sizing up individuals we think we can help. And there can be hundreds of criteria to make the decision to help or not to help—we essentially become judges.

It is this natural course of events that Jesus in now addressing. He is giving his disciple's an admonishment to not become judges of who is worthy of one's help. The context of this passage is still imbedded within the ongoing social justice themes of the beatitudes and Jesus' call for good works to those in need. The passage is still an extension of Jesus' implicit call for his followers to join the service of God and to not follow mammon. But the admonishment, here, addresses our human pride, prejudices, and even racial separations. I hope you can see how Jesus is addressing the unspoken questions that his listeners are developing as he speaks. He truly is a brilliant orator, in tune with his listener's thoughts and leading them step by step.

This context is also obvious when we look at the parallel verses of this sermon as presented in the Gospel of Luke.

Luke's record has the themes of equity and charity more strongly associated with the theme of withholding judgments regarding those being helped. Here is Luke's passage:

> *But love your enemies, do good, and lend, hoping for nothing in return; and your reward will be great, and you will be sons of the Most High. For He is kind to the unthankful and evil. Therefore be merciful, just as your Father also is merciful.* ***Judge not, and you shall not be judged.*** *Condemn not, and you shall not be condemned. Forgive, and you will be forgiven. Give, and it will be given to you: good measure, pressed down, shaken together, and running over will be put into your bosom. For with the same measure that you use, it will be measured back to you.*[353]

Notice how Jesus here precedes the phrase about not judging with statements of doing good, lending freely and being merciful, followed by statements of forgiveness and a willingness to give abundantly. So, the issue that Jesus is presenting is not a broad prohibition regarding the act of judging, but rather it is a caution that we are not to make unjust or discriminating judgments which prevent us from carrying out acts of kindness in line with the character of God. This is consistent with what Jesus has taught elsewhere in the Gospels. Following is one example:

> *Do not judge according to appearances, but judge with righteous judgment.*[354]

---

[353] Luke 6:35–38
[354] John 7:24

This verse from the book of John is plainly telling us to "judge," but is also telling us to look beyond the visible circumstances, investigate the situation and make a correct judgement. Both Matthew and Luke's Sermon on the Mount accounts imply that if we judge others, we should do it as we ourselves would like to be judged if the tables were turned.

Notice that in both Matthew and Luke's versions of the Sermon on the Mount, Jesus plainly shows that some form of judgment (distinguishing or evaluating) of a situation or person has already taken place. In Luke's account, Jesus has acknowledged that we have decided that someone is an "enemy", but Jesus is telling us to set that aside and do good for them and be merciful. In Matthew's case, the brother we are dealing with does have faults, but we are not to let those faults deter us from helping him, since our own faults can be greater than his. In addition, Matthew's whole passage is concluded with an instruction that requires us to discern (judge) situations that call for us to not be of assistance to some individuals—and by implication, to avoid them.

Taking both Matthew and Luke's passages into consideration, what then does Jesus mean when he says, *"judge not"* and *"condemn not"*? The Greek word for "judge" is a word we have looked at before. It is *krino*,[355] and it means *to distinguish* or *make a decision*, either mentally or judicially. The word translated into *condemn* is the Greek word *"katadikazo."*[356] It means to *adjudicate against*, or to *pronounce guilty*. Of course, in the context of these passages, Jesus is meaning we are not to see a person in need and make a decision as to whether or not they are worthy of assistance, or guilty of some sin. A person presently in need is a person presently in need, period! At that moment they have a problem that needs to be addressed. The

---

[355] Strong's Word NT:2919
[356] Strong's Word NT:2613

most appropriate action needed may be something that should be questioned and considered, but the person's need is still one that should be addressed.

In the passage *"Judge not, that you be not judged,"* the Greek word *krino* for the word "Judge" is in its present, active, imperative form. This means it is a command from the speaker, Jesus, to the listener, the disciple. So, we are being commanded to withhold our judgments regarding a person's situation, and the context of this discourse dictates that we are to take action to be of help. In the second part of this passage, the word "judged" again comes from *krino,* but this time *krino* is in its passive, subjunctive form. That means it is an action directed toward us that is contingent or probable, or is something that is eventual in the future, provided something else occurs. That "something" is our own judgment of whether a person in need of help should, or should not, be helped. In other words, *how we will be judged* is contingent upon how *we judge* and act regarding present, or future, situations facing us.[357]

In Matthew, Jesus' next statement adds to the understanding of what Jesus means. It reads as follows:

> *For with what judgment you judge, you will be judged; and with the measure you use, it will be measured back to you.*[358]

Most commentators explain this passage to mean that God will judge us in a similar fashion as we judge others. If we are harsh in our judgments, God will be harsh with us as well. If we are stingy with the help we give to others, God will be stingy in

---

[357] Luke's use of the additional words "condemn" and "condemned" follow the same grammatical structure as "judge" and "judged" with the first being imperative and the second being subjunctive.

[358] Matthew 7:2

the help He gives to us. And conversely, if we are generous to others, God will be generous to us. Note, that the results of our actions are the basis for how God returns merit to us. And this is important to remember! Jesus is speaking of how we will be treated by God and not by mankind. Keep in mind that earlier Jesus warned us that pursuing equity and social justice will lead to persecution, being reviled, and having evil spoken about us. The unfortunate truth is that our being non-judgmental and caring for those in need can result in very harsh judgment toward ourselves by our fellow man. We should act based on our desire to be cared for and rewarded by God the Father. Our loyalty is to Him, the opinions of men should not to us from doing good. Fortunately, true Christian brothers and sisters, and other good-hearted people of this world, will be supportive of our actions, so our generosity can have reciprocating results toward us in this life—at least from some sectors of mankind.

Jesus had earlier taught us in his instruction on prayer that we would be forgiven *"as we forgive others."*[359] But forgiveness from God is not our only benefit. Being generous reciprocates generosity from God as well. In both Matthew and Luke's record on this teaching, Jesus shows that if we act toward one in need, God is going to measure back that good to us. In Luke's account, however, Jesus makes it clear that we are not capable of out-giving God. When we give, God returns to us more than what we give. Our gift will return to us in abundance either in this life or the one to come. Luke, as does Matthew, says God will use the same measure that we use, but Luke implies that God will use it more often. For example, it is as if we gave someone a gallon of milk and then we were later given three gallons by someone else—same measure, just more of them.

---

[359] Luke also inserts this phrase into his recorded account of Jesus' teaching on *judge not* and *condemn not*. See Luke 6:37

Proponents of the prosperity gospel will often use these statements as proof that God will make generous Christians rich. I will not second guess God on how He may wish to reward Christians in this life for their generous use of the resources He has entrusted to His servants. However, I would remind those of a prosperity gospel mindset that with great wealth comes greater social equity responsibilities. Do not fill your barns and set about to take life easy. It could be your earthly undoing.

In both Matthew and Luke's record of this sermon, Jesus tells us to beware of trying to correct our brother of a fault—a speck of wood in their eye—when we ourselves are suffering from a much larger fault—a plank of wood in our own eye. Doing so is hypocritical. Jesus does not prohibit anyone from correcting a brother of their faults, but he makes it clear that we need to correct our own faults first. In short, nothing is secondary to our own relationship with God. We need to focus on being right with God before we can take on the role of leading others. This situation forms the basis as to why our judgment of others should be tempered. We ourselves have our own faults to overcome, and we ourselves need help.

This passage is given within the context of our service to God and not mammon. The context is about equity and social justice, and not sizing people up as to whether they are good candidates for assistance. It therefore implies we will see many people in need who have "specks" in their eyes, but their faults and shortcomings are not to be grounds for neglect. Social justice is, after all, about lifting people up. Many are fallen due to their own faults, ourselves included. If we look only at the faults of others and make them the justifications for not acting, there will be little action, and the expansion of the kingdom of heaven cannot be realized by Jesus' followers.

Having taken all this into consideration, the listeners of Jesus are suddenly given a concluding thought that appears to contradict everything Jesus has taught up to this point. Or does it? The concluding thought is as follows:

> *Do not give what is holy to the dogs; nor cast your pearls before swine, lest they trample them under their feet, and turn and tear you in pieces.*[360]

Although we have been instructed to not be judgmental of others in need, we find that we still need to be discerning of other's motives and attitudes. There is still a case for judgment. Jesus' statement is, of course, symbolic. He is not talking about four-footed animals here. Jesus is using the common derogatory terms of the day for people who are just plain offensive. The dogs and the swine represent people who present dangers to those of us who want to serve God. They are people who will misuse the resources we might make available to them.

Most commentators will explain this verse in symbolic terms and conclude that what Jesus is saying is we should not spend our time preaching the gospel to individuals who are hostile to the word of God and are not open to receiving it. Jesus does teach this very thing in other parts of the Gospel, and it is a prudent practice, but I have concluded that this is not what Jesus is instructing us here in this instance. It would not fit the context of Jesus' theme of serving God verses serving material wealth. It does not fit his instructions to be generous to the point that we need to depend on God for what we need to live—all worries set aside. Given the current context of Jesus' sermon, the most straightforward and logical explanation here is that Jesus is telling us there are individuals who should not be helped. Yes! There are

---

[360] Matthew 7:6

those who should not be given the resources that God has entrusted us with.

Let us take a closer look at the passage in terms of generosity. First, we need to understand that anything given to the service of God is considered to be "holy." In Old Testament times, this could be money, land, crops or animals, time, or even a firstborn child. Something set aside for the service of God was deemed holy. Jesus has shown in his sermon that service to God will require our actions, our time, our empathies, and material sacrifices for others in need. Every action given for this service of God is therefore "holy." Now, Jesus instructs us that these "holy" actions and efforts are not to be wasted on "dogs" or "swine."

Similarly, "pearls" in Jesus' time were a form of material wealth. They even served as a form of currency. So, it can be argued that Jesus is instructing us that our material wealth should not be wasted on swine. But does this negate the fact that we are to be generous with our wealth and willing to give our time, energy, and emotional strengths to people in need? How does this square with Jesus' teaching that we are not to withhold our service based on our prejudices regarding one's worthiness to receive aid? What does it mean that we should not deal with dogs and swine?

The answer is straightforward, and it regards the actions of the people who act like dogs and swine. Jesus' warning presents a truth that there are people in this world who will take the kindness of others and abuse those who are being kind. In some cases, the gift itself is not valued and is misused or destroyed. In other cases, the people receiving the gifts will turn on the generous giver and destroy them. Thieves, swindlers, and extortionists come in a variety of forms and disguises, and their motives are their own greed. The kingdom of heaven's goal is equity and social justice, for everyone's benefit. It is for a just society that lifts all individuals. However, there are still dogs and swine among us that have no interest in lifting others. They only want to benefit themselves even at the expense of others. These are the people we are to avoid. We are not to feed their greed.

This, of course, requires discernment, and frankly we sometimes cannot know who the "dogs" or "swine" are, until we have dealt with them and experienced their characters. I believe Jesus has outlined a process of generosity here in this passage. We should not be judgmental. We should give each person in need the benefit of the doubt. We should consider everyone worthy of aid until they prove themselves to be unworthy. Once it becomes plain that they are motivated by greed or are a danger to us, Jesus tells us to break off dealings with such people. And this is the key to Jesus' statement; generosity is not to be conducted in a situation that imposes dangers on the generous. Generosity is not to be blind. We are to be as harmless as doves, but as wise as serpents, as we are told by Jesus in other parts of the Gospels.

In trying to understand Jesus' statement, I researched other texts in the Bible to see if any might shed light on the use of the term "dogs." I found one that does help define the term, and surprisingly, it too has a social justice connection. It is found in the book of Isaiah in a passage that is believed to be a rebuke to Israel's irresponsible leaders. It reads as follows:

> *His watchmen are blind, they are all ignorant; they are all dumb dogs, they cannot bark; sleeping, lying down, loving to slumber. Yes, they are greedy dogs which never have enough. And they are shepherds who cannot understand; they all look to their own way, every one for his own gain, from his own territory. "Come," one says, "I will bring wine, and we will fill ourselves with intoxicating drink; tomorrow will be as today, and much more abundant."*[361]

---

[361] Isaiah 56:10–12

Notice in this passage, God is giving us a picture of shepherds in a field, watching their sheep with their dogs. The shepherds on watch are no better than sleeping watchdogs. In this analogy, the watchmen are those who are supposed to be protecting the sleep—leading and caring for the people. The blind and ignorant watchmen are first equated to greedy dogs, which are in turn equated to drunken shepherds. As you can see from these verses, "dogs" are analogous to the leaders who, rather than doing their work, want a life of ease. They are greedy and never have enough. And these dogs are just like their shepherd masters who are only concerned for themselves and their own gain. And what they do gain in the way of wealth is wasted on lust for being intoxicated and surrounded by abundance. The picture that this passage presents is one of individuals who would find the self-sacrificing tenets of membership in the kingdom of heaven abhorrent. The kingdom's lifestyle is the opposite of what they want to experience.

Keep in mind that this verse in Isaiah is defining the unacceptable actions of people within the Israelite community, and they are being called "dogs." Jesus will use a similar analogy later in this sermon when he refers to dangerous false prophets, who appear to be part of the Christian community, as *"ravenous wolves"*.[362] The word "swine," on the other hand, was a term sometimes used to refer to the "unclean" gentile people who oppressed the Jews.[363] In my personal opinion, I believe

---

[362] Matthew 7:15

[363] This appears first in Psalm 80:13 where Asaph laments the fact that Israel has been forsaken by God. Israel appears in the psalm as a vine brought out of Egypt. In verse thirteen Asaph makes the statement that swine/boars from the forest have uprooted the vine—Israel. Later in Jewish literature, many sages refer to Rome as a wild, destructive boar. (In Hebrew, the word for *swine* and *boar* is identical.) For a detailed discussion of the development of this trope in rabbinic literature, see Misgav Har-Peled, Har-Peled, *The Dialogical Beast: The Identification of Rome With the Pig in Early Rabbinic Literature* (Ph.D. Dissertation, Johns Hopkins University, 2013). The

that Jesus, in this passage, is giving us instruction that we should not give our resources to people within the kingdom of heaven's community (dogs), or outside that community (swine), who would use our gifts for their greedy, corrupt, or harmful living. These are individuals whose lives are not aligned in the direction that the kingdom of heaven wishes to move society. Giving to these types of individuals is damaging and therefore dangerous to the causes of justice, mercy and faith that motivate and grow God's kingdom. We are to be cautious and not aid their opposition to Christianity and its standards.

So what is the balance between impartiality and the withholding of aid? How do we follow Jesus' command to "judge not" and yet at the same time not give our God-given resources into the wrong hands? Perhaps it can be found by discerning a person's needs verses their desires. The two are not always aligned, and when we discern that they could be in opposition to each other, we need to exercise good judgement. We need to ask ourselves, "Is the situation or request for help being given to us truthfully."

For example, a person who is plainly an alcoholic or drug addict may request money for food. But is food what they really intend to use the money for. The individual does need help, but the help they truly need may be far beyond our skills to provide. Nevertheless, all individuals do need food and we should not be prejudice against the individual because of their addiction. We could respond to the request by doing exactly what the individual requested—offer to get them food. The truly hungry individual will accept the offer and we can have the opportunity to serve them. Those who have asked for the aid under a false pretense will most likely reject the offer.

---

book of 2 Peter in the New Testament also refers to "dogs" and "swine", using the term to refer to false prophets doing damage to the Christian church. See 2 Peter 2:22.

Jesus' concluding statement to avoid dogs and swine also implies something of importance. Those who should be helped will be individuals who value the aid they have received, as well as those who do not want to see harm done to those giving the aid. They will be individuals that take the assistance they receive and use it to improve their situation, to survive, to advance, to be positioned to help others. They may have a current disadvantage, but they are not irresponsible. They will not use the aid they receive to feed their greed or lust for worthless intoxications.

While it is true our generosity should be without prejudices, our preservation and proper use of our God-given resources for the aid of others will necessitate our discernment of other's motives and goals. This discernment may only be recognized by trial and error, but the character of the dogs and swine will be self-revealing in due course. Once known, we are to act within the directions given by Jesus to use our resources wisely.

CHAPTER 29

Asking, Seeking, Knocking

Ask, and it will be given to you; seek, and you will find; knock, and it will be opened to you. For everyone who asks receives, and he who seeks finds, and to him who knocks it will be opened. Or what man is there among you who, if his son asks for bread, will give him a stone? Or if he asks for a fish, will he give him a serpent? If you then, being evil, know how to give good gifts to your children, how much more will your Father who is in heaven give good things to those who ask Him! Therefore, whatever you want men to do to you, do also to them, for this is the Law and the Prophets.

Matthew 7:7–12

This passage of Jesus' is again one that cannot be understood correctly without taking into consideration the running context of his Sermon on the Mount. This is not a standalone passage, though it is often treated that way. It is connected to Jesus' preceding statements and should be viewed as part of a much larger whole. The promises of God's response to our asking, seeking, and knocking, are conditional upon the teachings of the Law and the Prophets, and the related context of Jesus' sermon. To see this, we will need to look closer at this message, but first, let us clear up a few details regarding the language and concepts within this passage.

Commentators on these verses often frame this passage as Jesus once again teaching us how to pray. I would have to agree since I view any communication with God as a form of prayer. Prayer was an earlier topic in the Sermon on the Mount, in which Jesus taught us not to be like actors in a play. We are not to be turning prayer into a public display of piety, but instead let it be a private, genuine communication with our Father in heaven. Jesus also taught us we should not use "vain repetitions" in our prayers. This implies that our prayers need to be genuine communication rather than the voicing of repetitive patterns that can become mindless utterances which allow our focus on God to drift, even while praying.

Jesus gave a model for prayer that directed us to have faith in our heavenly Father and his system of government that we should seek to put into action here on earth—as it is in heaven. That model also focuses our attention on themes of justice and mercy. We are to ask for our daily needs rather than asking to store up for the future. We are to ask God for forgiveness, but it is conditional on our reciprocal willingness to genuinely forgive the debts and wrongs that we have experienced from others.

Now Jesus directs us to make petitions to God by asking, seeking, and knocking. Notice I did not use the words "ask", "seek," and "knock" as they appeared in the verses above. There is a good reason for this. The words in the Greek language are in a form and mood that means our requests and searches and attempts to enter are not to be a single event, but rather an ongoing, focused action. Some translations of this Bible passage use the words "keep asking," "keep seeking," and "keep knocking" to more accurately communicate the intent of Jesus' words. Likewise, the promised responses are also arranged in words that show the desired result comes to those who "keep on" asking, seeking, and knocking.

When you stop and think about this, a persistent prayer to God is an act of our faith. It demonstrates our continued reliance on God as the ultimate source of help. If this were not so, we would stop asking for His help. Instead, we do not abandon our communication with God just because He did not quickly reply. We have faith that God is listening to our prayers and that He will give us a suitable result in His good time. We also recognize the fact that God might have His own solution to what we need, and He may be leading us to a solution that will give us a better understanding of His care, as well as help us understand God's plan for our lives. We are not to give up simply because God has not acted quickly, but we are to continue to follow His leadings until we realize our quest or find He has directed us to an even better resolution. Praying in faith will lead to our faith being rewarded and strengthened.

Keep in mind that prayer is not just an opportunity to speak to God. It is also a way for us to come into his presence and hear what he has to say to us. And for frail humans as we are, this might be the more important reason for us to "keep on" praying. It helps us stay in communion with God, and gives Him the opportunity to continue to reassure us He does have everything under his control. We need to be reassured more than once, so keep praying and keep listening to what God has to say to us.

Jesus makes clear this appeal to faith by giving his listeners several examples. If we have a child that asks for bread, we do not give him a stone. If he asks for a fish, we do not give him a snake. Even as sinners we are capable of caring correctly for our own families, and doing what we can to see that they are nourished and safe. Jesus uses these examples to argue that our heavenly Father—who is good—is even better equipped to give good things to those who ask him. We should have the trust of a child approaching our father for our needs, and know that he is both able and willing to meet our request.

Now, I said earlier that I agree with Bible commentators that this passage is further instruction from Jesus on how to pray. However, let me now take a position of disagreement, because this teaching by Jesus is much broader than just having the confidence to approach God the Father. It is also a guide on how we should make our needs known to others, and have confidence to approach our neighbors or those in authority.

Notice, if you will, that Jesus never says that our asking, seeking, and knocking is to be solely directed to God. In fact, his following examples are ones which first point out that humanity is capable of correctly meeting requests from others. In Luke's record of this teaching about asking, seeking, and knocking, Jesus prefaced the discussion with a story of a man going to his neighbor's house late at night in order to get bread for an arriving guest. The neighbor is reluctant to get up, but Jesus tells us he will help, if not for the sake of friendship, at least for the persistence of the one making the request.[364]

The Sermon on the Mount does not preclude us from asking, seeking, or knocking within human realms in order to obtain a desired result. In fact, the very essence of the kingdom of heaven, being revealed by this sermon, is directing that humanity work together, justly and in mercy, to meet each other's needs. If the kingdom is working properly, seeking help from human agents should be understood as a viable pathway to addressing

---

[364] Luke 11:5–13

any issue that may arise. However, the issue, the need, or the problem would first need to be made known if others are to be aware of it and take proper actions.

I learned this lesson well during my years in Africa. Being the administrator of a water well drilling project meant I regularly had people coming to me seeking my consideration of their village as a candidate for a much-needed water well. Many of these requests came from areas that were outside of the region my donors had assigned me to work. Nevertheless, the requests, and justifications for consideration, gave me the ability to design additional projects with greater scope of work that could be submitted to a donor for consideration on future projects. Many of these projects became funded, and today there are water wells and farms in areas that would have none if the request had never been made. And this lesson was not limited to my duties as an administrator. The resolution of other needs on many levels—education, medical care, transportation, food, and so forth—would never have been addressed without someone first making the need known.

The truth is that genuine members of the kingdom of heaven are, by nature, very generous individuals who are willing to share with others. Generosity, however, needs an outlet, and if needs are not made known, resources may not move to an area of need. Problems get addressed when the generous seek those in need or when those in need make known their plight to those who are generous. Inaction is often the result of not being aware of a need, rather than insensitivity to a need. Jesus' instruction for us to keep "asking, seeking, and knocking" is more than a teaching on how to approach the Father in heaven; it is also a teaching on how we need to communicate our needs to each other as well. In doing so, we work with our neighbors and secure help, find solutions, and have doors of opportunity opened to us.

This is also evident from the closing passage within this section. Jesus concludes with what is famously known as the Golden Rule. It is as follows:

Therefore, whatever you want men to do to you, do also to them, for this is the Law and the Prophets.[365]

The Golden Rule is about interactions between mankind, not between man and God. Therefore, if we have a question, we should ask it; if we are seeking something, we should search for it high and low; if we need a door opened, we should knock on it. Jesus' examples assure us that humanity is capable of doing the right thing and that God is ultimately the one who will coordinate our efforts and see that good comes from our pursuit.

Notice that Jesus states this Golden Rule by prefacing it with the word "therefore." What came before was his discussion that the Father is more willing to be generous than man is to his fellow man. This information is then used as the basis for why we should follow the golden rule of doing for others what we want done for us. In short, Jesus is saying, "Look you guys, God is very generous to you, so you should be generous to your fellow citizens as well." So, in essence, Jesus' punch line is a teaching that is less about praying to God, and more about our being willing to help those who are seeking our help. Jesus is saying, "Help them, just like God would help you."

We should be willing to help others in their pursuits since we would want them to help us in our pursuits. When someone has a question for you, answer, because you will want your questions answered when you ask. Likewise, we should be willing to see what others seek, and give opportunities to those who knock for them—just as we ourselves would like done

---

[365] Matthew 7:12

for us. This is a lifting of humanity; a process of ensuring that one's needs and security are met; helping each person reach their potential. This is the ultimate purpose of the Law and the Prophets—the creation of a just and merciful community concerned with the advancement of everyone.

There is an important point to remember in this process that Jesus has just revealed. He has structured the pathway as one that requires repeated attempts in order to be successful—*keep on* asking, seeking, and knocking. The need to repeat our actions implies initial failure. And this should be accepted as a fact of life—ideas are often initially rejected, but their acceptance can be realized after persistent effort in convincing others of their value. Individuals or agencies that can be the solution to a problem may not initially comprehend their role or potential in being part of the solution. Jesus teaches that we will need to be persistent in order to realize the change we seek.

Now, having made that pitch, I would like to qualify my statements a bit. I do not want you to believe we do not need to approach God with our request. Quite on the contrary, I believe we should go to God as our first resort. It is God who can best coordinate the efforts of brothers and sisters who want to work together to fulfill the principles of God's kingdom.

In Luke's account of this teaching, Jesus ends the passages with the following words:

> *If you then, being evil, know how to give good gifts to your children, how much more will your heavenly Father give the Holy Spirit to those who ask Him!*[366]

Here again, we see humanity capable of dealing correctly with those we love; nevertheless, a far greater gift is the Holy

---

[366] Luke 11:13

Spirit given by the Father. It is the Holy Spirit that will help cultivate the traits needed to extend our love to others beyond our circle of family and friends. The Holy Spirit also helps fashion our petitions to God, even when we do not have a complete knowledge of what we should pray for.[367] I firmly believe that as we approach God first with our petitions—asking, seeking, and knocking—God will either act Himself or direct our minds to earthly resources and willing human collaborators who will help us accomplish our request. More often it is the latter because the kingdom of heaven is about humanity working together, within the design of God, for the benefit of humanity. God wants us to work together and have meaningful relationships with each other. What better way to do this than to have us solve problems together?

I began this chapter by mentioning that this passage of Jesus' cannot be correctly understood outside of the context of the sermon he has been giving. So, let us take a look at that context.

Jesus has opened his sermon with a list of blessings that reveal our social responsibilities to anyone that is disadvantaged or in need. He has called for the members of the kingdom of heaven to be the ones to take action to see that good is done in our communities—for the glory of God the Father. He has pointed out that the religious leaders are focusing their attentions on what the Law and Prophets prohibit rather than on the higher social good that the statutes are trying to achieve. He calls for us to reach higher standards of justice, mercy, and faith. Jesus has pointed out that our earthly resources are tools that are to be used to benefit those in need, and that doing so is an investment in heavenly riches of far greater value. He has asked us to adopt this mindset and choose to serve God, rather than a worldly accumulation of wealth for our own pleasures. From there, he has assured us that taking such a course of action will have a

---

[367] Romans 8:26

cost, but it will not leave us destitute. God the Father knows our needs, and we will be fed, clothed, and sheltered as needed. Our generosity to others is not to be prejudiced regarding whether someone in need is worthy to be helped; we should only avoid those who disguise their greed in order to get more, and misuse the resources God has given us. Those truly in need, regardless of their status, or race, or religion, are to be assisted if we can do so.

It is in this context that Jesus then tells us we should ask, seek, and knock, having faith that answers are available; that what we seek can be found; that opportunities do exist and will open up before us; and that God's kingdom here on earth can be established. The preceding, intricately tied together points of social action, justice, mercy, and faith bring us essentially to this current position where Jesus is telling us not to act on our own. Rather, we should seek answers from God and from those whose have more knowledge than we do; we should turn to others for help in finding solutions to our societies' dilemmas, and finally create opportunities by knocking on doors—that is, take an initiative to get things done, rather than waiting for something to happen. If God meant for us to work alone, Jesus would not have instructed us to "ask," "seek," or "knock." He would have just said "pray to the Father."

The justification for this collaborative activity is that we ourselves would want someone to do this for us if we were in need, so we should do the same for others when they are in need. Jesus has outlined a course of action in this passage. He is giving us a pathway to follow to accomplish change, and has directed us to have faith that this is right, it will lead to success, and that God will ultimately coordinate that success. The pathway is one that calls for coordinated efforts to address society's needs. We are to ask for help, seek willing support, and knock on the doors of possible opportunities. People will respond as the Holy Spirit leads and softens hearts, and the problems that God wants us to address will be resolved.

In the two previous sections of Jesus' sermon, he defined "faith" in a light that is quite foreign to most Christian's way of thinking. Faith, for most, is taught to be a "belief" in Jesus and his ability to forgive our sins and give us eternal life. In the Sermon on the Mount, however, Jesus is framing faith as the act of accepting the kingdom of heaven and its equity themes, and believing that if we put them into action, the Father will meet our needs. Faith is the willingness to separate from our resources for a just cause and depend on God to care for us. It is not a distant hope regarding what God will do for us in the eternity to come, but rather, it is willingness to act, here and now—to be a representative of the kingdom of heaven here on earth. This is an active, working, faith—not a passive "belief-only" faith. Faith is one's belief in, and acceptance of, the kingdom of heaven being put into action "now," regardless of the cost. It is a faith to treat others as we want to be treated.

The Sermon on the Mount is about the weightier matters of the law—justice, mercy, and faith—and this "faith" is a far different faith than many Christians want to have. The theme of the Sermon on the Mount centers on the fact that this kind of faith is what is needed to enter the kingdom of heaven, and the lack of it will result in not being part of this kingdom. Serving God is being equitable; failing, or refusing to be equitable, is serving mammon. It takes faith to serve God, because it takes faith to be equitable and depend on God as your resource for life's basic needs.

For those Christians who think these ideas are out in left field and that these verses in Matthew are only about how we should approach God the Father in prayer for spiritual needs,

I would like to point out that the Bible explicitly demonstrates that social action, justice, and mercy are prerequisites to God answering our prayers. The Prophet Isaiah opens his book with a revelation as to why God is not responding to his people and not hearing their prayers, and it comes down to a social justice issue. In part, it reads as follows:

> *When you spread out your hands, I will hide my eyes from you; even though you make many prayers, I will not hear. Your hands are full of blood. Wash yourselves, make yourselves clean; put away the evil of your doings from before my eyes. Cease to do evil, learn to do good; seek justice, rebuke the oppressor; defend the fatherless, plead for the widow.*
>
> *"Come now, and let us reason together," says the LORD, "Though your sins are like scarlet, they shall be as white as snow; though they are red like crimson, they shall be as wool. If you are willing and obedient, you shall eat the good of the land, but if you refuse and rebel, you shall be devoured by the sword."*[368]

As we have seen in earlier chapters, Isaiah also gives a similar revelation during his presentation of what constitutes an acceptable fast before God. It, too, shows that God answers our calls and is present when His people have addressed the social needs of their communities.[369] Not addressing those needs shuts down communication between God and humanity.

In light of the teachings of the Prophet Isaiah, the results that come from God when we ask, seek, and knock, would not

---

[368] Isaiah 1:15–20
[369] Isaiah Chapter 58

be possible if the verses of Matthew allow for us to not be socially involved in the justice and equity of our communities. However, the Sermon on the Mount is a social justice sermon, and those following Jesus' teachings will be able to have confidence that God will hear their prayers and act on their behalf. Treating others as we wish to be treated is, as Jesus says, an action in line with the teachings of the Law and the Prophets.

I would like to add a thought here that is a bit out of line with Jesus' context, but I feel it does have merit. Asking, seeking, and knocking need not be thought of solely as a broad response to solving social inequities. As I mentioned earlier, people with resources to help someone in need, though willing, may not be aware of the needs around them. People in need are often unwilling to make their needs known, and may not even be aware there could be a solution to a problem they might have. **Our asking, seeking, and knocking can be the simple application of us coming to our neighbors and asking them how things are going, and if there is something we can do for them.** Being in touch with our neighbors, communicating with them, lets us discover their needs and explore ways in which we can make their lives less burdensome. By asking, seeking, and knocking, not on heaven's door but rather the doors of our community, we find the avenues that help us do unto others as we would like them to do to us. Being aware of our neighbors' condition is the first step to expressing love for our neighbor—which is the second "great" commandment.

In closing this chapter, I would like to make one last observation. This concerns Jesus' presentation of the "Golden Rule."

> *Therefore, whatever you want men to do to you, do also to them, for this is the Law and the Prophets.*[370]

---

[370] Matthew 7:12

Detractors of Christ often argue that this thought is not original to Jesus and that he gets credit for it that he does not deserve. They point out that there existed similar "rules" before the time of Jesus. Confucius, for example, said, "Do not to others what you would not wish done to yourself." And within ancient Jewish literature we read, "Do not do to anyone what you yourself would hate."[371] But most similar to Jesus' saying is a quote from Hillel the Elder (Rabbi Hillel) from the first century BCE, saying, "What is hateful to you, do not do to anyone else. This is the whole law; all the rest is only commentary."[372]

Jesus' saying does have a similar structure and may very well be a response to Hillel's similar teachings. What is different with Jesus' rule is that he is not dwelling on what the law prohibits us from doing to others; rather he focuses on the ideals that the Law and the Prophets are trying to achieve. Hillel, and the teachings of the scribes and Pharisees that Jesus addresses in the Sermon on the Mount, are focused on what I would consider a negative orientation to God's law. Jesus, on the other hand, takes the same law and focuses our attention on a positive orientation. The rabbis and religious leaders were fixated on prohibitions; Jesus was focused on what is permitted, positive and possible.

Both sayings of Hillel and Jesus are true but are derived from different planes of view. It is this difference in how Jesus and the religious leaders of his day saw the law that led to the tensions between them. For example, when Jesus healed on a Sabbath day, the leaders saw him working and breaking the Sabbath. Jesus, on the other hand, saw it as an act of releasing someone from a burden—the very essence of what keeping the Sabbath is to be. The leaders looked at the law and saw a prohibition; Jesus looked at the law and saw permission.

---

[371] Tobit 4:15

[372] Talmud, Shabbat 31a

CHAPTER 30

The Narrow Gate

Enter by the narrow gate; for wide is the gate and broad is the way that leads to destruction, and there are many who go in by it. Because narrow is the gate and difficult is the way which leads to life, and there are few who find it.

Matthew 7:13–14

When I was a child, my mother read to me and my siblings John Bunyan's classic Christian tale, *The Pilgrim's Progress*. I have a rather vivid imagination, so the story came to life for me and was an exciting adventure. Bunyan's pilgrim, named "Christian," had found the narrow gate and the difficult way, and was determined to travel it all the way to the Celestial City that lay at the end of its course. No doubt, Bunyan's tale was sparked by this statement of Jesus.' I will have to confess, I have often wished that the way to eternal life was, indeed, a physical route leading from earth to heaven as presented in Bunyan's religious allegory. However, this is not the reality that Jesus is trying to convey. It is, of course, a word picture framed within our physical world to help us mentally grasp our spiritual walk with God. So, what is it that Jesus means by this statement of his?

Once again, context is the key to understanding where Jesus is going with this statement. This is not just a clever picture that Jesus is attempting to create with words for the benefit of his disciples and for the creation of captivating stories. It is deliberately stated and carefully synced with Jesus' ongoing theme of social equities, and the teachings of the Old Testament, which his listeners knew well. Keep in mind what Jesus said, immediately preceding this statement:

> *Therefore, whatever you want men to do to you, do also to them, for this is the Law and the Prophets.*[373]

This revelation that doing good for others is the message of the Law and the Prophets—the word of God—is therefore the basis of picturing the way to life as entering a narrow gate and proceeding on a difficult way. It is likewise the basis for picturing the loss of life occurring by entering a broad, easier way, that leads to destruction. Jesus is not changing his sermon to new subject matter; rather he is incorporating Old Testament word pictures to support his claim that doing good is the essence of God's word.

The Old Testament has many analogies that create a picture of following God's commandments as being akin to walking a safe pathway. Perhaps the best known, and most quoted, of these is the verse found in Psalm 119:105, which states:

> *Your word is a lamp to my feet and a light to my path.*

This verse taken by itself gives no explicit indication there is a need for one to love his neighbor via deeds of kindness, jus-

---

[373] Matthew 7:12

tice, or equity. However, in the much broader context of Psalm 119, it becomes abundantly plain that this pathway is one of obedience to God's law and everything the law implies. Earlier in Psalm 119, King David, the author, states:

> *Give me understanding, and I shall keep your law; indeed, I shall observe it with my whole heart. Make me walk in the path of your commandments, for I delight in it. Incline my heart to your testimonies, and not to covetousness. Turn away my eyes from looking at worthless things, and revive me in your way.*[374]

Notice in this passage that for King David, walking within the path of God's commandments and testimonies involves avoiding covetousness and a desire for worthless things. He has juxtaposed walking with God, with greed for material or even political gains.

King David's son, Solomon, also held a similar view. In his book of Proverbs, Solomon uses the analogy of wisdom being the reverence and obedience to God's statutes in our lives. Walking outside of God's ways was to walk in the ways of those doing evil. In one of his councils to shun evil, Solomon tells us:

> *My son, do not walk in the way with them* [the evil], *keep your foot from their path; for their feet run to evil. . . . so are the ways of everyone who is greedy for gain; it takes away the life of its owners.*[375]

Solomon has delineated two paths, just as Jesus has. One path leads to life, and the other leads to life being taken away. Interest-

---

[374] Psalm 119:34–37
[375] Proverbs 1:15–19

ingly, Solomon has also tied the actions of the evil—walking the wrong path—as being motivated by greediness for gain. As you can recall, "greediness for gain" is the definition of the Aramaic word "mammon," which Jesus had referenced earlier in his sermon as the wrong master to follow.

Solomon goes on to inform his "son" with counsel that is more direct and broader in application, saying:

> For the Lord gives wisdom; from His mouth come knowledge and understanding; He stores up sound wisdom for the upright; He is a shield to those who walk uprightly; He guards the paths of justice, and preserves the way of His saints. Then you will understand **righteousness** and **justice, equity** and **every good path**. (emphasis added)[376]

Notice Solomon's connection to wisdom, words from God, walking in the right way and a resulting understanding of "*every good path*." Notice especially that he has grouped righteousness, justice, and equity as among "*every good path*." The implication is that there are other "good paths," but the most prominent and mentionable ones are the paths of righteousness, justice, and equity. None of these good paths are accomplished in a vacuum; they require a community, a set of problems and social inequities, and actions by individuals to make things right, just, and equitable.

By presenting these two teachings in parallel—the Golden Rule and the narrow path—Jesus is defining the Golden Rule as synonymous with the Old Testament's pathway to life teachings, namely obedience to the law, justice, equity, shunning greediness for gain. It is a link, paraphrasing well-known biblical illustrations, that his listeners could easily

---

[376] Proverbs 2:6–9

grasp. Jesus' analogy in the Sermon on the Mount, though far more concise, has added detail to the condition of this pathway. As with Solomon's proverbs, Jesus inserts warnings to those wanting to follow the right path, as well as to those who do not.

In this "narrow gate/difficult way" statement, Jesus uses a variety of words that does not sugar coat the prospects of what lies ahead for the travelers of each road. Let us briefly look at these.

First, the gate is said to be narrow. The word "narrow" here comes from the Greek word *stenos*,[377] which means *narrow*, as in narrow because of *obstacles standing close by*. It is passable, but it requires some navigation to get through it. The word from which our text derives the English word "difficult" is the Greek word, *thlibo*[378], which means *to crowd*. It comes from a root word that conveys the image of a narrow rut or worn track. *Thlibo* is often translated to mean *afflict, suffer, trouble* or *tribulation*.

Jesus' picture is clear; the road to life is one that requires a commitment to begin with; the gate at the start has obstacles that must be navigated. And then the road continuing beyond the gate is no walk in the park either; it will be crowded with obstacles as well. This is not new information coming from Jesus. His sermon has already shown us that being an active member of the kingdom of heaven means getting involved in helping others in need. That action will have a cost to us and will most likely make us more dependent on God for our basic needs. Helping to bear others' burdens, implicitly means taking part of the load upon ourselves; it is work, and it can be difficult. Jesus also concluded his beatitudes of social action with the revelation that those carrying out such actions will be persecuted. It is, no doubt, part of what will make the road to

---

[377] Strong's Word NT:4728
[378] Strong's Word NT:2346

life difficult. Not everyone will see the value of the justice, and mercy of the kingdom of heaven, and they will oppose those who uphold its values.

The wide gate and the broad way are the exact opposite of the way to life. There are no obstacles one must navigate around to get onto this road. The road itself is not rutted or difficult; there are no great sacrifices, and those on this path will experience little opposition as they stroll toward its final destination. Unfortunately, however, according to Jesus, this road leads to "*destruction.*" This word comes from the Greek word, *apoleia,*[379] and it means *ruin* or *loss*. It is used three other times in the New Testament[380] regarding living beings, and on all three occasions it is referring to those who have, or will, lose eternal life.

Jesus gives his listeners only two options: we are either on the difficult road to life or the easy road to destruction. The choice of which one to take does appear to be ours, however. Nevertheless, Jesus does instruct us on which way we should seek and take—he tells us "enter by the narrow gate."

Two options are all that Jesus ever gives in any of his gospel teachings. At the end of this sermon, he will divide the listeners into two groups; the wise who hear his words and follow, versus the foolish who hear and do not follow. Notice these two groups are derived from those who have been exposed to Jesus' words but react in opposite ways. Also, at the judgment at the end of the age, there will be found two groups: the sheep and the goats. In each case the two groups are faced with either life or the loss of life.

I would also like to point out one other piece of evidence that this statement of Jesus' has the social justice orientation that I have presented. It comes from the biblically recorded fact

---

[379] Strong's Word NT:684

[380] John 17:12 and Revelation 17:8,11

that the early Christian church movement was first known as the "Way." This fact is recorded in the book of Acts 9:2.[381] I do not think it is a coincidence that the term "way" came to describe early Christianity. Scripturally, the "way" was already synonymous with following God correctly. Jesus made references to himself being "the way, the truth, and the life." And as we have seen, he used the word picture of the path to life being a difficult "way"—one associated with social justice, mercy, and equity.

This early Christian church—the "Way" movement in its infancy—fashioned their conduct and relationships to others according to what they perceived Jesus had taught them. And how was this instruction perceived, and what kind of society of believers did it create? The book of Acts tells us what life was like for these early adherents of the teachings of Jesus. It states:

> Now all who believed were together, and had all things in common, and sold their possessions and goods, and divided them among all, as anyone had need. So, continuing daily with one accord in the temple, and breaking bread from house to house, they ate their food with gladness and simplicity of heart, praising God and having favor with all the people. And the Lord added to the church daily those who were being saved.[382]

These are the people, nearest to the time of Christ, accepting the Christian message from his closest disciples. What they learn and choose to do leads to the creation of a small society that is equitable to all its members, while seeking to eliminate

---

[381] See also Acts 19:9, 23; 24:14, 22
[382] Acts 2:44–47

need. This was the "Way" they chose to live based on their understanding of the words of Jesus.

In closing my comments on this passage, I would like to point out this is the third time Jesus has taught within this sermon, that following God and entering into the kingdom of heaven, requires discernment and decision. And, as Jesus has pointed out, the decisions are between life-or-death options. Jesus' first warning was near the beginning of his sermon; he told his listeners that entrance into the kingdom of heaven hinged on whether one loosened the commandments or did the commandments—obedience to God's law is important.[383] Shortly afterwards, Jesus taught the need to decide between serving God or mammon.[384] Jesus has now come full circle, by making the point with a new illustration. This time it is the path you choose; one leading to life, the other to destruction.

Jesus is emphasizing, and re-emphasizing, to his listeners that this message of his is of great importance. So great, in fact, that if they miss his points, or choose not to heed his instructions, they will forfeit their entrance into the kingdom of heaven, and forgo eternal life with God. He had already given a similar warning earlier when he demonstrated six times that the religious leaders were failing to teach the life-giving law correctly. Now he will give one more life-or-death illustration as he closes his sermon, but first he gives an additional warning to the crowd that this message of his will come under attack by people who want to alter his words and steer them away from the truths he has presented. This deception, Jesus warns, will once again be from within the apparent followers of the message itself. We will now turn our attention to this intriguing warning.

---

[383] Matthew 5:18–20
[384] Matthew 6:24

CHAPTER 31

Prophets, Wolves and Fruit

Beware of false prophets, who come to you in sheep's clothing, but inwardly they are ravenous wolves. You will know them by their fruits. Do men gather grapes from thornbushes or figs from thistles? Even so, every good tree bears good fruit, but a bad tree bears bad fruit. A good tree cannot bear bad fruit, nor can a bad tree bear good fruit. Every tree that does not bear good fruit is cut down and thrown into the fire. Therefore, by their fruits you will know them.

Matthew 7:15–20

From the analogy of "life" being a journey through a narrow gate and a difficult path, Jesus immediately warns his listeners to "beware of false prophets." This connection is not by accident but by design on Jesus' part. The Old Testament has frequently coupled the concept of following a prophet as being synonymous with the way one is walking with God, or without God. In either case, following a true prophet or following a false prophet brings one into a "walk" or "way" that either leads to life or some form of destruction. The book of Psalms is filled with many such examples. Its very first chapter and verse start with this theme and read as follows:

> *Blessed is the man who **walks** not in the counsel of the ungodly, nor stands in the **path** of sinners. . . . For the Lord knows the **way** [road] of the righteous, but the **way** [road] of the ungodly shall perish.* (emphasis added)[385]

Jesus' warning is meant to be understood as there are people who will try to direct you off the difficult way that leads to life and onto the broad way that leads to destruction. He refers to these people as "false prophets" and "ravenous wolves" and indicates that we will be able to identify them by their fruits. Since this is a life-or-death matter, I feel we should take a much closer look at these three elements—prophets, wolves, and fruit—so that we stay on the correct path. Let us begin our research.

A. Prophets

As Christians, we are familiar with the concept of prophets as mentioned in the Bible. We are familiar with the fact there are true prophets and false prophets. Most often, a "prophet" is thought of as someone having a close connection to God, and one who receives special revelations from Him. The revelations often come in the form of a voice, or a vision, or a dream. A prophet in the Bible does not need to be a shaman or someone with supernatural powers. They are generally regular human beings, spiritually inclined, through whom God chooses to communicate His word to the rest of us.

There is little mention of the position of "prophet" prior to the law given to Moses by God on Mt. Sinai. The book of Genesis

---

[385] Psalm 1:1, 6. Note: "Way" is translated from Strong's Word OT:1870, "road" or "course of life."

has King Abimelech making one passing reference to Abraham as a prophet.[386] The book of Exodus quotes God as saying He will give Moses his brother Arron to speak for him as if he was Moses' prophet.[387] And the book of Numbers makes two references to prophet(s). The first laments the fact that the camp of Israel in the wilderness had too few prophets,[388] and the second is God referring to Moses as being in a relationship with him that is superior to that of a prophet.[389]

It is not until the book of Deuteronomy that the Bible begins to spell out the role of a prophet and gives clues on how to spot a false one. The passage is quite important and reads as follows:

> *If there arises among you a prophet or a dreamer of dreams, and he gives you a sign or a wonder, and the sign or the wonder comes to pass, of which he spoke to you, saying, "**Let us go** after other gods"—which you have not known—"and let us serve them," you shall not listen to the words of that prophet or that dreamer of dreams, for the Lord your God is testing you to know whether you love the Lord your God with all your heart and with all your soul. You shall **walk** after the Lord your God and fear Him, and keep His commandments and obey His voice; you shall serve Him and hold fast to Him. But that prophet or that dreamer of dreams shall be put to death, because he has spoken in order to turn you away from the Lord your God, who brought you out of the land of Egypt and redeemed you from the house of bondage, to entice you from*

---

[386] Genesis 20:7

[387] Exodus 7:1

[388] Numbers 11:29

[389] Numbers 12:6

*the **way** in which the Lord your God commanded you to **walk**.* (emphasis added)[390]

This passage deals with false prophets, but the information given, when taken in reverse, also gives us some big clues as to the role of a true prophet. Notice that the primary goal of a false prophet is to entice the people of God away from their "walk after the Lord your God." This "walk" is framed by fearing (respecting) God, keeping His commandments, obeying His voice, serving and holding fast to Him. Anyone attempting to cause another to deviate from this God-given path is a false prophet. Taking this information in reverse would indicate that a true prophet would be one who is not enticing us away from God. Rather, they would be encouraging us to keep his commandments, obey his voice and be steadfast in our service to God. This closely follows the Prophet Isaiah's admonition which states:

To the law and to the testimony! If they do not speak according to this word, it is because there is no light in them.[391]

It should be noted that these false prophets have the ability to dream visionary dreams and to give signs or wonders that can, indeed, come true. They might not be true prophets, but they do have real powers. However, more notable than even this, is the fact that God reveals that these false prophets could be a test that He is sending, or using, to see whether or not we genuinely love Him with all our heart and soul. This fact is revealed in other parts of the Bible as well; followers of God will be tested for loyalty to God—both by God and by the enemies of God.

---

[390] Deuteronomy 13:1–5
[391] Isaiah 8:20

In Deuteronomy 18, Moses also reveals that God has said He is going to send a prophet in the future that will be like Moses. This likeness is found in the fact that this prophet will also be given God's words that he will speak to the people. These words will, of course, need to be in line with God's law and testimony, as conditioned in Deuteronomy 13, if this prophet is to pass the test of being a true prophet. Deuteronomy 18, however, also gives us more information concerning the identification of false prophets. The passage reads as follows:

> *I will raise up for them a prophet like you from among their brethren, and will put my words in His mouth, and He shall speak to them all that I command Him. And it shall be that whoever will not hear my words, which He speaks in my name, I will require it of him. But the prophet who presumes to speak a word in my name, which I have not commanded him to speak, or who speaks in the name of other gods, that prophet shall die.' And if you say in your heart, "How shall we know the word which the Lord has not spoken?"—when a prophet speaks in the name of the Lord, if the thing does not happen or come to pass, that is the thing which the Lord has not spoken; the prophet has spoken it presumptuously; you shall not be afraid of him.*[392]

In short, Deuteronomy 18 tells us that if a "prophet" presumes to speak in a name other than God's, or if he makes

---

[392] Deuteronomy 18:18–22. Note the English word "afraid" used in the last line of this passage is the Hebrew word *guwr* (Strong's Word OT:1481). It can mean "fear", but it also means to "turn aside from a road" or "sojourn". So, a more contextual translation of this word would be that we "should not travel in a false prophet's path."

a prediction in God's name that does not come true, he is a false prophet. This should not be confused with the passage of Deuteronomy 13, where the false prophet has powers to make signs and wonders come to pass. Here, the test of falseness is a prediction made in the name of God that does not come true—signs and wonders need not be predictions.

This passage in the law is, of course, the one that led the religious leaders in John the Baptist's day to ask him if he was, "The Prophet".[393] So, even in the time of Christ, the Jews were still looking for this prophet. In fact, many still are looking for him today.

I hope that the division between a true and a false prophet is beginning to become clear. True prophets have a limited scope of operation. What they have to say or teach must be in accordance with God's established word as given in the law, and if they make a prediction in the name of God it would have to come true. Their message is one that needs to lead the people toward God and his given words.

False prophets, on the other hand, have an unlimited scope of deceptive actions. They can say or do just about anything they want. They do not even have to be prophets; they can just claim that they have a word from God. Their visions can come from an evil source or, according to the Bible, be just made up within their own minds.[394] They may just be posing as enlightened leaders or teachers, possibly self-deluded, but their goal is to direct people to their opinions. Their message can be anything, but ultimately it is one that leads away from the true God and His words. Their message may also lead toward other gods, or to no god at all.

For many false prophets, their deceptive powers lie in their ability to carefully mix truth and error so that the error is cam-

---

[393] John 1:23–25
[394] Jeremiah 14:14 and Jeremiah 23:16

ouflaged by truth. They will convince people that they are on the difficult way, when in fact they have directed them onto the broad way. The first biblical example of this technique is plainly seen with Satan's deception of Adam and Eve in the Garden of Eden.[395] Satan, the serpent, questioned God's word, and was able to persuade Eve that God's words did not mean what she thought they meant. Eve took the serpent's bait and fell. Adam, in short course, tumbled after Eve.

The true prophets of the Bible give us more details concerning the identifying marks of false prophets. The Prophet Jeremiah pointed out that they contradicted his messages from God. If God, through Jeremiah, said there was going to be famine and no peace, the false prophets said there would be peace and no famine. He also reveals that the false prophets were committing adultery, walking in lies, and strengthening the hands of the evil doers.[396] The Prophet Micah tells us that false prophets made predictions in exchange for money.[397] And Ezekiel, in writing about the wickedness of Israel's leaders in his day, mentions how the prophets covered up the truth with falsehoods and did not guide the people back to the word of God. As a result, the people "*used oppressions, committed robbery, and mistreated the poor and needy; and they wrongfully oppress the stranger*".[398] Morality and love of neighbor quickly declines when a population is under the influence of false prophets.

Ezekiel's message is remarkably interesting in that it concerns the same issues being confronted by Jesus—social justice being thwarted by false prophets. The Sermon on the Mount is a social justice message founded on love for God

---

[395] Genesis 3; Revelation 20:2

[396] Jeremiah 23:13

[397] Micah 3:11

[398] Ezekiel 23:23–29

and love for our neighbors. Jesus is calling for full devotion to God and love for our neighbors with equity and justice. He has promised blessings to people who are taking actions to stop oppression, and helping the poor and needy, and freeing others of their burdens—the essence of God's law. It should come as no surprise that Jesus would use the term false prophet in his warning that we should beware of anyone who would teach or allow otherwise.

B. Ravenous Wolves

Jesus' reference to ravenous wolves and its connection to false prophets and teachers, is also very deliberate and biblical. The first biblical reference we have to a "ravenous wolf" is a surprising one. It is found in Jacob's blessing to his youngest son Benjamin. Generally, a blessing is a positive statement of hope regarding one's future and that of his family to come. Unfortunately, this was not the case for Benjamin. Jacob's blessing was short and quite negative; not at all what a son would like to hear from his dying father. It reads as follows:

> *Benjamin is a **ravenous wolf**; in the morning he shall devour the prey, and at night he shall divide the spoil.* (emphasis added)[399]

The word translated as *"ravenous"* is the Hebrew word *taraph*.[400] It means *to pluck off* or *to pull to pieces*. It gives us the mental picture of the prey being pulled apart and divided. This picture is reinforced by the blessing's repetitive structure and use of the words *devour* and *divide*.

---

[399] Genesis 49:27
[400] Strong's Word OT:2963

Sadly, the tribe of Benjamin frequently fulfilled this pronouncement of Jacob's. The book of Judges records a story regarding how the sins of one of the villages of the tribe of Benjamin results in civil war and a large loss of life within Israel.[401] It is also reflected in the failed monarchy of King Saul, a Benjamite. Saul was originally handpicked by God to be Israel's first king. Eventually, however, he departed from following God and God's commands, and his kingdom experienced divided loyalties between himself and God's anointed replacement—King David.

The Hebrew word *taraph* also appears in the book of Ezekiel the prophet, and it once again depicts the wayward people of God as divided, or being torn in pieces, due to the sins of their leaders. The list of errors provided by Ezekiel closely matches the themes that Jesus' Sermon on the Mount is seeking to correct. Notice as many of these errors as you can, as you read Ezekiel's message, which follows:

> *And the word of the Lord came to me, saying, "Son of man, say to her: 'You are a land that is not cleansed or rained on in the day of indignation.' The conspiracy of her prophets in her midst is like a roaring lion **tearing the prey** [taraph]; they have devoured people; they have taken treasure and precious things; they have made many widows in her midst. Her priests have violated My law and profaned My holy things; they have not distinguished between the holy and unholy, nor have they made known the difference between the unclean and the clean; and they have hidden their eyes from My Sabbaths, so that I am profaned among them. Her princes in her midst are like*

---

[401] Judges chapter 19 and 20

*wolves **tearing the prey** [taraph], to shed blood, to destroy people, and to get dishonest gain. Her prophets plastered them with untempered mortar, seeing false visions, and divining lies for them, saying, 'Thus says the Lord God,' when the Lord had not spoken. The people of the land have used oppressions, committed robbery, and mistreated the poor and needy; and they wrongfully oppress the stranger."* (emphasis added)[402]

Wow! Is this not this the flip side of the Sermon on the Mount in a nutshell?

The reference above to *"conspiracy of her prophets"* appears in different forms in ancient texts. Some texts indicate "princes" rather than prophets, while others make reference to "scribes." In all cases, the passage would be referring to leaders of the people—political or religious—and pointing out their characters and failed leadership.

Ezekiel's above list of failures closely reflects many of Jesus' themes. It presents injustices to the people, robberies and inequities, violations of God's law, the law being incorrectly taught by the religious leaders, and they have lost the ability to understand what is holy and unholy. The social justice and equity mandates of God's Sabbath systems are being ignored. Love of neighbor is replaced by the desire to get dishonest gains, and oppression follows. Robbery, mistreatment of the poor and needy, and oppression of strangers is the resulting condition of the nation. The weak become the prey of the strong and are being ripped apart and devoured. Are not these the very things that Jesus is calling for his listeners to stop and to reverse?

Matthew uses a Greek word in his record of the sermon to describe the "ravenous" wolves. The Greek word translated

---

[402] Ezekiel 22:23–29

"ravenous" is *harpax*,[403] and it means *rapacious* or *aggressively greedy or grasping*. While the Greek word may be a good equivalent for the Hebrew word *taraph*, it does not fully picture the division being caused by the actions of the wolves. If Jesus is intentionally using Old Testament symbolism of ravenous wolves as destroyers of God's designed social structure, and I believe he is, then the divisions to society that they cause are part of what he is trying to convey. Yes, wolves are greedy and aggressive, but this greed and aggression is leading to the pulling apart of God's people—just as the Hebrew word conveys.

Stop and think for a moment about the implications of Jesus' warning, considering what we have learned regarding false prophets and ravenous wolves. Jesus' Sermon on the Mount has been calling for social justice considerations. He has addressed the need for members of the kingdom of heaven to help the poor and the suffering. We are to seek what is right and to relieve the burdens of oppression. We are to share our wealth even to the point that we need to depend on God for our basic needs. We have been plainly told that we cannot serve both God and a desire to accumulate material wealth. Jesus' message has not deviated from the goals of God's Old Testament laws to love our neighbors. His message has mirrored the sabbatical themes of social justice and equity—rest and release from burdens and periodic economic redistribution. In the context of this message, Jesus warns us to beware of people who are trying to take us away from this pathway because they are greedy and materialistic—seeking control over the weak and getting dishonest gains. The wolves are those individuals who will direct us onto the broad pathway and will tear the kingdom of heaven apart if not seen for what they truly are.

This is a very solemn warning and one that we Christians may not have heeded. Have false prophets—

---

[403] Strong's Word NT:727

wolves masquerading as sheep—influenced Christianity? Has Christianity suffered from division? Is our focus on something other than our obligations to love our neighbors, to seek justice and equity, and lift the poor and comfort the needy? Have we been too focused on increasing the number of sheep while missing the message concerning how we are to be treating the sheep, and the world as a whole? We should not focus on one and exclude the other. Jesus' parting command to his followers is to "go" into all the nations and make "disciples" who "observe all things that I have commanded you."[404] Yes! This is a call to expand the kingdom of heaven, but it is equally a call to live the tenets of the kingdom as well. Can one truly be a disciple of Jesus' if they do not follow his words?

Today, there are well over three hundred different Christian denominations even though we all have only one king—Jesus Christ. Each denomination feels that their version of Christianity is best, and there is a focus on recruiting "Christians" from other denominations. Sadly, the Bible and various interpretations of its messages have become a point of division that can isolate and paralyze Christians from working toward a common goal. The divisions can cause suspicion toward others and a feeling of superiority—a kind of Christian bigotry. Each denomination focuses resources on maintaining and building its own individual institutions, and too often their leaders begin to concentrate on internal empire building. And as institutions grow, their resources are directed inward, and the denominations focus on their survival rather than the plain truths of Jesus' words.

Jesus' desire was, and still is, for a unified Christian body that is an active force for change in its families, communities, nations, and the world at large. This change was not just to be a

---

[404] Matthew 28:18-20. This parting command is often referred to as Jesus' "Great Commission" to his followers.

spiritual model; it was to be a template to put love of neighbor into action, to cultivate social justices, correct inequities, and be a conduit to meet the needs of the poor, wounded, and oppressed. Christians are to be the "pure in heart" of the earth, and to be its peacemakers–working toward a just society that the followers of mammon do not want, or cannot see the wisdom of its presence. Where would the world be today if Christianity had remained unified and focused on Jesus' teachings? Heaven only knows.

C. Fruits

Besides the Old Testament precedence that helps us comprehend the meanings of the terms "false prophets" and "ravenous wolves," Jesus gave us one more clue on how to discern who might be a false prophet, of which to beware. The clue is to look at the fruits that a person bears. Jesus says:

> *You will know them by their fruits. Do men gather grapes from thornbushes or figs from thistles? Even so, every good tree bears good fruit, but a bad tree bears bad fruit. A good tree cannot bear bad fruit, nor can a bad tree bear good fruit. Every tree that does not bear good fruit is cut down and thrown into the fire. Therefore, by their fruits you will know them.*[405]

This clue, unlike the previous two, has no Old Testament pattern or symbolism to draw upon. The analogy appears to be one drawn from Jesus' time. The closest reference we can turn to is that of the sermons of John the Baptist. John used the analogy of fruit trees and their productivity as a symbol of obeying the

---

[405] Matthew 7:16–20

will of God. Jesus' message in this passage closely parallels that of the sermons of John. We find the references in both the Gospels of Matthew and Luke, but Luke's Gospel also reveals what John meant by "*good fruit*." The quote is as follows:

> *Then he* [John] *said to the multitudes that came out to be baptized by him, "Brood of vipers! Who warned you to flee from the wrath to come?* **Therefore, bear fruits worthy of repentance. . . . And even now the ax is laid to the root of the trees. Therefore, every tree which does not bear good fruit is cut down and thrown into the fire.**
>
> *So, the people asked him, saying, "What shall we do then?"* [John] *answered and said to them, "He who has two tunics, let him give to him who has none; and he who has food, let him do likewise."*
>
> *Then tax collectors also came to be baptized, and said to him, "Teacher, what shall we do?" And* [John] *said to them, "Collect no more than what is appointed for you."*
>
> *Likewise, the soldiers asked him, saying, "And what shall we do?" So,* [John] *said to them, "Do not intimidate anyone or accuse falsely, and be content with your wages."* (emphasis added)[406]

John's use of the fruit tree analogy plainly points to "good fruits" as being actions of care for one's neighbor, equity, and justice in society. We can conclude from this that "bad fruit" would be the disregard for one's neighbors, greed, and injustice, to name a few.

Jesus used the fruit tree analogy on one other occasion in his ministry, and within that context the fruit represents the good or

---

[406] Luke 3:7–14. Also see Matthew 3:7–12

bad words we speak. There the words function as a revelation of the condition of our hearts, and the words we speak become the basis on which we are judged on the day of judgment.[407]

In addition, Jesus also uses an analogy of a vine, branches, and fruit in the book of John. This analogy parallels that of his message in the Sermon on the Mount, but here in John it refers only to the relationship between God, Jesus, and the followers of Christ, and has nothing to do with false prophets. It does have elements in common: followers of Christ are to bear fruit, and God works to help those who abide in Him to bear much fruit. Anyone who chooses to not abide in the vine (and thus bear no fruit) is removed and burned—the same fate as the trees with bad fruit in John the Baptist's message.[408]

This is the explanation of "fruit" in the Gospels. Its main meaning focuses on the righteous actions of the followers of Christ toward all mankind. Good fruit in the context of the Sermon on the Mount will be the fulfilment of the equity, justice, and love of neighbor mandates that Jesus is presenting as the theme of his sermon. Later in the New Testament, the analogy of fruits is extended to traits of good character. This is a logical extension, after all, a godly character and good deeds do go hand in hand. However, this extension does tend to dilute the original intent of the Gospel meaning.

So, what can we say in conclusion regarding Jesus' warning to us? As we can see, Jesus' warning to beware of false prophets who come in sheep's clothing but are actually ravenous wolves, is simple enough, but failing to understand the correct path to life as presented by Jesus in the Sermon on the Mount, will blind us from discerning who the false prophets are. His warning shows us they will appear to be Christian leaders, but rather than leading us toward God's law and its love for God

---

[407] Matthew 12:31–37

[408] See John chapter 15

and neighbor and its resulting unity, they will be motivated by forms of greed and control. Our God-given resources will be solicited and secured for purposes not within the confines of Jesus' message. The use of those resources will fail to address the justice and equity goals that Jesus has indicated as the difficult way. I do not care to define how this might be manifested, since each situation is unique. Rather, I will let the reader, under God's direction, be guided to avoid the danger of which we are being warned. Keep in mind, the wolves will be directing you away from the words of Christ. Be alert and beware!

Chapter 32

You Who Practice Lawlessness

> Not everyone who says to Me, "Lord, Lord," shall enter the kingdom of heaven, but he who does the will of My Father in heaven. Many will say to Me in that day, "Lord, Lord, have we not prophesied in Your name, cast out demons in Your name, and done many wonders in Your name?" And then I will declare to them, "I never knew you; depart from Me, you who practice lawlessness!"
>
> Matthew 7:21–23

Jesus' disciples and a crowd of people eager to hear this new rabbi, had gathered that day long ago on a mountainside, anticipating a new revelation of spiritual truths. Word had been circulating that John the Baptist had endorsed Jesus as the new spiritual leader of a coming kingdom of heaven. The people had questions on their mind and were eager for answers; "What is this coming kingdom of heaven? How do I enter it? What will it require from me, and how will it benefit me?" For some time now they have sat on the hillside listening to Jesus and have learned that "they" are this kingdom if they put into practice the laws of God which they have possessed for over a thousand years.

These laws, according to Jesus, have been misunderstood, incorrectly taught, and improperly applied, and often just plain ignored. Jesus has revealed that the essence of the law is to extend love to one's neighbor, to respect others' families and property, and to ensure the weak and disadvantaged among society are cared for and given the means and opportunity to succeed. And remarkably, to a Jewish mind of Jesus' day, he has also taught that this love is to be extended to one's enemies, not just neighbors. A major theme of the sermon has been that the law requires devotion to God and love for our neighbors, and not a devotion to the accumulation of material wealth. Love, along with faith in God to put that love into practice, is the narrow gate and the difficult way that few find and follow to eternal life.

Moments before uttering the above passage we are currently investigating in this chapter, Jesus had warned his listeners they needed to beware of false prophets. These prophets would be integrated among the members of the kingdom of heaven. They would appear like sheep within the flock, but this would only be a disguise. They would instead act as hungry wolves dividing and destroying the sheep, and trying to direct the true followers away from the tenets of the kingdom. Jesus, however, gave a clue on how to identify them—by their fruits you will know them.

From our study in the last chapter, we learned that Moses, within the law itself,[409] also warned of false prophets. He, too, gave clues on how to identify them. It was revealed that they can have powers to work successful signs and wonders. However, their ultimate end is to entice the followers of God away from keeping his commandments and obeying His voice—that is, to entice them to love other gods and to not love one's neighbor as himself. This is the bad fruit that will eventually ripen and reveal the identity of those who are not walking in God's path.

---

[409] Deuteronomy 13:1–5; 18:20–22

Jesus' words in Matthew 7:21–23 parallel Moses' warning about false prophets. It is not word for word, but it is thought for thought. Jesus is still on the topic of false prophets and is adding one more layer of identification regarding them. They address him as "Lord, Lord," therefore identifying themselves as his sheep. In fact, they themselves believe they are his sheep, but Jesus reveals to them that they are not. These fake Christians—false prophets—have done signs and wonders and prophesied in Jesus' name just as Moses warned. And Jesus concludes, just as Moses did, that these individuals are operating outside the requirements of God's commandments and voice, and are enticing God's people to follow a wrong path. As Jesus says, they are practicing lawlessness—they are not doing the will of his Father and are denied entrance into his kingdom.

The parallels between Moses' and Jesus' warning should not go unnoticed. Both deal with the subject of false prophets. Both indicate that the false prophets are within the company of God's people. Both are working signs and wonders. Both are enticing members of the kingdom away from God's commandments and voice. Both reference false prophets in the context of leading God's people into a walk on the wrong "way." It is difficult for me to believe that Jesus is not intentionally constructing this passage with the words of Deuteronomy 13 in mind.

I should point out that these failed Christians who have done signs and wonders in the name of Jesus are identifying themselves with the characteristics of the false prophets spoken of by Moses. They may not necessarily be leaders and teachers in the church who actively steer the flock away from God's commandments and words, but they have, at the very least, been self-deceived into thinking they are true Christians. Like the scribes and Pharisees Jesus warned about earlier in his sermon, they, too, have loosened the law's requirements to the point that they have a Christianity that is, for all intents and purposes, a practice of lawlessness. These two points—signs and wonders, and departure from the law of God—identifies them as being among the class of false prophets.

This passage of Matthew 7:21–23 also parallels Moses' prediction of the rise of another true prophet, and for the first time, Jesus has revealed to any astute listener that he is indeed that Prophet. This parallel comes from Moses' prediction found in Deuteronomy 18. Here, too, Moses speaks of both the true prophet to come, and of false prophets. The false prophets will be identified by their making predictions that do not come to pass. This would appear to indicate that the true prophet will make predictions that do come true, though it is not explicitly stated.

What is stated about the true prophet to come is that he will have God's words in his mouth, and he will speak them to the people. Whoever hears and does not obey these words will have to answer to God Himself.[410] Beginning with Matthew 7:21 and to the conclusion of this sermon, Jesus clearly reveals that he is the one in this role. He identifies himself as having God as his Father; he indicates that in the day of judgment to come, he is the one that the lost will appeal to for reconsideration of their denied entrance into the kingdom of heaven. He reveals that their fates are in his hands and that he is the one who evaluates the motivations and correctness of their actions based on God's law. And finally, as we shall cover in more detail in the next chapter, Jesus states that the words he is speaking need to be heeded, because they will determine the outcome of one's future. Those who hear his

---

[410] Deuteronomy 18:18–19

words and do them will be saved. Those who hear his words and fail to do them will be lost.

A. The Will of My Father Versus Lawlessness

Jesus' use of the phrase, *"he who does the will of my Father"* is used in contrast to those who say *"Lord, Lord"* but do not enter into the kingdom of heaven. These Christians, who are told to depart from Jesus, are therefore ones that failed to do the will of the Father, or as Jesus states at the end of the passage, they "practice lawlessness." The connection is plain; doing the will of the Father is therefore practicing *law-full-ness*, while not doing the will of the Father is the practice of *law-less-ness*.

The implication is also plain; the message that Jesus has been giving to the crowds has been outlining the will of his Father—delineating the purpose and true goal of God's law. Failing to understand and implement this message could result in being asked to depart from Jesus during the day of judgment. It is this failure to carry out true lawfulness that leads to the exclusion from heaven for the Christians who appeal for reconsideration.

Jesus earlier made two references to doing the will of his Father, but not with the same words. He used instead the parallel phrases *"sons* [or children] *of God"* and *"sons* [or children] *of your Father in heaven."* These phrases are from Matthew 5:9, the beatitude concerning peacemakers, and Matthew 5:45, referencing those who love their enemies. The tie between Mathew 7:21 and the phrases in Matthew 5 is found in Jesus' teaching located in Matthew chapter twelve, which reads as follows:

> *Then one said to Him, "Look, your mother and your brothers are standing outside, seeking to speak with you."*

*But he answered and said to the one who told him, "Who is my mother and who are my brothers?" And he stretched out his hand toward his disciples and said, "Here are my mother and my brothers! For **whoever does the will of my Father in heaven is my brother and sister and mother**."* (emphasis added)[411]

Jesus has made it plain that anyone doing the will of his Father is a child of God. The references to being sons (or children) of God found in Matthew 5 can therefore be equated to those who are doing the will of the heavenly Father.

In chapter eleven of this book, we have already looked closely at the character traits and conduct of the "peacemakers" who are privileged to be called the sons (children) of God. These are the followers of the will of the Father. These are those who practice lawfulness. Recall that we discovered a long list of actions common to "peacemakers' and "sons of God." For convenience, I have listed many of the traits below. They are:

- Pure (as in pure in heart, Matthew 5:8)
- Gentle
- Willing to yield
- Full of mercy and good works
- Impartial, non-hypocritical
- Bearing fruits of equity
- Calling for justice
- Pleading for truth
- Defending the poor, fatherless, afflicted, and needy
- Freeing others from the hand of the wicked
- Practicing the law
- Loving to neighbors

---

[411] Matthew 12:47–50

This, according to Jesus' Sermon on the Mount, is what constitutes a child of God—one who does the will of the Father. This is practicing the law and revealing one's love for God by their love for neighbors and enemies alike. Matthew 5:45 reveals that this kind of love directed toward enemies, is the exercise of God's perfection and His mercy.[412] In no uncertain terms, Jesus has stated in Matthew 7:21 that this is a requirement for entrance into the kingdom of heaven.

Jesus' model prayer given within this sermon also revealed that the "will of the Father" is practiced in heaven, and we are to pray that this will of the Father will be practiced here on earth. His model prayer then focuses on themes of justice, mercy, and faith—what Jesus calls the weightier matters of the law.[413] Given this information that God's will is being done in heaven, it should come as no surprise that those entering the kingdom of heaven are those who have adopted the "will of God" as their way of life. The Christians who have not done the will of God, have somehow missed the social implications and social justice obligations of God's will, which the peacemakers and those who love neighbor and enemy have lived.

The book of Luke is more direct in stating who the failed Christians are. Luke's Sermon on the Mount also ends with Jesus' story of two houses: one built on stone, the other on sand. However, immediately prior to beginning this story, Jesus makes the following statement:

> But why do you call Me "Lord, Lord," and not do the things which I say?[414]

---

[412] See chapter 20 of this book.

[413] See chapter 22 of this book.

[414] Luke 6:46

Jesus goes on to show that those who are obedient to his words will be saved, and those who hear his words but do not obey them will fall. By comparing these two parallel accounts, it is logical to conclude that not doing the things that Jesus says—disobedience to his word—is the same as practicing lawlessness and not doing the will of the Father.

B. In That Day

Throughout Jesus' ministry, he often used the phrase "Lord, Lord" in conjunction with stories concerning those who do not make it into the kingdom of heaven. "Lord, Lord" is the common appeal to him as individuals attempt to identify themselves as one of his followers, therefore deserving to be granted entrance into the kingdom. In Matthew 7:22, Jesus uses this phrase in conjunction with an event that is still future. He says, "*in that day*," meaning the day has not yet arrived when people will say to him "Lord, Lord."

Luke's Gospel account also uses the phrase "Lord, Lord" in a similar message where Jesus asked his followers to enter the narrow gate. Here, Luke does not mention two different paths, but rather two different ways in which individuals seek to enter a house. The story's teaching closely parallels the one in Jesus' Sermon on the Mount, and reads as follows:

> *Strive to enter through the narrow gate, for many, I say to you, will seek to enter and will not be able. When once the Master of the house has risen up and shut the door, and you begin to stand outside and knock at the door, saying, "Lord, Lord, open for us," and He will answer and say to you, "I do not know you, where you are from," then you will begin to say, "We ate and drank in*

Your presence, and You taught in our streets." But He will say, "I tell you I do not know you, where you are from. Depart from Me, all you workers of iniquity. "[415]

This story is also similar to Jesus' parable of the ten virgins—a story dealing with the events of five virgins being unprepared for the future coming of the Son of man. In this story, five of the virgins arrive to the house after the bridegroom has arrived for a wedding, and they find themselves locked out. The virgins call out to the master of the house and ask him to open the door saying, "*Lord, Lord.*" Likewise, the master of the house does not open the door but tells the virgins "*I do not know you.*"[416]

There are other future connections as well. The verses of Luke quoted above continue with Jesus speaking of the "*weeping and gnashing of teeth*"; when the lost see Abraham, Jacob, Isaac and the prophets in the kingdom that they, themselves, could not enter. The "weeping and gnashing of teeth" phrase is itself a term connected to events concerned with the time of the end. It is used by Jesus in this context in six different stories.[417]

This interconnectedness of the phase "Lord, Lord" used in conjunction with future end-time events proves it is being used as a refrain of the lost during the future return of Jesus. The reason this is important to understand is because Jesus is declaring in his sermon that he will be present during those end-time events, and that he is the one who will reject those

---

[415] Luke 13:24–28. Note: The word "iniquity" comes from Strong's Word NT:93 *adikia*, which means *injustice*.

[416] Matthew 25:1–13

[417] See Matthew 8:12; 13:41; 22:13; 24:51; 25:30; Luke 13:28. Note: In the Matthew 13:41 story containing this topic, the "*weeping and gnashing of teeth*" is experienced by those who "*practice lawlessness*" and are destroyed.

who have not done the will of the Father. It is also important because Jesus' parting words to the lost are that they have been *"practicing lawlessness,"* or as in the account of Luke, *"injustice."*[418] The implication is that the law, the will of the Father, and the obligatory words of Jesus, are still standing at this future time and serve as the basis for rejection of a class of individuals who believe they are Christ followers.

This is the second time Jesus has made this point in his Sermon on the Mount. The first time was his reference to those who "loosened" the law to the point it no longer served as an adequate guide for entrance into the kingdom of heaven. Contextually, his words imply that this was the nature of the incorrect teachings of the scribes and Pharisees.[419] In the second appearance of this problem, we have believing Christians who are self-deceived into thinking they are doing what is expected, even though they have pushed aside the requirements of the words of Jesus and the law, and no longer practice them. Both groups are guilty of concluding that the law of God does not apply as it is written. Both have misunderstood the expectations that Jesus and the law of God places on its followers.

C. Can Believers Be Lost?

You might recall that in chapter twelve of this book, when discussing John 3:16 and its following verses, I mentioned that Jesus in his dialog with Nicodemus does not mention the fates of one category of people. That would be the people who believe in Jesus but are not given entrance into the kingdom of heaven, that is, eternal life. John 3:16 plainly tells us that *"whoever believes in [Jesus] should not perish but have eter-*

---

[418] Luke 13:27. Strong's Word NT:93, *iniquity, injustice.*
[419] Matthew 5:17–20

nal life." However, Jesus' Sermon on the Mount and other Gospel references, as we have seen, are equally clear there is a category of individuals who believe that Jesus is Lord, have worked signs in his name, and yet they are excluded from the kingdom of heaven. And as we saw earlier, entrance into the kingdom of heaven is the same as receiving eternal life.[420] Is Jesus giving us two different messages, or is there a way to reconcile this conundrum?

There are theologians who feel that the Synoptic Gospels (Matthew, Mark, and Luke) have a different message than the Gospel of John, but I am not one of them. I see all four Gospels as having a consistent salvation message, howbeit John presents it with different details and language. Let us solve this conundrum by establishing a few facts. In the Sermon on the Mount, Jesus has been speaking of the kingdom of heaven and showing his listeners how to enter it. The message has clear social equity and justice obligations. It calls for members to be active agents for good, to both neighbors and anyone they might consider to be an enemy. This kingdom and its membership requires action—or we can easily say "work"—and it has a cost to its members.

Further, Jesus will point out in his concluding words (to be covered in the next chapter) that his words—spoken in the Sermon on the Mount—are to be followed if we want to be saved. The sermon also shows us that there can be individuals who believe they are followers of Christ, but Christ does not recognize them as members fit for the kingdom. Their failing relationship to Christ hinges on one basic point—failure to obey and implement the words of Jesus. Belief in Jesus, by itself, was not enough to save them. Luke quotes Jesus as saying:

---

[420] See Matthew 25:31–46. Note in particular, verses 34 and 46.

*But why do you call Me "Lord, Lord," and **not do the things** which I say?*[421]

Matthew adds more detail and has Jesus stating:

*I never knew you; depart from Me, you who **practice lawlessness**!*[422]

This is not inconsistent with the teachings of Jesus in the book of John. Jesus repeatedly told his disciples that his words were to be followed and would lead to life. For example:

Most assuredly, I say to you, if anyone keeps my word he shall never see death.[423]

And:

If anyone loves me, he will keep my word; and my Father will love him, and we will come to him and make our home with him. He who does not love me does not keep my words; and the word which you hear is not mine but the Father's who sent me. These things I have spoken to you while being present with you. But the Helper, the Holy Spirit, whom the Father will send in my name, he will teach you all things, and bring to your remembrance all things [the words/teachings] that I said to you.[424]

These are just two examples. It is clear from John that the

---

[421] Luke 6:46

[422] Matthew 7:23

[423] John 8:51. See also John 5:24

[424] John 14:23–27

words of Jesus (which are really the Father's words) are to be followed and implemented in our lives. Doing so is a demonstration of our love for Jesus, and his words do lead to eternal life.

Having eternal life is the subject of Jesus' discourse with Nicodemus in John 3. So, if believing should result in eternal life, and keeping Jesus' words results in eternal life, it should be easy to deduce that the "believing" of John 3 would also incorporate a love for Christ that results in our "keeping" his words. Belief, therefore, includes obedience to Jesus' words. Any belief that is only an intellectual ascent or void of devotion and faithful duty to his requested service, would be a non-saving, non-lifegiving, endeavor. Such believers would be the individuals who find themselves outside of the kingdom of heaven crying "Lord, Lord." Unfortunately, Jesus has repeatedly indicated by sermon and parable that such a class of followers does exist, and they will find out too late that they failed to keep his words and do the will of the Father. They have practiced lawlessness and will not be allowed to enter eternal life.

This is not a concept inconsistent with the teachings of the John 3 discourse. The *NIV Theological Dictionary of New Testament Words* states the following about the Greek word *pisteuō*, (i.e., believe) and its variations, which is used multiple times in the John 3 discourse and throughout the book of John:

> *Pisteuō* means to trust something or someone; it can refer to and confirm legendary tales and mythical ideas. **With reference to people, *pisteuō* means to obey**; the [passive] to enjoy trust. The [adjective] *pistos* means trusting or being **trustworthy**. The [verb] *pistoō* has the meaning of binding someone or oneself to be **faithful**." (emphasis added)[425]

---

[425] Verlyn D. Verbrugge, ed., *NIV Theological Dictionary of New Testament Words* (Grand Rapids, MI: Zondervan, 2000), page 1027.

Notice all the action in the above definitions: *obey*, *trustworthy*, and *faithful*. The English word faithful means, "strict or thorough in the performance of duty."[426] This fits the concept of *believing* meaning *obey* and Jesus' numerous references that we need to "do" his words. I do not see any misalignments between the Synoptic Gospels and the Gospel of John once we understand that believing encompasses the need to "do" what Jesus teaches.

An interesting note is that the Gospel of John uses the verb *pisteuō* with the Greek preposition *eis*, which means *to* or *into*. This pairing is unique to the New Testament. It is never used in secular Greek.[427] So, in John 3:15, 16, and 18, Jesus is literally saying that "whosoever believes *into* him should not perish." To me, this also shows that Jesus is trying to emphasize that our believing will direct us to enter "into" living his exemplary life. His actions are to become our actions.

It is also especially important to note the role of God's Holy Spirit in this active relationship "into" Jesus. Jesus' discourse with Nicodemus begins with the concept that we need a new life, and that that life comes about by repentance (a change of direction) and the Holy Spirit. Both are needed to enter the kingdom of heaven.[428] And, according to Peter, the Holy Spirit is given to those who are obedient to God. His comments were recorded shortly after the resurrection of Christ, while Peter was defending his actions (teaching the doctrines of the early "Way" church) before the counsel in Jerusalem. He states, in part, the following:

> *We ought to obey God rather than men. . . . Him [Jesus] God has exalted to His right hand to be*

---

[426] https://www.dictionary.com/browse/faithful

[427] See https://www.preceptaustin.org/1thessalonians_213

[428] John 3:5

Prince and Savior, to give repentance to Israel and forgiveness of sins. And we are His witnesses to these things, and so also is the Holy Spirit whom God has given to those who obey Him.[429]

The Holy Spirit is a gift from God to bring our own minds into alignment with the will of God. He also brought about the remembrance of Jesus' words so that they could be recorded, and we could have them today as our guide. Amazingly, Jesus also tells us that the Spirit and his words are one in the same.

It is the Spirit who gives life; the flesh profits nothing. The words that I speak to you are spirit, and they are life.[430]

This might come as a surprise to some Christians. Jesus' words are spirit. His words are life. This is what he has been saying all along; that following his words will save us—they lead to eternal life. His way is the way to life. Those words—spirit—are given to be obeyed.

Living the life that Jesus asks us to live is not possible without the Spirit and without his words. The study of the Holy Spirit and his complete role in our lives is an important one but it is beyond the scope of this book. Suffice it to say that perhaps the Christians to whom Jesus refers as not entering into the kingdom of heaven are spiritless, wordless, Christians—they have an interest in Jesus, but they do not heed the obligations of his words.

---

[429] Acts 5:29–32. See also John 17:6; Acts 1:8

[430] John 6:63

D. Lawlessness Equals Love Growing Cold

We have already looked closely at what Jesus meant by *"the will of the Father"* and have seen that the phrase *"practice lawlessness"* is a term synonymous with not doing the will of the Father. We have also seen that God's will and His law form the foundations of how we express our love to Him. And our love for Him is evident by how we exhibit love to our neighbors and even our enemies. There is no need to expand on this further. However, what I would like to point out is a misconception many Christians have concerning the connection between lawlessness and a lack of love. To do this, let us first look at one of Jesus' predictions of end-time events. It reads as follows:

> *Then many false prophets will rise up and deceive many. **And because lawlessness will abound, the love of many will grow cold.** But he who endures to the end shall be saved. And this gospel of the kingdom will be preached in all the world as a witness to all the nations, and then the end will come.* (emphasis added)[431]

The common misconception of far too many Christians is the belief that our world is in a spiritual decline, increasing in every kind of sin and discord, because the *"love of many is growing cold."* I hear it taught that as the people of the world lose their love for each other, lawlessness increases and abounds. It sounds logical and plausible, but Christians, look closely, this is not what Jesus is saying! It is, rather, the increase of lawlessness that causes the love of many to grow cold. And lawlessness increases due to the deceptions of false prophets, teachers, and leaders that, according to the Sermon on the

---

[431] Matthew 24:11–14

Mount, are directing us away from the narrow gate and the way to eternal life—away from the words of Jesus.

Stop and think about it for a moment! Does not the pattern that Jesus has laid out make more sense? Take for instance our earlier example of a society that is free of theft.[432] The belief and mutual agreement by everyone that stealing is wrong could lead to a secure and peaceful community—no need for locks; employees are receiving fair wages, and credit is given where credit is due. But what if someone begins to challenge this belief and starts to steal just a little, or skimp on an employee's wages—i.e., starts to become *lawless*. Their actions of breaking the law will begin to affect another person in a negative way. It will cause confusion initially. And as the dishonesty continues, it will lead to people becoming suspicious of, or fearing, that individual. This will lead to distrust, and distrust will lead to disrespect. These feelings will cause avoidance and an active disassociation from those who are becoming dishonest. Members within this society will start to detach from each other, and the distance that grows between them will make the hearts less fond of each other. Love will begin growing colder, and an interest in the wellbeing of others will diminish. Finally, the diminished interest in the wellbeing of others serves to demotivate the society to practice lawfulness. And the cycle continues a downward spiral to societal chaos. Lawfulness breeds respect and promotes love. Lawlessness breeds disrespect and cultivates animosity—love grows cold. And cold love breeds more lawlessness.

The opposite is also true. It is when we are interested and involved in the welfare of others that our interest and love for an individual grows. Being interested in the welfare of others is at the heart of God's law, therefore the pursuit and practice of God's law, which calls for us to foster a just and equitable

---

[432] See chapter 4

society, germinates love. This is the direction that God's law is pushing us toward. It is the voices of the false prophets, leaders and teachers that defame the law and direct us away from keeping it properly that starts the cascade of evil leading to love growing cold. They lead us away from life and toward destruction. It is why Jesus told us to beware of them as ravenous wolves and to understand that they hide among us.

E. An Intriguing Structural Pattern

What I am about to present to you in closing this chapter is a bit of a detour from the running verse by verse commentary. It stems from a stepping back and a looking at the overall structure of Jesus' sermon and noticing something interesting. You can call me a wonk if you wish, but I see a rather intriguing pattern in the layout of Jesus' Sermon on the Mount. Feel free to skip this section if you are not interested in peculiar details and want to move on. Are you still here? Fine!

Look closely at this sermon and you will notice that Jesus has not given us his message once. He has given it twice in the same sitting, and both messages have followed the same pattern. Jewish poetry and literature are filled with verses that use a repetitive structure to re-emphasize one's point. Jesus has done this same thing by delivering his message twice in one afternoon. The first message is shorter, while the second covers the same information in greater detail. Let me show you how.

Jesus begins this sermon with a series of nine blessings that outlines the benefits of the kingdom of heaven, and calls for its members to be socially just, equitable, and involved in benefiting the lives of others. These beatitudes reveal a deeper understanding of the Old Testament teachings and serve as a pattern for how members of the kingdom should view their roles and live their lives. The last two blessings point out that living such a life will be met with persecution. Jesus then directs his listeners to be the salt and light of the world, doing good works for others and thereby glorifying the Father in heaven. Service to God is to be our motivation for all the good we do for others.

Jesus then points out to his listeners that this is not a destruction of the Law and the Prophets; on the contrary, this is a fulfilment of the goal of their message. Jesus then states that this message—the Law and the Prophets as written—will last as long as there is a heaven and earth. He then warns that whoever breaks this law, and teaches men to do likewise, will not enter heaven. However, those who do keep the Law and Prophets, and teach others to do so, will be great in the kingdom of heaven. Finally, Jesus points out to the crowd that there are those among them who have not been leading and teaching them correctly—they are giving wrong information that can cause them to be excluded from the kingdom if they cannot exceed their misguided standards.

This message is covered by Matthew 5:1–20 and serves as the first of the two parallel sermons. The second begins at Matthew 5:21 (and continues to the end of Matthew 7) and repeats the themes of the first message. Here, Jesus begins by outlining six examples regarding how the people have been incorrectly taught the Law and Prophets. Jesus corrects the incomplete information of each theme and reveals a deeper understanding of how the teachings should be applied to one's life. The last of these six examples deals with extending love to enemies and those who persecute you. The first sermon begins with nine blessings elevating our standards and ends by warning of persecution. The second parallel message gives six antitheses, that likewise, cover teachings that are misunderstood and need to be raised to new standards. The last of these teachings ends by telling us to love our persecutors.

Jesus then turns the listeners attention to three areas where what we do is to be done for others but not openly. This deals with how we should be charitable, how we should pray and how we should fast. All three are things we should do, but we are to do them for God's rewards and not for the rewards of men. Imbedded within these three themes are actions of kindness, generosity, forgiveness, social justice, and faith. The message closely parallels Jesus' first message where he calls on his listeners to be salt and light and to do good works for the glory of the Father.

Jesus then expands on this theme of living a life of service to God. He teaches that by self-sacrifice, we are laying up treasures in heaven. This requires a whole new mindset; a new paradigm on how we live life. There are only two choices in life; we can serve God and be generous as God is generous, or we can serve ourselves and hoard our wealth for our own benefit. We cannot do both.

Jesus then teaches that when we choose to follow God, we do not need to worry about how we will survive—God will care for us. We are to be generous and know that all our basic needs will be met. Our generosity is to be without bias; we are not to judge whether a person in need is worthy of help. Living this way will take resources beyond our abilities at times but Jesus tells us to ask, seek, and knock, and solutions will be manifested. We are to do for others what we would want them to do for us. This simple motto is the foundation of God's law and the message of His prophets. It is a narrow gate and a way that leads to life. It is the path of following the will of the Father and the practicing of His laws.

Jesus' first message concluded by warning his listeners that the scribes and Pharisees among them are giving wrong information regarding the law of God, such that it could lead them away from the kingdom and the life it has to offer. Jesus also points out that the law is valid far into the future and should be correctly followed. Likewise, Jesus concludes his parallel second message with the same information. He warns the listeners to beware of false prophets who will lead them away from God's path, away from the will of the Father and into the practice of lawlessness. Jesus reveals that the will of the Father and the following of the law is still a relevant issue at the end-time judgment. In so doing, Jesus reveals he is God's prophet, predicted by Moses, and that he will be the one to accept or reject humanity based on which path they chose to follow.

Finally, Jesus' first message ends with a pronouncement regarding a contrast between those who loosen verses those who keep God's word as being either lost or saved. Likewise, Jesus ends his second message stating that one's being saved or destroyed depends on whether or not they hear and keep his words. This is the parable of a house being built on rock or sand, and it is what we will look at next.

CHAPTER 33

The House of Jesus

Therefore whoever hears these sayings of mine, and does them, I will liken him to a wise man who built his house on the rock: and the rain descended, the floods came, and the winds blew and beat on that house; and it did not fall, for it was founded on the rock.

But everyone who hears these sayings of mine, and does not do them, will be like a foolish man who built his house on the sand: and the rain descended, the floods came, and the winds blew and beat on that house; and it fell. And great was its fall.

Matthew 7:24–27

The significance of Jesus' words and his choice of words as he concludes his sermon, should not be taken lightly. Within this analogy of two houses withstanding storms, Jesus has identified himself as the prophet predicted by Moses. He has made his sayings equal to the law of God, likening them to the wisdom of the proverbs of Solomon. He has pronounced that following them, or not following them, is the difference between safety or destruction, and revealed that his teachings are the paramount school of thought that should be followed. It is no wonder that by the conclusion of this sermon, the people are said to be "astonished" by his teachings. They are brash and even blasphemous if they are not true.

Jesus has just warned the crowds to beware of false prophets—teachers and leaders—or even assumed followers of Christ leading one to a wrong path. He has given clues on how to unmask their true characters. He has identified his teachings as being those of the will of God in heaven, and has proclaimed that he is a son of the Father. He has elevated himself to the judge of mankind at the time of the end; the one who will direct their fates based on their faithfulness or unfaithfulness to the law. And now, as Jesus concludes his sermon, he uses the word "therefore" to connect his sayings to the words of God's "law", which will determine the fates of men.

The word "therefore" in this passage is translated from the Greek word *oun*.[433] It is a Greek conjunction joining two thoughts together. Our English word "therefore" functions the same way and is merely a bridge that connects a thought that has just been stated, to a thought that is about to be stated. "Therefore" is an indicator of cause and effect. When teaching, I am fond of telling my students that "There can be no 'therefore' if there is no 'before.'" In the context of Jesus' concluding words, the "before" is the loss of one's entrance into the kingdom of heaven due to a practice of lawlessness. The "therefore" that follows is a safe and secure shelter and life resulting from one's hearing and doing Jesus' sayings. In short, Jesus' words are the practice of lawfulness; they are the will of the Father; they are life.

These sayings of Jesus, as recorded in the Sermon on the Mount have, as we have now seen over the past chapters, threshed out the core principles and objectives of God's law and His prophets. These principles lead to the establishment of a fair and equitable society based on justice and mercy, that cares for the weak with

---

[433] Strong's Word NT:3767

the resources of the strong. This is not to be a society where the law is enforced by strong controls; rather, the ideal is that the members of the community embrace the goals of the law because of their love for God and neighbor. The members of the kingdom of heaven willingly give of their time, energy, and resources to ensure the provision and safety of the whole community—even to those who are strangers or enemies. It is social justice because of love combined with the faith of knowing that God will bless such a society and meet its needs.

Throughout this sermon, Jesus has repeatedly connected his sayings to God's law or to teachings of the prophets. Each topic has been founded on new and more complete interpretations of a law, and the redirecting of the minds of the listeners toward God's concerns for the wellbeing of every member of society, as proclaimed so often by the prophets. We have learned that "love your neighbor" means "love your neighbor and your enemy" as well. We have seen that caring for the poor and needy, the fatherless, and widows is self-sacrifice that is acceptable to God. Social justice is the freeing of people from their burdens, and giving rest, which is the object of the sabbatical laws and feasts. And Jesus concludes that these teachings are a practice of the law, and will lead to spiritual safety and entrance into the kingdom of heaven.

Jesus, in elevating his sayings to such a high level of importance, has assumed the characteristics of the promised "prophet" spoken of by Moses in the book of Deuteronomy. He has taught in accordance with the commands and voice of God, as a true prophet is required to do, and he now speaks the words that God has given him and states that not following these words will subject a person to God's judgment.

To help emphasize this statement, Jesus uses the analogy of two different individuals building a house in which to live. One is a "wise" person building a house on a secure foundation of "rock"; the other is a "foolish" person building a house on an insecure foundation of sand. The imagery of a "rock" being a place of safety is one that the Jewish mind is familiar with. Old Testament literature pictures the law of God being delivered to them on tablets of stone. Multiple psalms reference God as being a "rock of salvation" and a safe place in which to hide. Several of these references reveal that this safety is, in part, due to the commandments given by God and being faithful to His will. Rock represents God's word. For Jesus to connect his words to being a secure foundation of rock, is to say that his words are God's words.

Jesus' use of the words "wise" and "foolish" are also familiar themes to the Jewish mind. King Solomon's book of Proverbs makes multiple contrasts between the wise and the foolish, and those with wisdom versus those who lack understanding. The wise are those who have learned to "walk" in God's ways (revealed in His word), while the foolish are those who rebel and reject the sound council of God's path. By using these words, Jesus equates following his sayings to the security of the wisdom of Solomon, while rejecting his sayings leads to the fate of fools.

Jesus' reference to storms, wind, rain, and rising flood waters against both houses draws on the imagery of the flood story in the book of Genesis. In this story, God laments the growing injustice and evilness of mankind and finds it necessary to judge the earth and destroy it with a worldwide flood. God, however, provides a place of safety, in that He instructs Noah—a righteous man—to build an ark which will preserve him and his family. Thus, the imagery of the two houses subjected to a destructive flood foretells a future worldwide judgment from God, which Jesus earlier revealed he presides over as the decider of people's fates. As before, the saved are those who are following God's word, and those who perish are those who are not following His words.

Jesus' use of the imagery of houses is also one that is familiar to the Jewish mind. As we learned earlier in this book, in Jesus' day there were many rabbis who taught the law of God. Instruction usually took place in one's home—or "house." A house was, therefore, a place of instruction; to learn the ways of God and the sayings of the teachers. In Jesus' day, two prominent schools of thought regarding the interpretation and application of the law—God's word— were being propagated by two renowned religious leaders. Their established schools were known as the "House of Shammai" and the "House of Hillel." By combining the imagery of a safe house being one based on Jesus' sayings, Jesus was establishing a third "house" or schooling of the law. In short, the "House of Jesus." Jesus, however, does not offer it to his listeners as a third philosophy or competing educational opportunity. His house—his words, his teachings—is the only one that will give safety.

Early on in Jesus' sermon, he detoured from his main themes to tell his confused listeners that he had not come to destroy the Law and the Prophets, but to fulfill them. This was followed by warnings regarding the type of instruction they were being given by the scribes and Pharisees, and Jesus' revelation that these teachings were incomplete and could lead to one's exclusion from the kingdom of heaven. He now equates his sayings—his instructions to the people—as the ones able to save, the ones in line with the will of the Father, and the true practice of the Law and the Prophets. He has given us a fuller interpretation and application of what the Law and the Prophets has always intended. He has fulfilled (made complete) the Law and the teachings of the Prophets. He completes this thought with the imagery of a house—a place of instruction—that has the correct teachings and will stand the storms of judgment.

In Luke's record of the Sermon on the Mount, Jesus prefaces this parable of the two houses with the question, *"But why do you call Me 'Lord, Lord,' and not do the things which I say?"*[434] The question and the preceding two-house parable make it clear; Jesus is "Lord," but truly accepting him as Lord requires accepting and living his words.

---

[434] Luke 6:46

CHAPTER 34

Astonished

And so it was, when Jesus had ended these sayings, that the people were astonished at His teaching, for He taught them as one having authority, and not as the scribes.

Matthew 7:28–29

If you have come this far in this book, it should come as no surprise to you that, as Jesus concluded his Sermon on the Mount, Matthew records the above reaction by the people. They were "astonished"! Indeed!

The listeners of that day believed that poverty and suffering were judgments from God that verified his displeasure with them. Jesus takes the position that the poor and suffering are the objects of God's mercy, and that as followers of God, we are the tools in God's hands to alleviate their poverty and suffering. We, as the members of the kingdom of heaven, are the conduit of God's mercy to them. Astonishing!

The listeners of that day may have seen it as useless to try to intervene on behalf of the poor and suffering, since they were believed to have fallen from God's favor. Jesus takes the position that those who hunger for a just world will receive mercy from God, they will be His children, they will see God, and their hunger for righteousness will not be unfilled. Astonishing!

The listeners of that day may have had the belief that if one follows God and obeys His commandments, God's blessing will be upon them, and they will live comfortable, secure lives. Jesus teaches that living a life of obedience to God and being active in the pursuit of righteousness, especially for His name's sake, will result in persecution and the need to flee for one's safety. Astonishing!

The listeners of that day may have believed that change in their world required the concerted effort of a strong, united force to fight the evils that prevailed against them. Jesus takes the position that change can occur with only a candle of light and a pinch of salt. He teaches that an individual has power to change the world for the better. Astonishing!

The listeners of that day had trust in their religious leaders. After all, they were highly educated, literate men of pious dispositions, blessed by God. It was their responsibility to guide the nation in the ways of truth. Jesus takes the position that these leaders' teachings were incomplete at best, and at times wrong. To back up his position he gave the listeners six examples of how the leaders had failed them and left them short of the goals that God wanted them to achieve. Astonishing!

Jesus teaches that God's law and the message of the prophets as he had come to present it in its complete and fulfilled form, will continue in existence to the end of heaven and earth. Astonishing!

The listeners of that day had been taught by the religious leaders that they should love their neighbors but hate their enemies. Jesus takes the position that they should love both neighbor and enemy. He went on to say that God, Himself, shows kindness to those who hate Him, so if we want to share the character of God—His perfection—it requires that we love our enemies, too. Astonishing!

The listeners of that day had been taught that there are three ways to approach God in an attempt to avert a negative divine decree against them. In short, God's heart might be swayed by one's charity to others, or one's prayers to God, or by one's self-denial. Jesus addresses each of these topics. He does not state that these three are of no value, but he warns that if they are done in an attitude of self-aggrandizement, there will be no recognition from God. Astonishing!

The listeners of that day thought they knew how to pray. One could approach God and tell Him what they needed, or ask for forgiveness. Jesus reinstructed them that prayer to God is to start with our desire to be a partaker in faith of God's heavenly tenets here on earth. We are not to seek for wealth or an easy life; we should only ask God for what is enough for today. There should be no greed in our requests. We should ask God for forgiveness, but only expect it if we ourselves are forgiving to others. Jesus' simple, yet profound, prayer highlights the three weightier matters of God's law that should be the template of our lives—justice, mercy and faith. Astonishing!

The listeners of that day believed that wealth was a sign of God's favor. Wealth was also seen as a way of guarding oneself from future harm. It guaranteed comfort and safety. As a result, many had an aggressive desire to accumulate material wealth. Jesus takes the position that greed to accumulate wealth is a misuse of the resources given by God. It undermined one's willingness to help the poor and having faith in God to provide for your daily needs. Jesus taught that you cannot serve both material greed and God. Astonishing.

Jesus directed that the way to become truly rich and store up treasures in heaven—the wealth that really matters—is to be willing to be an active member of the kingdom of heaven and seek justice and equity within your sphere of influence. These are the works that glorify God. The pursuit of these works will require one to invest his own resources. The cost could be high, but we are to have faith that God will care for us. These works are to be done without prejudice and in concert with others as God will direct. Astonishing!

Jesus teaches that these instructions of his are the pathway to eternal life. They are the path to godly living. They are the practice of lawfulness. His spoken words, if heard and followed, would guarantee safety in the times of trouble that lay ahead. Astonishing!

Part of Jesus' conclusion that day, was that the followers of the kingdom of heaven would be subject to deceptions from within the ranks of those who claimed to be followers. These false followers, however, would have teachings and actions that were meant to separate the true followers from the words of Jesus. Their actions would be a form of lawlessness that will result in their loss of entrance into the kingdom to come. It is the lawlessness of failing to do the words of Christ their Lord. Astonishing!

In this book, I have presented to you what I believe to be a very literal interpretation of Jesus' sermon. As you have read, you have discovered that Jesus views the kingdom of heaven as a body of followers of his words. You have also discovered that Jesus' words as presented in this sermon are a completed revelation of God's law, and that the law is in effect to the end of the world. Jesus' words explain more fully what God wants us to do, rather than what He wants us to not do. Jesus' words are the pathway that leads to eternal life. His words define what it means to love one's neighbor as oneself. His words teach us that love has social obligations to his followers. To love one's neighbor, enemies included, is to care for others who are in need—friend or foe. Astonishing!

Jesus' teachings obligate us to be mindful of others' physical, social, and civil needs. Jesus' message is infused with social justice and social equity calls to action. And he concludes by teaching us that if we see him as our Lord, then his teaching of justice and equity, mercy and forgiveness, is to produce actions based on our faith in his Father. Faith that our sacrifices for the good of others will not destitute ourselves and will be blessings to our society. Active followers will be lights of direction and the salt that makes life worth living.

Jesus' whole Sermon on the Mount has been about the kingdom of heaven and how to be part of it. While a kingdom of heaven might make one consider the realms above us, Jesus' message has dealt predominately with life on present-day earth, and specifically on how to make that life better for those who need help. He has addressed issues pertaining to physical needs, emotional needs, social justice, wealth distribution, conflict resolution, debt forgiveness, faith in God, and much more. These are the steppingstones in the pathway to the kingdom. Nevertheless, these are rarely the issues that most Christians are directed to when taught the Sermon on the Mount. Astonishing!

Most Christians are taught that the kingdom of heaven is a future utopia. In the future, it will be. However, Jesus was introducing the kingdom of heaven as something to be present on earth in his day and continuing beyond the time of the end. Jesus made it clear that today's kingdom is far from a utopia. The teachings within Jesus' kingdom of heaven show that it operates in a sphere of poverty, hunger, depression, injustice, inequity, and persecution of those seeking to resolve or alleviate these conditions. He shows that the followers of the kingdom's tenets will pay a cost, they may be deprived of the luxuries of life, and they may suffer opposition so severe that they will need to flee for their safety. However, he promises that God will meet all their basic needs, and they are assured of His care, as well as current blessings and future rewards.

The very fact that Jesus asks us to share of our means, anticipates that we will be living in a world that has disparities in wealth and other inequities. But it also anticipates that his followers will have means to respond to others' needs. Wealth is therefore not the problem. Wealth is a means to solve the problem. The problem of disparity rests in the human heart, and Jesus' sermon was an address to every listener to take to heart the goals of his kingdom. It is a call to be a remedy for injustices, not one of its causes.

In modern applications social warriors generally confront governments and their laws when fighting for their causes of social justice. Some feel that the cause is capitalism. Some feel that it is socialism, communism, dictators or kings, or racism that foster systems that deprive others of justice and basic needs. In truth, it is the inhumanity and greed in each one of us that is the root of the problem. Governments will fail. They have "specks" in their eyes, while the people who reside in them have "planks" in their eyes. Social justice issues are corporate ones, and social justice warriors cannot make meaningful progress until we, as individuals, corporately remove the planks from our eyes. It is our lack of love for our neighbors, and our enemies, and our disregard for God that breeds injustice. God will hold us accountable for these failures and the social ills they have caused.

Jesus, in his Sermon on the Mount, addressed this root cause. He does not speak of the Roman nation, or their oppression of his nation. Instead, he focuses on the single most basic unit of social justice and equity within the world—the individual and how he relates to others. Jesus demonstrated by use of parables in other parts of the Gospels that the kingdom of heaven was like a small seed, or a measure of leavening. Each is only a small part of the whole, but they both grow to influence and shape their worlds. Likewise, he sees the individual as lights of the world and salt of the earth, both playing vital roles in making life livable and enjoyable. Social disparities will disappear as more and more individuals heed his words and become lights and salt. In this way, the kingdom grows and becomes an increasing benefit to humanity.

The kingdom of heaven has grown on earth since the preaching of the Sermon on the Mount. It has been of great benefit to many who were, and still are, in need. Christian organizations throughout history have been the most active of the world religions to create hospitals, schools, shelters, orphanages, food and clothing distribution centers, economic development agencies, and on and on. Christianity should continue to do so. It is a part of Jesus' gospel message to his followers. It is a part of his call to Christian service. And it is part of his assigned pathway to eternal life. Participating in the care of others and defending them from evil is a work assigned by God, and it is one way we demonstrate our loyalty to God.

Many Christian view the Sermon on the Mount as a relic of an old covenant. They think that the ideals that Jesus presented are unobtainable and no longer necessary. They treat the sermon as one having great moral ideals, but it is no longer needed to obtain salvation. In fact, some teach that following Jesus' sermon is an act of self-righteousness and a lack of faith, and that following Jesus' words as presented in this sermon could cause one's loss of salvation.

I roundly and vigorously disagree! You have now seen Jesus' sermon in a literal, direct interpretation. He has not given any indication that his words can be ignored. He has instead put his words on par with the Law and the Prophets and indicated that they will remain to the end of time. He has shown that his teachings form the basis of judgment of those who are, or claim to be, his followers in the time of the end. If his words are not to be heeded, why does he give them so much weight?

The straightforward answer is that Jesus' words are to be heeded. The kingdom of heaven here on earth, today, is to be a force of good among the nations. Jesus has outlined a course of action for his followers. He has outlined the framework of the love that is to be displayed to others by his followers. Those of us who follow his words will be a blessing, and will be blessed, because of our love in action. Our implementation of Jesus' teachings gives glory to the Father in heaven. Our actions are motivated by our faith that there is a Father in heaven, and the king of the kingdom—Jesus—has directed us to be agents of change in this world. Inaction would be unfaithfulness to the God we believe in and serve. If we believe in the Father and His assigned king—Jesus Christ, our Lord and Savior—then we must also be active as He has directed us to be. The Sermon on the Mount is the way our king would have us go.

Are you astonished? Now what?

CHAPTER 35

Shamar:

The Call to Action

Can you recall the first recorded question asked by man in the Bible? Would you know where to find it? It is a short, simple question, but it has deep and profound meaning. Its answer is one that few of us have fully comprehended, or one we have chosen to ignore. The question strikes at the core of God's intended purpose in His creation of humanity. God—a loving and giving being—made man in His own image. Man was to be like the "us" of the Godhead—a loving and giving being. That one question, answered correctly, tells man what the character of that "us" is. It defines God's association within the trinity, His relationship with the unfallen host of heaven, His bond to man, and God's intended relationship of man to his own kind.

The answer to that first question asked by man forms the basis of nearly all the teachings of the Old and New Testaments of the Bible—the Law, the Prophets, and the teachings of Jesus and his disciples. In fact, it is a core principle taught by many of the world's religions. It would be good to always have it in our minds. It should be a question we ask ourselves whenever we face a moral decision.

Have you recalled the question yet? Do you know the answer? That question is: *"Am I my brother's keeper?"* It is found in Genesis chapter four. It is uttered by the murderer Cain, who had earlier killed his brother, Abel. He thought the killing had not been observed. God, however, had seen the crime, and He approached Cain with His own question, *"Where is Abel your brother?"* Cain's callous response was intended to cover up his crime, *"I do not know. Am I my brother's keeper?"*

"Keeper" is the English translation for the Hebrew word *"shamar."*[435] It means to protect, guard, to attend to. English renderings of the word can take the form of *to take heed, guard, protect, preserve, regard,* or *save.* All of which indicate that the thing to be *shamared* is of great value to the one doing the *shamaring.* Cain's question to God is implying, "Is my brother supposed to be of value to me?" "Is my brother supposed to be my responsibility?"

God answers this question with one of His own, *"What have you done?"* He then tells Cain that He knows Abel has been murdered, and He pronounces a curse on Cain that he will have to live with for the rest of his life. The implied answer to Cain's question of, *"Am I my brother's keeper?"* is "Yes"! He was, according to God, and his failure to "keep" his brother led Cain onto a path of disregard, and to his eventual murderous act, and to a lifelong curse.

This story in Genesis concerns the relationship of two brothers from the same mother and father. However, the Hebrew word for brother, *ach,*[436] can be extended to other relationships that are not directly connected by blood. It can be one's cousin, kindred, tribe, or nation. The relationship, however, can extend even further. The Old Testament and the teachings of Jesus include non-relatives as "brothers." They go as far as to include

---

[435] Strong's Word OT:8104 *shamar* (shaw-mar'); a primitive root meaning properly *to hedge about* (as with thorns), i.e., *guard* and generally, *to protect, to attend to*, etc.

[436] Strong's Word OT:251 *'ach* (awkh); a primitive word meaning *a brother* (used in the widest sense of literal relationship and metaphorical affinity or resemblance to those of like kind)

foreigners as "brothers." Jesus even extends the relationship to one's enemies, and anyone in need of *shamar* is to be considered a neighbor in need of love.

Many Christians study the Gospels with the filter of what God is doing for "me." As in how much God loves "me" and wants to save "me." They see salvation primarily as a revelation of God's relationship to themselves. This, however, is a blinding filter. Remove it and look closer, and notice that the majority of the Gospel is taught in the context of how we are to relate to mankind—our brothers. The Gospels hold instruction for being a brother's keeper. They reveal that the "keepers" are those who walk with divinity and have unity with God—being considered children of God and sharing in his blessings. The Gospels reveal that the keepers are those who receive salvation.

The teachings of Jesus that we have explored in this book ultimately center on a belief that all humankind is connected to each other, and we are to be our brother's keeper to all those on our planet. We have taken an in-depth, literal look at Jesus' epic Sermon on the Mount, and have seen that its themes are based in love for others, and our responsibilities to care for those who are suffering or disadvantaged. The sermon gives direction to those who want to be members of the kingdom of heaven. It instructs them concerning their roles in practicing social justice, social equity, and faith in God—their king. It has laid out a pathway to heaven for the members to follow. It is a pathway that practices justice, mercy, and faith in God.

It is my hope that as you have read the previous chapters, you have seen Jesus' teachings more clearly than before. I hope you have seen the justice and equity themes of the Sermon on the Mount that flow from its beginning all the way to its end. I hope you have seen that Jesus' sermon is a call to duty. It is asking members, and would-be members, of the kingdom of heaven to put into action the tenets of a heavenly kingdom.

These tenets are the weightier matters of love—justice, mercy and faith in God, and faith in His wisdom regarding the ways of love.

Notice, however, that Jesus' concept of social justice is different from the concept of today's social justice movements. While activists today seek government support in the distribution of others' wealth, Jesus calls on individuals to voluntarily see the needs around them and give of their wealth to address those needs. Today's activists make distinctions (often inconsistently) between who are the wealthy or powerful that should be forced to give of their wealth or power, and who should receive that wealth or power. They delineate between who is responsible for the care of others and who is not. Jesus, however, teaches that we are all responsible for the care of our brothers, and that one's wealth, power, or influence is subjective and relative. He does not ask for only billionaires or millionaires to respond to others' needs. Instead, even a person with only two coats has something to give to a person who has none. The responsibility to care for others is the responsibility of anyone who can respond to others in need.

Social justice and equity begin within each of us. It is our response to those within our reach. Each of us has our own sphere of influence, and the kingdom of heaven asks us to be mindful of the needs within that sphere and to respond to those needs as our abilities allow. For some, the response can be in the form of monetary or material support. For others, the response may be emotional support. While others may serve best by communicating and coordinating efforts that can address a need. In all cases, the justice is from one or more responsive individuals to another. True justice and equity come from within the hearts of individuals. There is no need to encourage it into action. It does, however, need to be taught, supported, and given direction.

Social justice activists seek a state of equality among all individuals. The kingdom of heaven, as it operates here on earth, and as taught by Jesus, anticipates that this equality will never be realized. It understands that disparities will continue to exist and that one of the kingdom of heaven's functions is to balance these disparities.

The kingdom of heaven understands that not all individuals can be equal. It allows for diversity of talent, opportunity, and one's given status in life. It realizes that there will be diversity in achievements and in the establishment of personal wealth. Wealth, power, and position are not the problem. It is the greedy desire to accumulate material wealth or power at the harm of others that is a problem. The just accumulation of resources, in and of themselves, are tools that can balance inequities, and in the hands of God's faithful, they will be used mercifully and justly.

The kingdom of heaven, as taught by Jesus in the Sermon on the Mount, sees a world of continued injustice, disparity, and tragedy that necessitates the calling into action of its members to respond to the sufferings of its brothers—family, friends, neighbors, strangers, and enemies. The response should be ongoing and should continue until our king returns to make a new heaven and new earth. Prior to that time, there will be no utopia. Disparities and injustices will always exist, and so will the need to address them. The nature and the degree of social injustices and social inequities in this world will remain an ever-changing situation, morphing from ever-changing conditions. Those in need today may be those in power tomorrow, and vice versa.

The simplest and most basic unit of social justice and equity is, and always has been, the individual, not government. Jesus' Sermon on the Mount speaks to the individual and their responsibility to love their neighbors and to love their enemies, and to improve the world around them. Jesus did not advocate the establishment of an earthly government to accomplish social justice goals, rather, he called upon his followers to join a preexisting heavenly kingdom that already held social justice and equity as foundational pillars. Followers are asked to give their loyalties to this heavenly kingdom and to implement these pillars beyond the confines of the earthly governments in which they reside. They are to cultivate justice and equity where earthly governments fall short.

In this book, I have outlined how Jesus' Sermon on the Mount is an extension of the Old Testament Laws and Prophets. Jesus' sermon incorporates and continues the wisdom and instructions that the God of heaven has communicated since the fall of man. He reminded his audience what God does not want, yet at the same time he explained the goal that God is wanting to achieve among His followers. That goal is for us to live a life of mercy and justice, and to have faith that God will bless our actions of mercy and justice. It is for us to put love for our neighbors and even our enemies into action. The Sermon on the Mount is the illumination of a pathway that leads to heavenly social justice and equity.

What this book has not done, is tell you specifically how this new knowledge is to be implemented. The reason is simple. Your situation is unique. You know best your abilities and what resources you have to contribute. For some individuals, the exercise of Jesus' teaching may extend to only the confines of one's immediate community. For others, in this age of worldwide connectivity, their response and influence can reach the far ends of the earth. My only hope is that you have seen the meaning of Jesus' Sermon on the Mount and that you will seek and find how God wants you to be a light to a dark world, and that you will be that light for the glory of the Father.

By this we know love, because He laid down His life for us. And we also ought to lay down our lives for the brethren. But whoever has this world's goods, and sees his brother in need, and shuts up his heart from him, how does the love of God abide in him? My little children, let us not love in word or in tongue, but in deed and in truth.

1 John 3:16–19

ACKNOWLEDGMENTS

First and foremost, I would, of course, like to thank Jesus Christ, my Lord and Savior, for what he has done for me. I have been fortunate to have come to know and trust him at an early age, and thus been able to see his guiding hand many times in my life. He has granted me many opportunities to cultivate a knowledge of his Word and world, and has given me many life adventures that have shaped who I am today.

I would also like to express my great appreciation to individuals that have helped shape this book. This includes Rick Steele of *Rick Steele Editorial Services* and Victoria Brock of *The Word Tank*. It also includes my good friend, a.k.a. anonymous, who provided invaluable input. These individuals have done an excellent job of correcting my writing deficiencies, and at times my disjointed thoughts. They have made me look a lot smarter than I really am. Without them this book would just be a file lost in my computer. They have helped make my thoughts a tangible reality. Thank you!

Finally, I would like to thank my wife and family for allowing me the space and hours of isolation needed to accomplish this project. For what it is worth, this project has been your accomplishment as well. Thank you!

Made in the USA
Columbia, SC
28 June 2021